Patient-Centered Care Series

Series Editors

Moira Stewart,
Judith Belle Brown
and
Thomas R Freeman

Challenges and Solutions in Patient-Centered Care

A case book

Edited by
Judith Belle Brown,
Moira Stewart
and
W Wayne Weston
Centre for Studies in Family Medicine
The University of Western Ontario

Radcliffe Medical Press

Radcliffe Medical Press Ltd
18 Marcham Road
Abingdon
Oxon OX14 1AA
United Kingdom

www.radcliffe-oxford.com
The Radcliffe Medical Press electronic catalogue and online ordering facility.
Direct sales to anywhere in the world.

British Library Cataloguing in Publication Data

A catalogue record for this book is available from the British Library.

ISBN 1 85775 986 9

Typeset by Aarontype Ltd, Easton, Bristol
Printed and bound by TJ International Ltd, Padstow, Cornwall

Contents

About the editors

Judith Belle Brown, PhD in Social Work from Smith College, is a Professor in the Centre for Studies in Family Medicine, the Department of Family Medicine, at The University of Western Ontario (UWO) and in the School of Social Work at King's College, London, Ontario, Canada. She has been conducting research on the patient-centered clinical method for over two decades. Dr Brown has presented papers and conducted workshops both nationally (Canada and the United States) and internationally (UK, Holland, Spain, Hong Kong, Sweden, New Zealand, Denmark) on the patient-centered method. Dr Brown co-ordinates courses on patient-centered communication at UWO at the undergraduate, postgraduate and Masters levels. Dr Brown is a co-author of the book *Patient-Centered Medicine: transforming the clinical method*. She has also published papers dealing with patient–doctor communication in *Social Science and Medicine, Family Practice: An International Journal, Canadian Medical Association Journal* and *Canadian Family Physician*. Dr Brown was a recipient of the American Academy on Physician and Patient Award for Outstanding Research in 1996. In the same year, she was made an Honorary Member of the College of Family Physicians of Canada.

Moira Stewart, PhD, is a Professor in the Department of Family Medicine and Director of the Centre for Studies in Family Medicine at The University of Western Ontario, London, Ontario, Canada. She is an epidemiologist who, for the past 25 years, has conducted research on primary care health services and on communication between patients and doctors. She has published numerous articles in *Social Science and Medicine, Medical Care, Journal of Family Practice, Family Practice: An International Journal, Canadian Medical Association Journal, Journal of the Royal College of General Practitioners* and *British Medical Journal*. She has been particularly active in fostering an international network of teachers and scientists of communication in medicine, and has published two books on the topic: *Communicating with Medical Patients* and *Patient-Centered Medicine: transforming the clinical method*. As a leader in the application of a wide variety of research methodologies in primary care, she was part of a team which sponsored five international symposia and edited five widely used books in a series called Foundations of Primary Care Research. She is an Honorary Member of the College of Family Physicians of Canada (1991), received a Woman of Distinction Award for London, Ontario (1993) and is a recipient of the American Academy on Physician and Patient Award for Outstanding Research (1996).

W Wayne Weston, MD, CCFP, FCFP, is a Professor of Family Medicine in the Faculty of Medicine, The University of Western Ontario, London, Ontario, Canada. After graduating from The University of Toronto in 1964, he practiced in Tavistock, Ontario, for 10 years before joining the faculty at Western. He has a special interest in patient–physician communication and faculty development and has been a leader in the development of two large educational projects involving the five Ontario medical schools – the EFPO (Educating Future Physicians for Ontario) Project and Project CREATE (Curriculum Renewal and Evaluation of Addiction Training and Education). He has published over 120 articles and book chapters in such journals as *Canadian Family Physician*, *Canadian Medical Association Journal* and *Academic Medicine*. He has led over 200 workshops for faculty on patient-centered interviewing, problem-based learning and clinical teaching in Canada, New Zealand, Scotland and the United States. He received the Award for Excellence in Teaching from the University of Western Ontario, the Dean's award of excellence for teaching, the prestigious 3M Award for Excellence in Teaching in Canada and is the first recipient of the McWhinney award for education presented by the College of Family Physicians of Canada and the first family physician to receive the Canadian Association for Medical Education award for distinguished contributions to medical education.

List of contributors

Martin J Bass, MD, MSc, CCFP
(deceased)
Professor and Director, Centre for Studies in Family Medicine (1986–96)
Department of Family Medicine
The University of Western Ontario
London, Ontario, Canada

John Biehn, MD, CCFP, FCFP
Professor Emeritus, Department of Family Medicine
The University of Western Ontario
London, Ontario, Canada

Lynn Brown, MSW, RSW
Lecturer (part-time), Department of Family Medicine
St Joseph's Family Medical and Dental Centre
London, Ontario, Canada

Neil R Campbell, PhD
Assistant Professor, Departments of Psychiatry and Family Medicine
LHSC-VC
London, Ontario. Canada

June C Carroll, MD, CCFP, FCFP
Associate Professor, Department of Family and Community Medicine
Sydney G Frankfort Chair in Family Medicine
Mount Sinai Hospital
Toronto, Ontario, Canada

Thomas R Freeman, MD, MClSc, CCFP, FCFP
Associate Professor and Chair, Department of Family Medicine
The University of Western Ontario
London, Ontario, Canada

Toula M Gerace, BScN, MSc
Assistant Professor (part-time), Department of Family Medicine
Byron Family Medical Centre
London, Ontario, Canada

Sharon Graham, MD, CCFP
Strathroy Medical Clinic
Strathroy, Ontario, Canada

Jo-Anne Hammond, MD, MClSc, CCFP
Assistant Professor (part-time), Department of Family Medicine
London, Ontario, Canada

Dorothy E Haswell, MB, BS, CCFP (retired)
London, Ontario, Canada

Brian K E Hennen, MD, CCFP, FCFP
Dean, Faculty of Medicine
University of Manitoba
Winnipeg, Manitoba, Canada

Lynne Hughes Marsh, BScN
Palliative Care
LHSC-WC
London, Ontario, Canada

John Jordan, MD, MClSc, CCFP, FCFP
Associate Professor, Department of Family Medicine
Byron Family Medical Centre
London, Ontario, Canada

Diana Lemaire, MSc
Department of Pediatrics, Faculty of Medicine and Dentistry
Children's Hospital of Western Ontario
London, Ontario, Canada

Barbara Lent, MD, CCFP, FCFP
Associate Professor, Department of Family Medicine
Victoria Family Medical Centre
London, Ontario, Canada

Cathy MacLean, MD, CCFP, FCFP
Associate Professor, Department of Family Medicine
Director, Undergraduate Program
Dalhousie University
Halifax, Nova Scotia, Canada

Susan M McNair, MD, CCFP, FCFP, MClSc
Associate Professor, Department of Family Medicine
St Joseph's Family Medical and Dental Centre
London, Ontario, Canada

Ian R McWhinney, OC, MD
Professor Emeritus, Department of Family Medicine
Centre for Studies in Family Medicine
The University of Western Ontario
London, Ontario, Canada

Carol L McWilliam, MScN, EdD
Professor, School of Nursing
The University of Western Ontario
London, Ontario, Canada

Christine Millman, MD, CCFP
Family Physician
Alexandria, Ontario, Canada

Joseph Morrissy, MB, ChB, CCFP, FCFP
Professor Emeritus, Department of Family Medicine
The University of Western Ontario
London, Ontario, Canada

Juan Muñoz, MD, CCFP, PhD
Assistant Professor, Department of Family Medicine
McMaster University HSC
Hamilton, Ontario, Canada

W E (Ted) Osmun, MD, MClSc, CCFP
Associate Professor, Department of Family Medicine
Southwest Middlesex Health Centre
Mt Brydges, Ontario, Canada

Marie-Claude Raymond, MD, CCFP, MClSc
HMR Unite de Medecin Familiale
Montreal, Quebec, Canada

Morrison Reid, MSW
Lecturer (part-time), Department of Family Medicine
Victoria Family Medical Centre
London, Ontario, Canada

Leslie Rourke, MD, MClSc, FAAFP, CCFP, FCFP
Assistant Professor (part-time), Department of Family Medicine
Goderich, Ontario, Canada

Bridget L Ryan, MSc
Project Co-ordinator
Centre for Studies in Family Medicine
The University of Western Ontario
London, Ontario, Canada

George Sas, MD, CM, CCFP
Assistant Professor, Department of Family Medicine
Wortley Village Family Medical Centre
London, Ontario, Canada

Tammy L Schilbe, MSW, RSW
School Social Worker
London District Catholic School Board
London, Ontario, Canada

W Peter Scott, BA, MDiv
United Church of Canada
London, Ontario, Canada

David Snadden, MB, ChB, MClSc, FRChP
Director, Postgraduate General Practice Education
Senior Lecturer
Tayside Centre for General Practice
University of Dundee
Dundee, Scotland

Mary Pat Tillmann, MSW, MD, CCFP
Consultant in Family Medicine
King Faisal Specialist Hospital and Research Center
Riyadh, Saudi Arabia

Stephen J Wetmore, BSc, MSc, MD, MClSc, CCFP, FCFP
Associate Professor, Department of Family Medicine
Victoria Family Medical Centre
London, Ontario, Canada

John Yaphe, MD, MClSc
Lecturer, Department of Family Medicine
Rabin Medical Center and Sackler School of Medicine
Tel Aviv University
Tel Aviv, Israel

Acknowledgments

This book represents the accumulation of patient stories over a span of many years. Without question, they are stories that challenge us and make us reflect on clinical practice. We are grateful to our colleagues who have been willing to share with us their experiences with patients, both positive and negative. We have also been the proud recipients of patients' stories which are reflected in other cases.

Sincere thanks are extended to Dr Brian K E Hennen, Chair of the Department of Family Medicine (from 1987 to 1999), The University of Western Ontario, and the late Dr Martin J Bass, Director of the Centre for Studies in Family Medicine (from 1986 to 1996), for creating an environment which encouraged our writing.

We thank Magda Catani for her secretarial co-ordination of this project; her devotion and thoroughness have been outstanding. The editorial expertise of Pat Morden, of Morden Communications Inc, has enhanced this manuscript. The assistance of the Canadian Library of Family Medicine in this project has been exceptional. Andrea Burt's aid in the final stages of preparing the manuscript is greatly appreciated.

Finally, we would like to thank the Committee on Medical Care and Practice of the Ontario Medical Association (OMA) and the *Ontario Medical Review*, the official publication of the OMA, for providing us with the opportunity to share the patients' stories in the column 'A Time to Talk, A Time to Listen' over an eight-year period and for supporting the publication of this book.

Dedication

This book is dedicated to Dr Ian R McWhinney, our mentor, whose wise counsel has lead us to a greater appreciation of the patient's illness experience.

Introduction

Patients often complain that doctors don't listen. This book is an attempt to help doctors listen and, as a result, to be more effective.

The book presents case examples of the many problems encountered in patient–doctor interactions and provides some ideas for dealing with these problems more effectively. It does not address every concern but highlights those common in day-to-day practice. What makes these vignettes important and useful is that they are based, in large part, on real situations – situations that we have all encountered and wondered how to handle. The 'solutions' we offer are not particularly new or novel but they are, we believe, a picture of how medicine needs to be practiced today. We hope to challenge you, to stimulate you to think and, most of all, to listen, in a new and fruitful manner.

For 20 years, the Patient–Doctor Communication Group at the Centre for Studies in Family Medicine, Department of Family Medicine, The University of Western Ontario (UWO), has been developing and testing a method of practice that integrates the traditional medical model with a patient-centered approach that endeavours to understand the patient's unique experience of illness. The patient-centered clinical method was initially introduced to our department at UWO by Dr Joseph Levenstein, who was a visiting professor in 1982. A subsequent program of education, research and conceptual development led to a body of work described in *Patient-Centered Medicine: transforming the clinical method* (Stewart *et al.*, 1995). The patient-centered method, first described in Stewart *et al.* (1995), is outlined below and consists of six interactive components to be considered in every patient–physician interaction.

Component I: Exploring Both the Disease and the Illness Experience

The first component is to assess the two modes of ill health: disease and illness. In addition to assessing the disease process by history and physical examination, the doctor explores the patient's illness experience. Specifically, the doctor considers how the patient feels about being ill, what the patient's ideas are about the illness, what impact the illness is having on the patient's functioning and what he or she expects from the physician.

Component II: Understanding the Whole Person

The second component is to integrate the concepts of disease and illness with an understanding of the whole person. This includes an awareness of the patient's position in the lifecycle and the social context in which they live.

Component III: Finding Common Ground

The third component of the method is the mutual task of finding common ground between the patient and the doctor. This consists of three key areas: mutually defining the problem; mutually defining the goals of management/ treatment; and mutually exploring the roles to be assumed by the patient and the doctor.

Component IV: Incorporating Prevention and Health Promotion

The fourth component is to use each visit as an opportunity for prevention and health promotion.

Component V: Enhancing the Patient–Doctor Relationship

The fifth component is that each encounter with the patient should be used to develop the patient–doctor relationship. The trust and respect that evolve in the relationship will have an impact on other components of the method.

Component VI: Being Realistic

The sixth component requires that, throughout the process, the physician is realistic in terms of time, availability of resources and the amount of emotional and physical energy needed.

Why is practicing patient-centered medicine important?

Research has shown that the components of the patient-centered approach have positive relationships with a variety of worthy outcomes such as patient recovery, emotional health, physical function and physiologic outcomes (Stewart, 1995). Other outcomes documented in another review include: patient satisfaction, patient adherence, physician satisfaction, fewer malpractice complaints and time (Stewart *et al.*, 1996). Also, programs which encouraged patients and physicians to communicate in a more patient-centered way have resulted in improved patient outcomes (Evans *et al.*, 1987; Greenfield *et al.*, 1985; Kaplan *et al.*, 1989a, b; Roter *et al.*, 1995).

On a more practical level, the patient-centered method is valuable to physicians for several reasons. First, the model is a reasonable representation of the realities of medical practice. By providing a useful framework the model guides physicians in their complex work of caring for patients. Because the method grew out of medical practice, rather than being borrowed from other disciplines, it has immediate applicability for both novice as well as experienced physicians.

Secondly, the patient-centered method applies to the majority of interactions between patients and doctors. It is not geared only towards counseling or interviewing but can be employed with patients of all ages with a variety of concerns.

Thirdly, it describes what doctors do when they are functioning well with their patients and therefore it supplies a conceptual framework for physicians in their daily practice. The patient-centered method is more than an exhortation to be more caring; it describes specific behaviors that need to be learned and explains when and how to use them with patients. Because the model is explicit about the behavior of an effective doctor, it also provides a vocabulary and a focus for teaching and learning.

About the cases

While each case illustrates one or more of the components of the patient-centered clinical method, every vignette has within its story all aspects of the method. This reflects the interactive and dynamic nature of the patient-centered clinical method and illustrates how physicians must shift from one component of the method to another as they follow patients' cues. The analogy is with a dance: as one partner responds to the tempo and nuances of the music, the other follows and vice versa. The mutual rhythm that is created is influenced by the environment or context in which the 'dance' or interaction takes place.

The names and many identifying characteristics of the individuals portrayed in the vignettes have been changed to protect confidentiality. All these stories are based on real experiences, most often described by the healthcare provider. In some instances, the stories have originated from patients' or family members' own personal experiences. From our perspective these stories have tremendous validity and value; they exemplify the human qualities of suffering, conflict and perseverance. On many occasions we are privileged to witness the patient's triumph over tragic and troubled circumstances. Time and time again, we see the critical role of communication in these triumphs. When we take time to listen – to give value to people's stories, their fears, their angst and their sorrow – we gain a deeper and more thorough appreciation of their suffering and the listening ultimately provides direction in the process of healing.

Component I: Understanding Both the Patient's Disease and Illness Experience

Judith Belle Brown, W Wayne Weston and Moira Stewart

The basis of the patient-centered clinical method is to both understand and distinguish between two conceptualizations of ill health: disease and illness. Effective patient care requires equal attention to patients' personal experiences of illnesses as well as their diagnoses or diseases. Disease is diagnosed by using the conventional biomedical model but understanding illness requires a broader approach. Disease can be defined as an abstraction, explaining sickness in terms of pathophysiology: abnormal structure and function of tissues and organs. This model is a conceptual framework for understanding the biological dimensions of sickness by reducing sickness to disease. The focus is on the body, not the person. In contrast, illness is the patient's personal experience of sickness – the feelings, thoughts, experiences and altered behaviors of someone who feels unwell.

A particular disease is what everyone with that disease has in common but the illness experience of each person is unique. Disease and illness do not always co-exist. Patients with undiagnosed asymptomatic disease are not ill; people who are grieving or worried may feel ill but have no disease. Patients and doctors who recognize this distinction and who realize how common it is to feel ill and have no disease are less likely to search needlessly and fruitlessly for pathology. Even when disease is present, however, it may not adequately explain the patient's suffering, because the amount of distress a patient experiences refers not only to the amount of tissue damage but to the personal meaning of the illness.

Several authors have described this same distinction between disease and illness from different perspectives. Mishler (1984) described two contrasting

---

Note: Parts of this chapter were published in *Canadian Family Physician* 1989; **35**: 147–51 and in *Patient-Centered Medicine: transforming the clinical method*, Sage Publications, 1995.

voices: the voice of medicine and the voice of the lifeworld. The voice of medicine, on the one hand, promotes a scientific, detached attitude and uses questions such as: 'Where does it hurt? When did it start? How long does it last? What makes it better or worse?'. The voice of the lifeworld, on the other hand, reflects a 'common-sense' view of the world. It centers on the individual's particular social context, the meaning of illness events and how these may affect the achievement of personal goals. Typical questions to ask in exploring the lifeworld are: 'What are you most concerned about? How does it disrupt your life? What do you think it is? How do you think I can help you?'.

Mishler (1984, p. 192) notes that in order to understand, diagnose and treat patients' problems doctors must give priority to patients' experience of illness and not be blinded by their own technocratic perspective. Eric Cassell (1985) has a similar message, observing that the patient's story of illness has two aspects: the body and the person. Only when the physician understands both does the full meaning of the illness experience become known. Yet the danger, Cassell notes, is the growing reliance on both technology and knowledge about the pathophysiology of disease, which often divert the physician's attention from the patient's illness experience.

For over 20 years researchers have emphasized the importance that patients assign to the meaning of their illness (Galazka and Eckert, 1986; Katon and Kleinman, 1981; Kleinman *et al.* 1978). These 'explanatory models' represent the thoughts, ideas or theories that patients hold in regard to their experience of being sick. Specific questions can be used to elicit the patients' experience. For example: the physician might ask: 'How would you describe the problem that has brought you to me? Does anyone else that you know have these problems? What do you think is causing the problem? Why do you think this problem has happened to you and why now? What do you think will clear up this problem? Apart from me, who else do you think can help you get better?' (Good and Good, 1981).

The seminal work of the authors cited above has guided us in formulating four key dimensions of the illness experience and provided direction in how to inquire about patients' illness experiences.

Four dimensions of the illness experience

Patients often provide physicians with cues and prompts, which may be verbal or non-verbal, about why they are seeking help on that particular occasion. Patients may appear sad, sigh deeply or be short of breath. They may say directly: 'I am worried, Doctor. Could my headache mean I have a brain tumor?'. Or, indirectly, they may present a variety of vague complaints that are indicative of a significant illness such as depression. It is essential that doctors ask their patients: 'What brings you in today?'. Concurrently, doctors must ask themselves: 'What has precipitated this patient's visit?'.

Patient-centered physicians address four dimensions of the illness experience:

- patients' feelings, especially their fears, about their problems
- their ideas about what is wrong
- the effect of the illness on their daily functioning
- their expectations of the doctor.

When physicians explore these dimensions of the illness experience, patients are more likely to be satisfied with their doctors, more likely to comply with the treatment recommendations and also more likely to recover (Stewart, 1995).

What are the patients' *feelings*? Are they anxious that their symptoms represent the onset of a chronic illness such as multiple sclerosis? Patients often experience feelings of resentment, anger or guilt when they are ill. Others may feel a sense of relief and view the illness as an opportunity for respite from demands or responsibilities.

What are the patient's *ideas* about their illness? How do they understand what is happening to them? What meaning do they assign to this experience of being sick? Many persons endure illness as an unbearable loss; in contrast, it may be viewed as an opportunity to make significant changes in their life. Alternatively illness may be seen as a form of punishment or, perhaps, as an opportunity for dependency. Whatever the illness, knowing its meaning is paramount for understanding the patient.

What are the effects of the illness on *function*? Does it limit the patient's daily activities? Does it impair their family relationships? Does it require a change in lifestyle? Does it jeopardize their financial security? Does it impair their role in society? Knowing patients' level of function has implications for future management.

What are their *expectations* of the doctor? Does the presentation of a headache carry with it an expectation of an MRI? Do they want the doctor to do something or just listen? Are they seeking reassurance or an answer?

The following examples of patient–doctor dialogue contain specific questions that physicians might ask to elicit this information.

To the doctor's question: 'What brings you in today?' a patient responds: 'I've had these severe stomach pains for the last few weeks. I'm wondering if there is something that I can do about them'. The patient's feelings about the abdominal pain can be elicited by questions such as: 'What are your concerns about the abdominal pain? Do you think that something specific is causing the pain? Is there something particularly worrisome for you about these stomach pains?'.

To examine the patient's ideas about the stomach pains, the physician might ask (waiting after each question for the patient's reply): 'What do you think is causing the pain? Have you any ideas or theories about why you might be having them? Do you think there is any relationship between the stomach pain and current events in your life?'.

To determine how the abdominal pain may be impeding the patient's function, the doctor might ask: 'How are your stomach pains affecting your day-to-day living? Are they stopping you from participating in any activities? Is there any connection between the stomach pain and the way your life is going?'.

Finally, to identify the patient's expectations of the physician at this visit, the doctor might enquire: 'What do you think would help you to deal with these stomach pains? Is there some specific management that you want for your pain? In what way may I help you? Have you a particular test in mind? What do you think would reassure you about these stomach pains?'.

Certain illnesses or events in the lives of individuals may cause them embarrassment or emotional discomfort. As a result, patients may not always feel at ease with themselves or their physician and may cloak their primary concerns in myriad symptoms. The doctor must, on occasion, respond to each of these symptoms to create an environment in which patients may feel more trusting and comfortable about exposing their concerns. Often, the doctor will provide them with an avenue to express their feelings by commenting: 'I sense that there is something troubling you or something more is going on. Can I help you with that?'. Finally, identifying the key questions to be asked should not be taken lightly. Malterud (1994), in describing a method for clinicians to formulate and evaluate the wording of key questions, emphasizes that the wording of questions should be comfortable for the doctor and suited to the patient's context.

Preview of the cases

The following cases illustrate how doctors can explore both the disease and the illness experience. The initial case highlights the four dimensions of the illness experience from the perspective of a family grappling with the impact of a family member's chronic illness on their lives. The second case examines the role of religious faith in relation to the experience of being ill. The third case presentation explores how patients' prior experiences with illness influence their willingness to accept a diagnosis and the subsequent patient role.

In order to help chronically ill older patients retain their independence and dignity we need to understand their experiences of loss, as illustrated in case 4, and how the illness affects their relationships, as described in the fifth case.

The next three cases examine the patient's illness experience from quite diverse perspectives: the trauma of a woman who has been sexually assaulted;

the challenges of caring for a patient when the patient is a doctor; and the meaning of pain for a dying patient.

The final case is presented in two parts and serves as an introduction to the next component, understanding the whole person. It begins with the diagnosis of a chronic disease, diabetes, and examines the doctor's exploration of the patient's unique response to the experience of illness. In Part 2 we see how the diagnosis results in a serious crisis for the patient, which is ultimately resolved by the physician's understanding of the whole person.

Cases Illustrating Component I: Understanding Both the Patient's Disease and Illness Experience

The family's illness experience

Judith Belle Brown, Lynn Brown, W Wayne Weston and Moira Stewart

Understanding family members' experience of illness can be achieved by explor-
ing four key dimensions: their feelings about the illness; their ideas regarding the
diagnosis and subsequent management; the impact of the illness on the family's
functioning; and finally, each family member's expectations of the doctor.

When Shannon and Andrew, both from large, closely knit, Irish Catholic
families, decided to have their third child, life felt secure and positive. Both had
steady employment and their two children Robert, four, and Sean, nine, were
well and happy. The pregnancy was uneventful until the beginning of the third
trimester when Shannon experienced severe bleeding resulting in an emergency
caesarean section. Born prematurely, the baby underwent numerous medical
crises, including two cardiac arrests. Her recovery was slow and as the months
passed, her development seriously lagged. After many investigations a diagnosis
of cerebral palsy was confirmed.

The family had not experienced serious illness in the past and was devastated
by the diagnosis. The following are examples of questions which helped Dr Feldman, their family doctor, to understand the impact of the traumatic diagnosis
on Shannon and Andrew.

'Can you tell me how you're both feeling about what's been happening with
your baby?' Dr Feldman asked.

'I just keep thinking about how this is hitting Shannon,' Andrew replied. 'She
feels like it's all her fault.'

Turning to Shannon, the doctor inquired: 'Shannon ... how is it for you?'

'I know it doesn't make sense,' Shannon replied tearfully, 'but I keep thinking there must have been something I could have done to prevent this from
happening.'

Note: This case description first appeared in the November 1994 issue of the *Ontario Medical
Review* and is reprinted with the permission of the Ontario Medical Association.

From this exchange Dr Feldman gained initial insight into Andrew's protectiveness of his wife and Shannon's guilt regarding the diagnosis of cerebral palsy.

Dr Feldman continued: 'How are you making sense of all that has happened?'

'Well, I have this terrible feeling that it was the stress of work that brought on the bleeding,' Shannon replied. 'But my job is a thing of the past – all my time is now devoted to the baby.'

This understanding of the couple's ideas about the illness then lead the doctor to inquire about the impact of the illness on the family functioning.

'Problems like this often preoccupy parents so much that they have no time for each other,' she said. 'Has that been a problem for you?'

'It's hard,' Shannon replied, 'but we have found out how important it is to have time just for ourselves. In a way, this crisis has brought us closer together.'

'I'm really glad to hear that,' Dr Feldman replied. 'You both deserve a lot of credit for being so supportive of one another ... Please let me know if you find that this is putting a strain on your marriage. You said a moment ago that all your time is devoted to the baby. How are your boys responding to this change and to their little sister?'

'The nine-year-old is really trying to help,' Andrew replied. 'But Robert, who is four, just clings to me when I get home from work.'

These questions reveal that while the medical crisis has brought the couple together, the family, as a whole, has experienced some challenges.

Finally, Dr Feldman asked Shannon and Andrew about their expectations of her.

'Given everything you are facing and all the challenges ahead, I was wondering how I can best be of help to you.'

'Well, right now, just knowing that you are here and willing to help us through it ... that's what matters to me,' said Shannon.

'If you can help Shannon to stop blaming herself,' said Andrew. 'That would really make a difference.'

There are many common, and predictable, responses of family members to illness in one member. But each family is unique or may respond in unexpected ways. It is important to explore the impact of illness on each family member (Maurer and Strasberg, 1989). This can be achieved by inquiring about four key dimensions of the illness experience (FIFE):

1 the family members' Feelings about the illness
2 their Ideas regarding the diagnosis and its meaning to them
3 how the illness is affecting the family's Functioning
4 their Expectations of the doctor regarding management.

Families will demonstrate a wide range of feelings in response to the illness of a family member, such as fear, anxiety, shame, anger, loss and mourning.

Questions to elicit feelings about a family member's illness can be as simple as: 'How do you feel about what is happening? What worries you the most about the diagnosis? How will it change your family life?'. All family members need an opportunity to express their feelings and, most importantly, their fears about what the illness means to them.

Families will also have numerous ideas or theories about why the illness has happened. It will be determined, in many instances, by their beliefs, attitudes, opinions and values. The family's responses to the illness may be passive or proactive. For example, some families may be stoical and view the diagnosis fatalistically, while others may perceive the illness as an opportunity to change lifestyle behaviors. Families may react to the illness based on pre-determined cultural beliefs: the illness may represent punishment, relief, escape, loss of control, revenge or growth. Making sense of the family's illness experience must occur in the context of their belief system.

The impact of the illness on the family's functioning is also important. Specific questions which may help the doctor learn more about how the family is coping with the illness include: 'How is the illness affecting your family's day-to-day living? What changes has the illness imposed on your family? How has the illness altered your family's roles and responsibilities? What are you doing now that you didn't do before? What are you not doing that you used to do?'. Also, a question which focuses on adaptive family changes, depending on where the family is in the process of acceptance, might be: 'What have you learned about yourselves as a family in dealing with this illness?'.

Other questions include the family members' expectations of the doctor. Do they anticipate a cure for their family member or do they realize that the best the doctor can do is provide symptomatic relief and compassionate care? The doctor can inquire of the family: 'How can I help you with this problem? In what way can I be of help to your family? What would be the most helpful thing I can do for you at this time?'.

In the interaction described above, the doctor asked questions that addressed all four dimensions. By exploring the family's feelings, ideas, current functioning and expectations, she was able to develop an understanding of the family's experience of the illness.

Religious faith and the illness experience

*Judith Belle Brown, Moira Stewart,
W Wayne Weston and W Peter Scott*

To help a patient deal with the dying process, the physician must be aware of the patient's religious affiliation and beliefs. When these beliefs differ from those of the physician, she must be able to acknowledge and accept the differences.

'Doctor, God will not let me die. He will cure my cancer,' said Mary, a 62-year-old patient, on her admission to the palliative care unit. A woman of strong religious convictions, Mary firmly believed that God would perform a miracle and cure her. The purpose of the miracle, she explained, was not to save her life, as she was 'prepared for death', but to convince her husband of God's existence. She was reluctant to receive medical intervention but finally agreed to medication for pain control. The doctor responsible for her care found her refusal of treatment frustrating and difficult to accept.

Terminal illness frequently triggers spiritual questions such as 'Why me?' and 'What is life all about?'. A central theme of all religions is the mystery of human suffering. The patient's religious affiliation and beliefs may be most helpful at a time of great need and for this reason should not be ignored by the physician.

However, there may be a significant difference, or even a conflict, between the patient's beliefs and those of the doctor (Weston and Brown, 1989). This can cause discomfort for both and may severely impede their communication. The doctor, through self-awareness and understanding, must have the ability to acknowledge and accept differences in beliefs.

This can be difficult. Medical training and philosophical orientation have been directed toward scientific understanding and generally ignore questions

Note: This case description first appeared in the September 1990 issue of the *Ontario Medical Review* and is reprinted with the permission of the Ontario Medical Association.

about the meaning of the patient's suffering. Also, the physician's own personal struggle and search for meaning may blur the issues. Painful personal experiences or current spiritual concerns may hamper the doctor's capacity to listen and remain open to the patient's concerns.

Despite these powerful professional and personal influences, doctors believe that they have the right and responsibility to inquire about religion in medical practice, particularly in the context of terminal illness. Patients' religious beliefs are central to their well-being and can influence the patient's choice of a physician and the maintenance of the patient–doctor relationship.

In this case, were Mary's statements expressions of her faith or a reflection of her denial? The physician had been trained to look for pathology. He was concerned that the patient was using her religious beliefs or ideas as a form of denial. Although Mary said that she was prepared to die, the doctor wondered if her hope for a miracle was a way to avoid dealing with the pain of her own impending death. If doctors or other health professionals decide to confront patients about such denial, it must be done in a way that does not violate the patient's beliefs or show disrespect for her faith. We must guard against leaving patients defenceless at a time of such potential physical, psychological or spiritual catastrophe.

Buckman (1988), in a book written for lay caregivers, raises several pertinent points. He suggests that the caregiver:

- assesses the patient's needs from a physical, psychological and social perspective
- is reliable and consistent in providing time for the patient to talk and the caregiver to listen
- involves other people.

Buckman writes: 'This is no time to convert someone to your view of the world. If the patient's religious beliefs happen to differ from yours, as long as they work for the patient, honour and support them'.

In the case we are discussing, the doctor must be aware of Mary's religious beliefs and how these beliefs might help her and her family to cope with the dying process. If we are not comfortable in discussing religious matters with our patients, either because of unresolved conflicts or lack of knowledge, we have the responsibility to find someone who is. This may be a pastoral care representative, the patient's clergy or another member of the healthcare team.

Responding to the illness experience

John Jordan and Judith Belle Brown

Prior experiences with illness may result in some people being fearful of assuming the role of patient. Consequently, they may disagree with or even refuse the physician's recommended treatment. This is not a rejection of the doctor's expertise but rather a reflection of the patient's own anxiety. Doctors need to respond with flexibility and understanding.

A routine letter requesting health information for insurance purposes arrived on Dr Robertson's desk one morning, accompanied by the patient's signed authorization for release of information to the insurance company. Mrs Dubois, a 68-year-old woman in the practice for 10 years, had applied for some life insurance. As was his usual practice, Dr Robertson had the chart pulled for review, to forward on the appropriate information to the insurance company. The doctor noticed that Mrs Dubois had had an elevated random blood glucose four months earlier. A note on the chart indicated that Mrs Dubois had been asked to come to the lab for a fasting blood glucose determination. However, there was no record of a follow-up blood test in her chart, nor had Mrs Dubois been back to the office since that time.

Concerned by this information, Dr Robertson telephoned Mrs Dubois. He explained that before he could provide information to the insurance company, Mrs Dubois would need to have a fasting blood glucose test. Mrs Dubois asked why it was necessary, as she felt quite well. The doctor said this was the usual practice after an abnormal blood glucose result, such as the one she had had a few months earlier. Dr Robertson asked Mrs Dubois to arrange an appointment to see him later that week and then he would review the blood test results with her. Reluctantly, Mrs Dubois agreed to the doctor's request.

Note: This case description first appeared in the February 1996 issue of the *Ontario Medical Review* and is reprinted with the permission of the Ontario Medical Association.

Mrs Dubois came into the office as arranged, polite and courteous as always. A soft-spoken and somewhat shy woman, Mrs Dubois had been widowed three years earlier when her husband had a second stroke.

'How are you today, Mrs Dubois?' asked the doctor.

'I'm just fine, thanks,' said Mrs Dubois. 'I'm looking forward to spending the holidays with my daughter's family. The nurse took my blood pressure today and said it was good.'

'Mrs Dubois, I asked you to come in today because I was concerned about the results of the blood test you had done a few months ago,' said the doctor, 'and I thought it was important to re-check your blood glucose before breakfast. You had that test done yesterday morning and the result came back at 16. That's quite high. It suggests that you have developed adult-onset diabetes.'

'But how could this happen? I feel fine,' she said, sounding upset. 'There must be some mistake. I couldn't have diabetes!'

Dr Robertson explained to Mrs Dubois the meaning of an elevated blood glucose. He recommended that she increase her activity level and make appropriate changes to her diet in order to lower her blood glucose. He also speculated that Mrs Dubois would probably need to start oral hypoglycemics to bring her blood glucose into the normal range. He suggested an appointment with the diabetic education center to help Mrs Dubois in the management of her diabetes.

To his surprise, Mrs Dubois politely refused. 'I'm sorry Dr Robertson, but I don't want to go to the diabetic education center and I don't think I should take medication. It didn't help my husband.'

The doctor was puzzled by the patient's response. He had proposed what he thought was a reasonable plan of management: to receive diabetic counseling about diet and lifestyle modifications, as well as to begin oral hypoglycemics to keep her blood glucose at less than 10. He knew Mrs Dubois was quite familiar with the disease as her husband had been diabetic for several years prior to his death three years earlier. Yet, Mrs Dubois refused to be treated herself. Dr Robertson needed to understand her reluctance more fully. Mrs Dubois's husband had been chronically ill for several years, disabled by a stroke. In addition, he had suffered from diabetes, hypertension and coronary artery disease. Mrs Dubois had been her husband's primary caretaker, devoting all her time and energy to his care until the time of his death. She had come to believe that the treatment her husband received had not helped to maintain or maximize his health; in fact, she thought of it as a marker of poor health and declining status.

Mrs Dubois believed that to agree to treatment would signal that her health was failing and she feared that a decline in her health would be precipitated by the very fact of receiving treatment.

'I'm sorry I won't take the treatments you've suggested', she said to the doctor. 'I just don't want to think about diabetes right now.'

Aware of past experiences and present concerns, the doctor acknowledged it was perhaps too painful for her to contemplate the diagnosis of diabetes at this time. 'Will you still see me as a patient if I change my mind or decide at some time to come back to discuss the matter further?' Mrs Dubois asked.

Dr Robertson didn't hesitate. 'Of course I'll see you. In fact, I'd like to see you when you get back from holidays to see how you are doing.'

This case demonstrates several key communication issues. First, the doctor's approach was not to argue or coerce the patient into accepting the diagnosis or treatment plan. However, it was important for the doctor to provide the patient with the information necessary for her to know before making a decision. The doctor needed to understand the various factors contributing to her decision-making process.

Secondly, the doctor, armed with a deeper knowledge of the patient's personal experience with illness, was able to acknowledge and accept her difficulty in coming to terms with the diagnosis of a chronic illness. When patients disagree with or even refuse the doctor's recommended treatment, they are often fearful that the physician will respond with disapproval or rejection.

As this case demonstrates, the patient's reasons for refusing treatment are often rooted in past experiences. By validating the patient's emotional difficulty in 'becoming a patient', based on the hardships she experienced in relation to her husband's chronic illness, the doctor was able to provide the patient with support and understanding.

Thirdly, the doctor made it clear that he was willing to see the patient again, no matter what her decision about the proposed treatment. He was prepared to listen to her concerns, help her to reflect on her feelings about her husband's illness and explore the impact of this experience on her own healthcare.

In summary, doctors need to be responsive and flexible to patients, allowing some latitude as to how, when and to what extent they decide to accept medical care. This approach requires considering how past experiences of illness impact on present decisions.

4

Major life events and the illness experience

Carol L McWilliam, Judith Belle Brown and Susan M McNair

Patients' physical problems frequently overshadow a underlying contributor to their experience of illness. As a result, physicians can miss the vital connection between presenting problems and a prior life experience.

Mrs Farraday, a 70-year-old woman, had lived alone since the loss of her husband 15 years ago. Her widowhood had been lonely and over the years she had become more and more socially isolated. In the last year Mrs Farraday's many physical complaints, related to her chronic obstructive pulmonary disease, ischemic heart disease, diabetes and glaucoma, had intensified. While not requiring extensive medical treatment, the symptoms served as her ticket of entry into the healthcare system.

Mrs Farraday most often arrived in the emergency department by ambulance and quickly gained a negative reputation. She became well known to a great variety of health professionals, who described her as 'complaintive', 'dependent' or 'difficult'. A psychogeriatric assessment revealed that Mrs Farraday showed no evidence of acute psychiatric illness. Health professionals involved in her care believed that she 'just needed to get out and meet people'.

Treatment of Mrs Farraday's medical problems focused on immediate attention to presenting signs and symptoms. The attending internist explained:

'Her chest is chronic, and it is going to remain chronic. It is not really going to get much better, and it is not going to get much worse unless she gets pneumonia. So, she turns up in emergency, and we bail her out for a few days and discharge her as fast as possible.'

Mrs Farraday's family physician tried to keep her out of hospital, initially attempting to address her needs, both physical and emotional, through house calls. His comments reflect his concern and frustration:

> 'This particular case is very, very difficult. She has made the rounds to every hospital and had numerous admissions. None of those admissions were medically necessary. In making house calls, I have found that she just wants a person to sit and listen. But I cannot do that all the time. I just can't close the office door and drive down to visit with her for 15–20 minutes. My time is under pressure!'

This case seems to contain an insoluble problem, one that is not appropriately addressed through traditional medical interventions. However, understanding Mrs Farraday's illness in the context of the loss of her husband sheds new light on how her problems could be approached. Attending to her needs in a more meaningful and useful way might alleviate symptoms, reducing unnecessary office visits and the frequency of hospitalization.

Over a period of time, Mrs Farraday's family doctor, Dr Hasse, discovered that unresolved grief was part of her illness experience. She had been a very healthy and active woman, who enjoyed going for long walks and was involved in the local community center. Her health problems had begun when her husband died unexpectedly 15 years ago. They had relied heavily on each other and his death was a significant loss for Mrs Farraday. On the anniversary of his death her physical complaints were often exacerbated. Dr Hasse observed: 'She just seems to want to reach out and cling to someone'.

In talking to the doctor, Mrs Farraday confessed to a tremendous need for '. . . a true friend . . . someone who wants to really help and doesn't make empty promises'.

She also spoke of her anger and frustration with her various healthcare professionals. 'Old people are really sick or they wouldn't be here, and doctors and nurses should quit treating them like little children or senile people!' Although Mrs Farraday could not initially make the connection between her frequent demands for treatment of her symptoms and her need to be cared for as a human being, she was aware that her current medical care was not meeting her needs.

Dr Hasse persisted in exploring Mrs Farraday's life experience. He learned that she was used to being independent and assertive. As a young adult, Mrs Farraday had had the courage to leave an abusive marriage and set out on her own, supporting herself for many years as a clerical worker. In her middle adulthood, Mrs Farraday had remarried a 'kindred spirit' and lived happily with him for eight years. His death had shattered her and depleted her energy for living.

Working with this newly gained understanding, Dr Hasse was able to establish an appropriate plan of care, directed towards resolving her grief and re-establishing her independence. As a result, Mrs Farraday's illness experience was significantly modified, her signs and symptoms responded more readily to treatment and her energy for living was restored.

The doctor worked to understand the whole patient – her disease, illness and life experience. That allowed him to provide the missing connection and help her regain her interest in life.

Patients expect healthcare professionals to understand and therapeutically respond to their many interpersonal and relational needs (Montgomery, 1993). Patient-centered care fosters caring communication and promotes attention to all aspects affecting the patient's well-being. Such caring has been observed to help heal the pain and emotional anguish associated with loss, including the loss of loved ones (Montgomery, 1993). Among the requirements of caring, Mayeroff (1971) identifies the importance of acquiring knowledge of the other, understanding that person's needs, having courage to follow their lead into the unknown territories of need and offering hope that the person will grow through caring.

Only by using a patient-centered approach to assess a patient's illnesses in their larger life context can we hope to understand what at first glance appears to be a senseless abuse of medical services. Taking time to listen to the patient's story helps us to discover important connections, leading to improved care.

5

Chronically ill seniors

Carol L McWilliam, Judith Belle Brown and W Wayne Weston

Developing an effective plan of care for chronically ill older patients often requires that the doctor understand the meaning of the illness experience not only for the patient, but also for the patient's spouse. Frequently, the feelings and fears each has about the illness affect the dynamics of their relationship and how they deal with chronic problems. When the doctor elicits a mutual understanding of the illness experience, patient, spouse and doctor can share common goals for care.

Geoffrey Sampson, aged 86, had been greatly weakened by several severe bouts of colitis ultimately necessitating a colostomy. Repeated hospitalizations for dehydration and electrolyte imbalance, complicated by congestive heart failure, added to his problems. Once an accountant for a large corporation, over the course of his 26 years of retirement he had gradually withdrawn from outside interests, which had included playing the organ for his church and teaching organ lessons to several young people in the congregation. At home, Mr Sampson had long since completed the many do-it-yourself projects he had planned for his retirement and had given over all of the gardening and house-hold upkeep responsibilities to his eldest son. He spent most of his waking hours in a chair strategically placed for watching television or for observing the world go by his window.

Ada Sampson, aged 84, anxiously attended to all her husband's needs. She rarely complained about the demands his care placed on her or that her own needs were frequently neglected. Mrs Sampson had abandoned all her outside interests to devote all her energy to her husband's care. Initially, Dr Mai, their family physician, concluded that the situation was stable and relatively accep-table. The Sampsons made few requests for assistance and the doctor admired Mrs Sampson's devotion to her husband. While Mr Sampson did not appear to

Note: This case description first appeared in the February 1995 issue of the *Ontario Medical Review* and is reprinted with the permission of the Ontario Medical Association.

be making much effort to stay mobile, it seemed reasonable, given his age, that he was choosing to merely 'bide his time'.

Over the course of several office visits, however, Dr Mai began to understand the illness experience of this aging couple in a new light.

'How are you doing?' Dr Mai asked.

'Oh, I have no problem sleeping at night,' replied Mr Sampson.

'And during the day? How are you managing?' inquired Dr Mai.

'Ada always helps me get dressed. She feeds me well, tends to my colostomy, and makes sure I have everything I need,' Mr Sampson replied. He hesitated for a moment. 'I'm kind of a burden for her.'

'What makes you say that?' the doctor asked.

'Well, she has to look after me, do this and that for me.'

'Is that hard for you?'

'Well, I never had to depend on her before.'

There was a moment of silence before the doctor spoke again. 'Do you see yourself getting back to being more independent?' he asked.

'Well, I'd love to get my health back,' Mr Sampson replied, 'but there's not much I can do about it.'

Dr Mai explained the importance of attempting to walk a bit each day, hoping that Mr Sampson would follow through.

Soon after, Dr Mai saw Mrs Sampson and asked her how she was managing.

'Oh, fine,' she replied. 'I'm a very physical person, and can manage day to day, but sometimes I get a little tired and lose a bit of patience. But I meditate with the Bible, and that gives me strength. I'm not going to be sick, you know.'

Dr Mai made a mental note about the 'losing patience'. He decided to have Mr and Mrs Sampson booked in together for the next visit. Here's what happened.

'How are you two managing these days?' he asked the couple.

'Well, I took him up to the hospital for his blood work the other day,' Mrs Sampson replied, 'and they wanted to put him in a wheelchair. That's just too much! Too many people enjoy being pushed around! I think people are basically lazy, including myself, if I let myself be! When he was in hospital the last time, they told him that he was to move around more!'

'I don't understand why I should be moving around more,' said Mr Sampson resentfully. 'If I had something to move around for, okay, but to just move around for the sake of moving around! I need more rest than a young person does. It just seems at our house that there is no rest for the wicked!'

'Well, you do rest most of the day, honey,' Mrs Sampson chuckled. 'You sleep three-quarters of the day!'

'I suppose you, like that doctor in the hospital, would probably set the dog on me. That's what they do on the farm when the cattle won't move,' he said to the doctor, 'set the dog on them!'

'Oh really, Geoffrey!'

'Mrs Sampson, can you tell Geoffrey why it's important to you for him to move around?' the doctor asked.

'Yes,' she replied readily. 'I just want him to get the strength back in his legs. If you sit all the time, your muscles get weaker and weaker, and you'll never be able to do anything.'

'I don't want to sit all the time,' replied her husband huffily, 'but I don't like to be told continually to get going.'

'I don't think he gets told all the time!' said Mrs Sampson, addressing the doctor. 'Just when it's time to do it, like after he's slept for two hours.'

'I feel tired all the time,' said Mr Sampson. 'I don't have any energy. Maybe I need some pep pills.'

'I think what you, Ada, are trying to say is that a little bit of activity will help Geoffrey get stronger and maybe help him feel less tired too,' said Dr Mai. 'And I think what you, Geoffrey, are trying to say is that you would like to have more control over your own life.'

Mr and Mrs Sampson looked at one another and nodded.

Throughout these visits, Dr Mai had successfully listened to how the illness was experienced by the patient and his wife. He recognized their interdependent relationship and the importance of helping each of them to understand their problems. Subtly and sensitively, Dr Mai assisted them to understand the erosion of Mr Sampson's control over his own life as he became stuck in the sick role and his wife was caught in the caretaker role. He showed them that their married relationship had come to resemble a parent–child relationship. Finally, he helped them examine their potential and restore their usual mutually supportive relationship (Carlsen, 1991).

With Dr Mai's help, both Mr and Mrs Sampson came to see how their individual concerns and needs taxed their relationship and prevented them from working together on the problems at hand. With this newly acquired understanding, they worked out a schedule that gave Mr Sampson the dignity of control over his walking exercise. Mrs Sampson felt better, knowing they were together attending her husband's health needs. As Mr Sampson reported at a visit two months later, 'Well, I'm not out there running three-legged races, but I think I'm improving a little bit every day. And Ada seems happy again. It sure beats just biding my time!'

6

Acute assault victim

Susan M McNair and Judith Belle Brown

Sexual assault is a traumatic event for the victim, resulting in the need for immediate crisis intervention as well as attention to the long-term sequelae. Caring for acute sexual assault victims presents challenges, both short term and long term, for physicians.

Early one morning, 37-year-old Leah set out to deliver her son's newspapers. Concerned about her 13-year-old son's elevated temperature, she was anxious to complete the task quickly and return to his bedside.

Hoping to hasten the paper delivery, she set out across a dark footpath bordering an isolated field that ran behind a row of houses. Suddenly, Leah heard something behind her. Before she could respond, the assailant grabbed her and with one hand over her mouth and the other holding a knife to her throat, he told Leah to co-operate or he would kill her. She was pulled into the dark field and there, in the still of early dawn, the assailant vaginally and anally penetrated her, savagely punching her about the head and neck, then fled into the dark. Immobilized by the fear of being killed, Leah lay stunned in the wet grass. Eventually she summoned her courage and sought refuge at a nearby house.

Distraught and bleeding, Leah was brought to the local emergency department by police. Dr Anders met Leah five hours after the assault. She was exhausted and frightened. She had already related her story, in detail, to the police and seemed distressed by needing to tell her story again to Dr Anders and the nurse. Leah was overwhelmed by the complicated consent form she needed to sign for completion of the forensic examination and evidence collection. In response to her distress, Dr Anders proceeded slowly, allowing Leah an opportunity to talk about her disbelief, guilt, anger and profound grief regarding the assault.

Note: This case description first appeared in the November 1995 issue of the *Ontario Medical Review* and is reprinted with the permission of the Ontario Medical Association.

As Leah bravely told her story, she frequently broke into sobs of remorse and self-blame, questioning how she could have 'so foolishly' walked the dark path that morning. How would her husband and son ever forgive her? She seemed to tolerate the lengthy forensic examination and evidence collection remarkably well, until the pelvic examination. Then, as if she were re-experiencing the trauma, Leah fell apart, choked by uncontrollable tears. Gradually, in response to the patience and understanding expressed by both the nurse and physician, her crying eased and Leah was able to proceed with the examination.

Leah's lacerations were sutured and X-rays ruled out any facial fractures. She received medical prophylaxis for sexually transmitted diseases and pregnancy. The doctor gave her written information about the medical management she had received and offered details about follow-up. Leah was given telephone numbers of contact people who she could call if she needed support urgently. The doctor spent time discussing the myriad emotions – fear, anger, sadness – that Leah might experience in the coming days and weeks.

Leah insisted that her husband, Zack, remain at home with their ill son until her return. Although confused and concerned by the horrific attack on his wife, Zack agreed. In response to Leah's request, the staff contacted her sister to ensure that Leah did not travel home alone.

Over the next year Leah frequently saw both Dr Anders and the social worker at the hospital for support and education regarding the psychological sequelae of sexual assault. In the early weeks, she experienced insomnia, agitation and thoughts of suicide. She feared her assailant, never found, would return to find her and kill her. She also worried about her family's safety, especially that of her son. As the months passed, Leah began to recognize her own strengths and to experience the benefits of her social supports, including a close girlfriend who had previously experienced an assault. The counseling provided by the social worker also served as a central role in her healing process.

Leah's husband and son had their own special needs. They often felt alone and afraid and needed support and education about the spectrum of Leah's responses. They could not serve as her supports unless their own needs were met. Through sessions with the social worker, both husband and son were able to express their own experience of sadness, anger and confusion over the brutal and un-provoked attack on their wife and mother. With time they were able to under-stand her feelings, which promoted both their own healing and Leah's.

Treating victims of acute sexual assault presents physicians with several challenges. While knowledge and skills are required to successfully collect, document and preserve the forensic evidence, the ability to respond to the survivor's emotional turmoil is of paramount importance. The physician's response, at the time of crisis and in subsequent follow-up, plays an essential role in the patient's recovery (Calhoun and Atkeson, 1991).

In the immediate care of sexual assault victims, physicians must realize that self-blame presents a major barrier to recovery. This sense of self-blame is expressed by many victims of sexual assault and must be acknowledged and discussed, in both the short and long term. Physicians must reassure victims that their decisions were appropriate and that whatever they needed to do to survive was acceptable. Victims must not be rushed through the examination process: it may, in fact, be experienced as a further violation. Patients must be given time to make decisions about their own care and to gain some sense of control over what must seem an out-of-control experience. Finally, victims must be believed. The role of the examining physician is not to determine guilt or innocence but expertly to collect evidence and to offer compassion and high-quality care.

In the long term physicians must remain available to sexual assault survivors, to answer their questions and to offer psychological support (Cohen and Roth, 1987). Physicians must also insure adequate support and education for the family and friends of sexual assault survivors, who often struggle with their own fears, guilt, anger and profound sense of loss. Finally, physicians must remain available for one another. The fears and uncertainties that caring for acute victims of sexual assault can evoke in caregivers must not be ignored. Physicians must ensure adequate peer support and discussion to allow for continuing care of these most suffering patients.

7

Doctor as patient

W E Osmun, Judith Belle Brown and Juan Muñoz

When a doctor experiences an illness, it can be challenging for patient and physician. The patient may find it difficult to surrender control and yet still be subject to the anxieties and fears any patient experiences. The attending physician may feel uncomfortable caring for a colleague. Early in the process the attending physician should initiate an open and frank discussion to avoid confusion over roles and expectations.

Dr Ben Jorgenson had not felt well all day. What had begun as a vague abdominal pain had progressed to fever and loss of appetite. When the pain localized to the right lower quadrant, Ben feared appendicitis.

Although Ben had lived in Little Current for six years, he had never asked one of his colleagues to be his family doctor. He was, after all, a young man and had never been seriously ill. The few times he had needed medication, Jorgenson used the samples on hand in the office.

While Ben Jorgenson worked well with all his colleagues, some relationships had proven difficult, especially with Murray Myton. Hospital politics had caused a rift between them. They treated each other with a superficial politeness that fooled no one.

It was Sunday. Checking the call schedule, Ben groaned: Murray was on. Ben wondered if he could call in another physician friend, but then Murray might take offence. Ben did not want their relationship to deteriorate further. He had to work with the man.

By the time Ben arrived at the hospital he felt really ill. Ben was greeted by Rapinder, the emergency room nurse, who said, 'You don't look so hot'.

Reluctantly Ben confessed, 'I think I have appendicitis'.

Rapinder's eyebrows shot up. 'Come in, I'll get you a stretcher. Murray's busy upstairs doing a delivery...' Ben felt a wave of relief, only to have it dashed as Rapinder continued, '... but don't worry, he's almost finished.'

Note: This case description first appeared in the April 1996 issue of the *Ontario Medical Review* and is reprinted with the permission of the Ontario Medical Association.

Moments later, Murray appeared around the curtain, abruptly stating, 'I guess you want me to get someone else in'. Murray hoped Ben would say yes, admitting to his discomfort with Murray's care. Unfortunately Murray presented the question as a challenge rather than an option. Ben refused the offer of another physician.

Uncomfortable, Murray allowed Ben to control the interview. As a result Murray forgot key questions that were part of his usual routine. Not wishing to appear incompetent by returning to ask the questions, he assumed the responses would be negative. Certainly Ben, 'the patient', would have mentioned if there was anything important of note. 'After all,' Murray thought, 'he's had plenty of time to think about it, he waited long enough to come in.'

It was part of Murray's routine to ask his patients if they preferred to have their operations in Little Current or in the closest city. Murray himself would have been uncomfortable having his partners care for him and he assumed Ben felt the same way. Having a good relationship with the town's surgeon, Ben would have preferred to have stayed in Little Current but felt too ill to protest. Arrangements were made to transfer Ben by ambulance to the nearest tertiary center. Clothed only in a hospital gown, he felt surprisingly vulnerable.

Having deviated from his normal routine, Murray forgot to offer pain relief and Ben had an uncomfortable ride to the city. As a result of the delays, Ben's appendix had ruptured. He required a drain and intravenous therapy. His course of recovery was prolonged. Nevertheless, Ben returned to work 10 days after the operation. Eventually the malaise and fatigue caused him to take a further three weeks off.

Physicians find it difficult to be patients. The change in role is a challenge and a threat. Physicians' fears cause them to minimize symptoms and to self-medicate, resulting in late presentations and more complex and severe health problems.

Physicians are knowledgeable but we must remember that they are still patients with their own anxieties and fears (Pullen et al., 1995). They require the reassurance and the information needed by all patients (Ende et al., 1990). Physicians, too, are subject to irrational fears when vulnerable from illness (Stoudmeire and Rhoads, 1983).

All doctors need a personal physician. At the first interview, the treating physician and the patient should explore each other's expectations. Hurried 'corridor consultations' should be discouraged. The goal should be a relationship in which both individuals feel comfortable and trusting. Physicians do want to be treated as patients: they find it frustrating to have examinations avoided and assumptions made.

When treating a fellow physician, it is tempting to avoid the emotional component of illness and deal only with the biological aspects. Unfortunately, physicians are more prone to mental illness and addiction than the lay population. While aggressive probing into private matters may not be necessary, the attending physician should be open to discussing emotional difficulties.

The physician who is the patient also has a responsibility to the relationship. The patient should not unduly infringe on the treating physician's private time or discuss personal issues in corridors or coffee lounges. Instead of self-prescribing or ordering investigations on himself, he should discuss concerns with his personal physician.

To be chosen as a physician by a colleague is a great compliment to one's skills and knowledge. Still, some physicians may feel uncomfortable in the role, not wishing to expand a collegial relationship into a professional one. They may worry that in assuming care of another physician, their abilities will be under scrutiny by their knowledgeable patient. This can be especially difficult if the patient is a more senior or prominent physician.

If Ben and Murray had been open with one another, Ben's rocky postoperative course might have been avoided. Instead they acted on their own fears and preoccupations, bringing old emotional baggage to this new professional relationship. Murray failed to reach mutual agreement with his patient; instead he made assumptions based on his own wants. Murray identified with Ben and, seeing Ben as an extension of himself, made decisions that reflected his own concerns, not those of his patient.

A frank exchange of expectations, an adherence to routine and the courage to admit to their mutual discomfort may have resulted in a more satisfactory outcome.

8

Pain

Judith Belle Brown and Susan M McNair

Pain, particularly for the patient who is dying, may have multiple meanings. In order to understand and alleviate a patient's pain, doctors need to engage in a process of communication which includes listening, knowing, responding and taking time.

Mr Dukakis, age 78, had been a robust and active man until he was diagnosed with cancer of the prostate. The diagnosis of cancer had come as a complete shock to him; he had never imagined it could happen to him.

Mrs Dukakis was less surprised. She had known that something 'just wasn't quite right' with her husband. She described how her husband had complained for over two years of various 'aches and pains' which he had attributed to 'rheumatism'. On several occasions, she had urged him to visit the doctor but he always insisted he would be better when 'the weather got warm'. He had always enjoyed good health and held firm to the conviction that '. . . I'm not the kind of a man who runs to the doctor with such minor concerns'.

It was only when Mr Dukakis went into complete urinary retention and required hospital admission that the reality of his problem was confirmed: advanced prostatic carcinoma. When they learned the diagnosis, both Mr Dukakis and his wife responded stoically to the disturbing news. Following his discharge from hospital, the couple quietly attempted to put their shattered lives back together, making relatively few demands on the healthcare professionals involved in Mr Dukakis' care.

One day, in response to an uncharacteristic request from Mrs Dukakis, their family doctor made a house call. Dr Lewis found the patient diaphoretic and in obvious pain. He immediately offered an injectable analgesic. The patient firmly replied: 'Look Doc, I don't want any medication, it's not necessary. Give it to somebody else, not me!'

The doctor felt confused and bewildered by his patient's adamant stance. Mr Dukakis was clearly in pain. But this was not the first time the patient had

Note: This case description first appeared in the June 1994 issue of the *Ontario Medical Review* and is reprinted with the permissin of the Ontario Medical Association.

refused offers of help during the course of his illness. For example, even though it had become extremely difficult for Mr Dukakis to negotiate the stairs to their second-story bedroom, he saw no reason why a bed should be set up for him in the dining room.

'You don't sleep in a dining room,' he had exclaimed with exasperation. 'It's a place to eat, to visit with friends and family!'

A commode was out of the question but with great reluctance he had agreed to have a urinal at his bedside, 'in case of emergencies'. While Mrs Dukakis was obviously exhausted by the demands of her husband's constant care, Mr Dukakis saw no need for the services of a homemaker. 'We are managing just fine,' he would explain firmly. He finally allowed the visiting nurse to assist with his personal hygiene, but even this service he experienced as a humiliation and defeat. On several occasions Dr Lewis offered to speak to the Dukakis' adult children who lived out West. Each time Mr Dukakis said, 'Not a good time. They have busy lives and don't need to worry about us'.

Dr Lewis began to suspect a link between these rejections for help and Mr Dukakis' denial of the severity of his condition. Yet, Dr Lewis wasn't sure how to handle the situation. To openly confront Mr Dukakis' denial could be devastating and might result in deterioration of his condition. By not addressing the situation, the doctor was concerned that Mr Dukakis would continue to suffer severe and debilitating pain. In addition, Mrs Dukakis might be further compromised, both physically and emotionally, by the burden of her husband's care.

After serious consideration, Dr Lewis spoke to Mr Dukakis about his habit of refusing help. The doctor discovered that for Mr Dukakis, receiving professional help represented a loss of control. For him, accepting help and in particular taking medication was equivalent to inevitable death. Mr Dukakis explained: 'When I feel the pain, it means that I am still alive, that I have a chance'. This difficult but important interaction confirmed the suspected link between the patient's rejections of care and his denial of the illness.

The medical profession has come to recognize the dying process as a unique experience for each individual patient. However, we must continue to seek understanding of the personal meaning underlying patients' care decisions. As illustrated in this case, if we fail to understand the meaning, and potential significance, of the patient's pain we will not be able to take the necessary steps to ameliorate it.

In their qualitative study, Miller *et al.* (1994) reported the perceptions of pain by both patients and doctors. In addition, they examined the doctor's role in the 'treatment' of pain. Their findings revealed that both patients and physicians perceived the doctor's role to be a four-stage process which includes listening, knowing, responding and taking time.

This case reflects this process and emphasizes that it may take several encounters to put the process of caring into action. The doctor listened to the patient and to his own feelings. He came to know the patient beyond the expression of his physical pain and his refusal for help. The doctor's increased understanding of Mr Dukakis' experience of his illness and the significance of his pain provided alternative ways of responding and caring. Finally, the doctor took the time necessary for a quality interaction to occur. Through this communication process the patient's dignity was maintained and his pain alleviated.

9

Coming to terms with illness: 1

Cathy MacLean and Judith Belle Brown

Successful treatment of a disease is often dependent upon our ability to understand the patient and his or her experience of illness. Building trust, knowing the patient and facilitating mutual agreement about management are key elements in this process.

When Dr Carrothers walked into the examining room, she was shocked by what she saw. There sat her patient, Mr Haller, formerly a robust man of significant stature, now looking thin and defeated. Before the doctor could utter a word, the patient stated flatly, 'I have diabetes'. He went on to describe the classic symptoms of polyuria, polydipsia, increased hunger and weight loss. These were familiar symptoms to him. Both his father and uncle had been diagnosed with diabetes and had suffered from numerous complications related to the disease.

Two months prior to this visit, the patient's dentist had suggested Mr Haller make an appointment with his family physician after noticing the acetone smell of his breath. Despite this advice, marked weight loss and increasing nocturia, Mr Haller didn't make an appointment. Finally, after persistent urging from his wife, Mr Haller agreed to seek help. Examination of the patient revealed a 40-pound weight loss since his last visit and a blood sugar of 28 mmol/l.

As Mr Haller's family doctor, Dr Carrothers had come to know this 42-year-old man, his wife and their two children over the past several years. In recent months Mr Haller had experienced numerous medical problems. They began when he presented with a symptomatic inguinal hernia. Over the course of the diagnosis and referral for surgery, it became apparent that Mr Haller did not are for doctors, hospitals or 'anything to do with them'. He was afraid of needles, worried about his surgery and terrified of a general anesthetic. Mr Haller was most anxious to have Dr Carrothers assist in the surgery. Dr Carrothers

Note: This case description first appeared in the August 1995 issue of the *Ontario Medical Review* and is reprinted with the permission of the Ontario Medical Association.

readily agreed. This small act of support cemented the doctor's relationship with her patient. Developing this trust formed the basis of their ongoing relationship, which would prove to be indispensable in Mr Haller's care during the months ahead.

Mr Haller's recovery from his hernia repair was uneventful. However, a few months later, he developed abdominal pain. During the assessment of his abdominal pain, Dr Carrothers became aware of the incredible stress the family was experiencing. Their eldest child was healthy but making the transition from elementary school to junior high. Mr and Mrs Haller were facing the usual challenges of a child entering puberty. Their youngest daughter had been born premature at 34 weeks as a result of an abruptio and related complications had resulted in significant physical disabilities. In addition, Mr Haller had his own business and was often away on weekends, leaving his wife to care for the children. In order to establish the business, the family had relocated from the East, leaving them isolated from family and friends who had served as a major source of support in the past.

Remarkably, these stresses were not the underlying cause of Mr Haller's abdominal pain. The diagnosis was cholelithiasis and once again, within a few short months, Mr Haller faced another operation. He was able to undergo this operation without the presence of his family physician and recovered quickly following a laparoscopic cholecystectomy. However, it had been extremely difficult for him to face these two surgeries.

As these health problems developed, Mr Haller frequently expressed concern about losing his health, feeling vulnerable and out of control. He perceived himself as fit, powerful and athletic. He had played competitive basketball in his youth and continued to see himself as a strong, healthy man. He prided himself on his accomplishments in business, developing a reputation for being 'the best in his field'. Being married for 20 years, owning his own home and being a good provider for his family were major accomplishments for Mr Haller, who had come from a dysfunctional family. In response to his poor relationship with his own father, he was 'determined to be a good father and husband', giving his family everything he had been denied.

The diagnosis of diabetes was a catastrophic experience for Mr Haller. The reality of living with diabetes represented a crisis for this man. He was afraid, angry, depressed and overwhelmed. Mr Haller refused to be admitted to hospital and was terrified of using insulin because of his fear of needles. He had witnessed the effects of diabetes on his father and uncle and was convinced he would suffer the same long-term consequences of the disease. For Mr Haller, this was the 'final blow' from his father.

The trust established earlier in the patient–doctor relationship helped Mr Haller safely share his many feelings. By listening and encouraging discussion, the doctor assisted him in expressing his fears and concerns. In addition, she explored the impact of the diabetes on his ability to work and to fulfill his family responsibilities. Based on her prior knowledge of the patient, the doctor negotiated the management of his disease in such a way that Mr Haller was able to maintain some control in the decision making. It was critical for this patient to play an active role in this process. Initially, he agreed to be monitored carefully as an outpatient and to begin a trial of oral hypoglycemics. After this treatment approach was unsuccessful, Mr Haller began the insulin injections, despite his fear of needles. His diabetes rapidly came under control but his experience of the illness remained profound. He continued to feel unwell for several months as he grappled with the meaning of his illness. Control of Mr Haller's disease had been achieved quickly but attention to the impact of his illness was ongoing.

Mr Haller's story continues.

10

Coming to terms with illness: 2

Cathy MacLean and Judith Belle Brown

In order to respond to the crisis experienced by a patient with a newly diagnosed chronic disease, physicians need to understand the patient's life circumstances, including his or her family relationships and roles at home and in the community.

Following treatment of his diabetes, Mr Haller's blood sugars were under control within a few months. Concerned about maintaining his business, Mr Haller was anxious to return to work, yet, whenever he tried to start working again, he experienced 'reactions'. During these 'reactions', he became shaky and light-headed and felt as if he was about to pass out, despite normal blood sugars. These symptoms, coupled with the uncertainty of their origin, caused Mr Haller and his family tremendous anxiety.

Being in control had been a central objective in Mr Haller's life. Now he was struggling to control his diabetes. He was anxious to learn everything he could about diabetes. He requested literature at every office visit and attended diabetic education classes, voraciously consuming every available detail about the disease. His need for control was reflected in his decisions about when to start rotating his injection sites, when to use a pen for his injections and when to start a multidose regime. He grew extremely impatient with the diabetic nurse educator, who he viewed as 'sticking to the rules' and thus an obstacle to his goal of attaining ultimate control over his diabetes.

Mr Haller monitored his sugars four times a day and carried his glucometer wherever he went. He followed his diet to the letter, monitoring his intake in detail. Controlling everything in the past had always solved his problems: why couldn't he make this dreaded disease go away? Mr Haller was also frustrated with his endocrinologist. Often during his visits to the specialist, he was told he was managing very well. Later, Mr Haller would complain to Dr Carrothers, his family doctor, 'Why do I feel so lousy if I'm supposed to be doing so well?' Dr Carrothers listened and empathetically responded to his feelings of frustration.

Note: This case description first appeared in the September 1995 issue of the *Ontario Medical Review* and is reprinted with the permission of the Ontario Medical Association.

Mr Haller frequently expressed anger during visits with Dr Carrothers, saying, 'Why me? What have I done to deserve this? Why am I being punished?'. The coping strategies he had employed in the past were no longer effective. At times he would ask: 'Why can't this just go away? If I follow my diet and my sugars are good, does this mean that I don't have diabetes any more?'. Dr Carrothers' knowledge of the patient's past life experiences, including his role as primary caregiver and sole provider for his family, helped her understand his anger and despair (Weyrauch, 1994). It was extremely difficult for Mr Haller to accept that there was nothing he could do to make his diabetes disappear.

The diagnosis of Mr Haller's chronic condition had also been difficult for his wife. Although supportive and understanding, Mrs Haller was struggling to cope. She was exhausted from loss of sleep and overwhelmed by her concern about her husband's future. Further exploration by Dr Carrothers revealed that Mrs Haller was worried her husband was going to have a hypoglycemic reaction while asleep and die in bed next to her. Mrs Haller felt she had to 'stay on guard' and consequently was awake most of the night. She found it difficult to talk to her husband about her fears and was reluctant to reveal her terror that he might die.

Mr Haller desperately needed to regain some control over his life, to be the caregiver in the family rather than the one receiving care (Miller, 1992). Dr Carrothers arranged regular office visits and worked with Mr Haller to achieve these goals. She gave Mr Haller control over as many issues as possible in the management of his diabetes. She facilitated his return to work and helped have his driver's license reinstated (it had been revoked at the time of his diagnosis due to blurred vision). She agreed with his request to use a pen for injections and allowed him to control his blood tests, referrals and diet.

Over the weeks, as they talked at length about his family of origin, a strong link became apparent between Mr Haller's struggles with diabetes and his past relationship with his father. 'He never gave me anything until now. And now he's given me diabetes,' stated Mr Haller with emotion. Often these feelings fuelled his anger about the diabetes and his fear about the effects of the disease. His father had suffered many complications related to his diabetes. Given Mr Haller's excellent control of his blood sugar, Dr Carrothers was able to reassure him about the unlikelihood of complications in the future.

Dr Carrothers also met together with Mr Haller and his wife. As a couple they were able to openly share their fears and concerns. With the decline of Mr Haller's hypoglycemic reactions, Mrs Haller felt reassured and gradually was able to sleep peacefully.

Mr Haller returned to work and started to re-establish his routines. With these successes, he started to have fewer 'reactions'. In time, working through his many feelings, he was able to recognize how his relationship with his father influenced his experience of his illness. With the support of his family doctor, his friends and family, he was able to move on from his diagnosis of diabetes.

Component II: Understanding the Whole Person

Judith Belle Brown, W Wayne Weston and Moira Stewart

None of us is immune to the challenges and demands presented at each stage of development. The ascendancy to independence in adolescence, the creation of intimate partnerships in adulthood, the realignment of roles and tasks brought about by retirement are all examples of inevitable lifecycle changes. How we negotiate each subsequent stage will be influenced by prior life experience. For many individuals, the successful achievement of the tasks and expectations of each developmental phase propels them through life relatively unscathed. But for others each ensuing life phase may be marred by past failures and previous losses. For them, life's challenges are experienced as overwhelming and often unachievable.

Thus, the person's position in the lifecycle will influence how they respond to illness. For example, the exacerbation of an elderly man's COPD may compromise his ability to care for his wife who is suffering from Alzheimer's disease, necessitating her placement in a nursing home. His failure to fulfill his responsibilities may result in a loss of sense of purpose and a further decline of his health. Conversely, illness can impede the patient's negotiation of tasks specific to a particular stage of development. For example, the onset of a chronic illness such as juvenile-onset diabetes may create difficulty for an adolescent attempting to negotiate the turbulent process of becoming independent.

The second component of the patient-centered clinical method is the integration of the concepts of disease and illness with an understanding of the whole person, including an awareness of the patient's position in the lifecycle and his or her life context. The patient's position in the lifecycle takes into consideration the individual's own personality development, as well as the family's various stages of development. The patient's context includes, for example, his or her

---

Note: Parts of this chapter were published previously in *Patient-Centered Medicine: transforming the clinical method*, Sage Publications (1995).

family, friendship networks, employment, school, religion, culture and the healthcare system.

The person: individual development

Understanding patients' diseases is only one aspect of their personhood. They are children, partners and parents who have a past, a present and a future. The motives, attachments, ideals and expectations that shape their personality evolve as they negotiate each developmental phase. Healthy individual development is reflected by a solid sense of self, positive self-esteem and a position of independence and autonomy, coupled with the capacity for connectedness and intimacy (Eagle, 1984; Erikson, 1950, 1982; Jordan *et al.*, 1991; Mishne, 1993). Their lives are greatly influenced by each developmental phase which may be isolated and lonely for a homeless adolescent or vast and complex for a middle-aged man, recently diagnosed with diabetes and facing the multiple responsibilities of husband, father, son and worker. Thus their position in the lifecycle, the tasks they perform and the roles they assume will influence the care they seek.

Understanding the patient's current stage of development and the relevant developmental tasks which need to be accomplished can assist doctors in several ways. First, knowledge of the possible life-stage crises that occur in individual development helps the doctor recognize the patient's problems as more than isolated, episodic phenomena. Also, being aware of prior losses or developmental crises assists the doctor to identify vulnerable junctures in the patient's life. For example, knowing that a patient has minimal family interaction or limited social supports alerts the physician to an individual at risk. Second, it can increase the doctor's sensitivity to the multiple factors that influence the patient's problems and broaden awareness of the impact of the patient's life history. Third, an understanding of the whole person enhances the physician's interaction with the patient and may be particularly helpful when signs or symptoms do not point to a clearly defined disease process or when the patient's response to an illness appears exaggerated or out of character. On these occasions, it is often helpful to explore how the patient is dealing with the common issues related to his or her stage in the lifecycle. Finally, understanding the whole person may also expand the doctor's level of comfort with caring as well as curing.

The person and the family lifecycle

Illness is a powerful agent of change. The burden of illness, either acute or chronic, may cause severe disruption to the most functional family system

(Ransom, 1993; Rolland, 1989). Illness in the family causes a major disruption, altering how families relate, and may ultimately impede their ability to overcome the ramifications of the illness experience (McDaniel *et al.*, 1990). Illness may demand a change in the family role structure and task allocation. Changes in routine, such as care of an elderly parent or visits to the hospital, may be required.

The family disequilibrium resulting from illness can also alter the established rules and expectations of the family members, transform their methods of communication and substantially alter the family structure. The changes imposed on families by illness are limitless and accompanied by a host of feelings: loss, fear, anger, resignation, anxiety, sadness, resentment and dependency.

How families have coped previously will influence how they negotiate the impact of the illness on their family roles, rules, patterns of communication and structures. Therefore, in understanding the impact of the illness on the family, some key questions can guide the doctor's inquiry. At what point is the family in the family lifecycle (e.g. starting a family, retirement)? Where is each member in the lifecycle (e.g. adolescence, middle age)? What are the developmental tasks for each individual and for the family as a whole? How does the illness affect the achievement of these multiple tasks? What kinds of illnesses has the family experienced? What kinds of support have they mobilized in the past to help them cope with illness? Is there currently an established support network? How has the family dealt with illness in the past? Have they responded with functional or dysfunctional patterns of behavior? For example, has the family demonstrated potential maladaptive responses, such as rejection of the sick person or overprotection that stifles responsibility for self-care?

These latter questions are important because they elicit how families may contribute to or perpetuate illness behavior in their members. The family may represent a safe refuge for the ill person or, conversely, may aggravate the illness through maladaptive responses.

Context, systems and culture

Context includes the disease, the illness, the person and the environment. Each person is part of multiple and interlocking systems including his or her family, ethnic group, peers, social contacts, work and school environments and religious group. The healthcare system represents another significant system as the patient interacts with the doctor and other members of the healthcare team. Relationships and connections with each system may change when the patient becomes ill and the role assumed by the patient within each of these systems can be significantly altered depending on the severity of the illness. Also, the nature and quality of these interlocking systems can facilitate or impede how the patient responds to illness.

Culture, perhaps more than any other aspect of the patient's context, has a profound impact on their healthcare. How patients conceptualize and interpret their illness is strongly determined by cultural affiliation. Cultural norms and values influence how patients experience illness, seek care and accept medical interventions (Kleinman *et al.*, 1978).

There are several cultural features to consider for each of the four aspects (disease, illness, person and context) of the whole person in this model. Although disease is explained by the conventional medical model, it is not immune to the influence of culture. The conventional medical model and the scientific method are both products of Western culture. Thus, our cultural 'filters' affect how we, as clinicians, understand and manage diseases (Payer, 1988). Just as the approaches to medical practice differ, the venues employed by patients in meeting their healthcare needs also vary.

Patients' experience of illness will be profoundly influenced by cultural beliefs about 'appropriate' illness behavior and models of care. What counts as a symptom of illness and when to consult family members, lay practitioners, healers or traditional healthcare professionals are all prescribed by culture.

Culture has a fundamental effect on the psychological development of the person. A move from one culture to another involves major upheaval and loss, which may have serious effects on self-esteem. Such a transition may be compounded by the trauma of torture and the humiliation of refugee status. Language barriers make it even more difficult to articulate needs and to receive support.

There are different cultural responses to transitions in the family lifecycle such as pregnancy, labour, childbirth and care of the elderly and dying. Cultural differences in family roles and rules may come into conflict with the expectations of the doctor. In some cultural groups, the sharing of personal and family concerns with an individual outside the family network is prohibited (Germain, 1984).

What strategies can the doctor use to learn more about the patient's culture? It is the doctor's responsibility to attempt to bridge the cultural gap by becoming as familiar as possible with the patient's cultural traditions and beliefs. For example, it may be useful to explain to patients that it would help the doctor, in caring for them, to know more about them, their home situation and the country from which they came. Doctors can point out that they are not experts in other cultures and that they need patients' help to understand them better. The doctors might ask for tolerance if they say or do something that would be inappropriate in the patient's homeland and encourage patients to inform them so that they do not repeat the same mistake. This disclosure may be difficult for some patients if they are accustomed to viewing doctors as authorities or if their life experiences have socialized them to respond to authority figures with deference, submissiveness or fear.

It is important to avoid stereotyping people; every culture is complex and diverse. Often, more differences exist between individuals within a particular culture than between the cultures of the patient and doctor. The most important and relevant information about patients' cultures will come from the patients themselves. They are the experts on what cultural uniqueness means to them.

Conclusion

Over time, doctors gain an understanding of the social and developmental context in which their patients live their lives. Usually, this information is not gathered in a single encounter as part of a formal social history but rather is accumulated during many visits that can span many months or years. As patient and doctor share life experiences, this understanding becomes richer and more detailed. With certain patients such information may help the doctor understand the patient's complex dynamics and idiosyncratic responses to illness or demands for care. Specific aspects of the patient's family dynamics or developmental difficulties may not be necessarily shared with the patient but may guide the doctor in the management and care of the patient. In other instances, facilitating the patient's awareness of the origin of their conflicts or distress may help them make sense of their struggles and pain. Finally, understanding the whole person can deepen the doctor's knowledge of the human condition, especially the nature of suffering and the responses of persons to sickness (Cassell, 1991; Mayeroff, 1971).

Preview of the cases

The following cases illustrate the challenges and rewards that doctors experience in understanding the patient as a whole person.

We begin with two adolescent women whose lives are dramatically different. The common thread that binds the two stories is the importance of understanding and respecting their unique worlds. The third case examines the struggles of a young woman as she attempts to fulfill the multiple roles of wife, mother and daughter-in-law, in the context of significant losses. The physician's attention to her past history and current life circumstances highlights the importance of understanding the whole person.

In the next case we observe how assumptions about a patient's life context may mislead the physician's inquiry about the source of the patient's concerns.

Violence against women is a serious problem in our society. Often doctors are the first point of contact for victims of abuse in their search for help and understanding. The two cases presented provide a snapshot of the impact of abuse on women at two different stages of the lifecycle. The first case illustrates the need for physicians to respond to victims of childhood sexual abuse with sensitivity and hope at both the time of the initial disclosure and throughout the healing process during the months ahead. The second case demonstrates how the disclosure of a long history of abuse may be revealed under unusual circumstances, in this instance during the care of a dying woman.

Understanding elderly patients' life experiences, both past and present, can help make the vital connection between current concerns and symptoms and prior life events. This knowledge of the whole person, as case 17 illustrates, can assist doctors in promoting the patient's fullest potential, in spite of their serious physical limitations. The experience of illness may have a devastating impact on a family as demonstrated in the eighth case in this section.

Culture plays a powerful role in how we experience life and death. A case of a dying man, presented in two parts, emphasizes the need for promoting hope and developing an understanding of cultural differences. This case views these issues from the perspective of both the dying patient and his family.

Cases Illustrating Component II: Understanding the Whole Person

11

Needs of the adolescent patient

David Snadden and Judith Belle Brown

Doctors must understand symptoms in the full context of the patient's situation and family system. As with any patient, consultations with adolescents will be most successful if the doctor builds trust with the patient and shows respect for her ideas, concerns and expectations.

'I don't really need to be here but my dad thought I should see the doctor,' said Zoe. 'I'm okay.'

Sixteen-year-old Zoe sat in the office, her hands tightly clenched, and stared at the floor. Like many teenagers her answers came slowly and hesitatingly. For the last three weeks she hadn't felt like getting up in the morning or going to school and her appetite had diminished. She had felt this way since one of her classmates had died from meningitis.

Before Zoe arrived her father had phoned Dr Randall. He said that Zoe was really not herself. He and his wife were very worried about her, their only child, and felt that something had to be done about her symptoms.

The doctor felt trapped between the father's insistence on action and Zoe's unwillingness to communicate with him. The doctor thought of depression and anorexia and appropriate treatment for these flitted through his mind. Realizing that some of these ideas had been generated by his conversation with Zoe's father, Dr Randall decided it would be important to find out what Zoe thought was wrong and how she thought she might be helped.

'Tell me more about how you're doing, Zoe,' he said.

To break down the barriers and gain some trust, he started asking general questions about school and how the others in the class had been affected by her friend's death. It was fairly easy to move from this safe factual area to ask how Zoe had felt and how she was coping with her feelings during this difficult period. It transpired that she had a supportive network of friends and that they

Note: This description first appeared in the November 1991 issue of the *Ontario Medical Review* and is reprinted with the permission of the Ontario Medical Association.

had spent a lot of time talking about the problems that had arisen from their friend's death. Zoe had not been able to talk to her parents the same way, but realized that her symptoms were due to grief. She was not unduly worried by her symptoms and had already accepted them as part of the grieving process. In fact, she thought she was adjusting to the loss reasonably well. She had only come to the doctor's office at her father's insistence.

Zoe noted that her father had become increasingly protective of her since her classmate's death. Before that, Zoe had felt that her parents viewed her as responsible and mature, thus affording her a fair degree of autonomy and independence. Now she felt that both her parents had become overly solicitous about her welfare. The doctor asked Zoe why she thought this change had happened. Zoe was really not sure at first, but after a while began to wonder if her parents were worried about losing her. The doctor agreed that it was a possibility. Understanding this, Zoe was then able to reflect on some of the mixed emotions that may have been influencing her parents' behaviour. In the end, she decided to go home and discuss her thoughts and feelings with her parents. She declined the doctor's offer of further help, saying that she would be happy to return for a chat if things were not going well for her in the future.

This case illustrates the importance of not taking symptoms in isolation but looking at them in the context of the patient's situation and family system. When dealing with bereavement in adolescent patients it is important to find out if the patient has support appropriate to their age group: they should be encouraged to seek out peers for support (Siegel, 1975). In this respect, the doctor needs to support and encourage the patient's individuation and autonomy (Ney, 1987).

In this example the patient had already found support among her peers but was having difficulty understanding her parents' attitude towards her. While supporting and encouraging her independence and exploring her parents' emotional responses, the doctor helped Zoe to deal with her father's insistence that there must be a physical reason for her symptoms. By respecting her ideas, concerns and expectations, the doctor reached a mutually satisfactory conclusion to the consultation. By reaching a mutual understanding of the problem with the patient the doctor helped trust to develop in their relationship, thus allowing the young patient to feel that she could easily return in the future if she needed further help or advice.

12

Homeless youth

Tammy L Schilbe, Judith Belle Brown, Morrison Reid and Stephen J Wetmore

Homeless youth face a wide array of social problems, often marked by a pattern of repeated victimization, and are particularly vulnerable to serious health problems such as unplanned pregnancy, drug abuse, depression and suicide. To develop a rapport with homeless youth and engage them in the treatment process, physicians must suspend their preconceived ideas, slow down and listen.

As part of her probation order, 17-year-old Jessie attended counseling sessions with Dr Clarke, arranged through her community's homeless youth drop-in center.

Jessie was extremely open about her life and discussed several significant problems during the initial session. She had a lengthy criminal record consisting of more than 17 convictions including theft, assault, breaking and entering, possession of narcotics, assaulting a police officer and breach of probation. She described her mother as a severe alcoholic who frequently left Jessie unsupervised as a child. Jessie indicated that she had been abused by several of her mother's partners.

During the initial counseling session Jessie disclosed that she had been raped by acquaintances on five separate occasions, once as recently as two weeks ago. She talked of the assaults as though they were a disturbing but expected part of street life. She was adamant that the legal system could not help her and had no interest in talking to the police.

Jessie went on to say that she had struggled with her decision to have two abortions in the past two years. It was also evident from her description of her current lifestyle that Jessie was still heavily abusing drugs and alcohol and putting herself in dangerous situations. Jessie, however, viewed her current lifestyle as a considerable improvement on her previous habits.

Dr Clarke felt overwhelmed by the seriousness of Jessie's problems and inadequate to address them. How could she establish common ground with a patient whose life experiences were so different?

Her first impulse was to refer Jessie for residential treatment. But she resisted jumping to any conclusion, taking the time to listen to Jessie's descriptions of previous experiences. She learned that Jessie had lived in several treatment settings and was determined never to return to a similar setting.

At-risk adolescents are considered one of the most difficult groups to engage in a helping relationship. Physicians may be wary of working with street youth for a number of reasons. Although there is no 'typical' street youth, many have poor health habits, have difficulty keeping scheduled appointments and may be reluctant to accept the advice of adults (Farrow *et al.*, 1992). Troubled adolescents can be very negative, even belligerent. Many have had poor or no social skill modeling and mask their insecurity with verbal aggression. Others, like Jessie, are severely emotionally damaged, depressed and actively abusing drugs or alcohol.

This is a population which is largely misunderstood. Street kids are stereotyped as selfish, highly resistant, even dangerous. There is also a tendency to assume they are transient by choice.

What you see is not what you get. Many street youth have been abused by their families and are victimized further on the streets. For homeless adolescents, the difficulties of their developmental stage are multiplied by the absence of secure attachments and productive coping mechanisms. This is exacerbated by the lack of basic necessities.

One of the first tasks is to develop a rapport by finding common ground with young people. This may sound simple but homeless youth live in a world nothing like our own. Very few helping professionals have experienced homelessness and many of our biases and values are based on upper- or middle-class views of the world. Lecturing about nutritious food choices or other healthcare issues, while necessary, may be irrelevant for someone who is never sure where they will sleep or eat. This group is much more concerned with everyday survival than long-term healthcare. Sometimes the only common ground is the mutual acknowledgment that the youth is the expert when it comes to his or her situation. This attitude can have great transformative power in the relationship-building process.

Jessie's story is one of intense and repeated pain. Her multiple disclosures during the course of a one-hour interview made it difficult to avoid becoming overwhelmed. The issues seem to warrant intense and immediate intervention. However, what youth like Jessie need most is to be heard. From Jessie's description of her relationships with professionals, it was apparent that too much direction would frighten her away. Jessie had a limited ability to accept direction from others, possibly because she had no experience in this area. Other troubled youth have had too much direction in the form of controlling and rigid parenting styles.

Helping professionals naturally tend to provide intervention which is based on adult assumptions about what is best for youth. When we see a young person living transiently from one dangerous situation to another, we feel we must educate him or her about safe alternatives to street life. In Jessie's situation, residential treatment seemed like an appropriate referral. However, the physician was careful not to prescribe solutions prematurely, without first hearing the patient's story.

For many street youth, the authority associated with traditional shelters and institutions is even more frightening than life on the street. Given that many have experienced early dysfunctional relationships, they find it difficult to believe that giving up their personal freedom today will improve their future. For Jessie, her freedom was all she had left.

Most homeless youth need and want the listening ear of an adult but, because of their background, find it difficult to trust. Physicians need to focus energy on the communication between themselves and street youth and remember that listening is one of the most important tools they have. The task of engaging homeless youth must be undertaken with understanding, patience and positive regard. Many adolescents need a lengthy period of interaction before being able to trust enough to accept help. Any direction which is overly negative, resembles lecturing or feels confining is rarely accepted. A confrontational, authoritarian style of intervention which reminds the youth of his or her inadequacies will be ineffective because it may remind him or her of previous negative experiences with adults. Expecting homeless youth to complete tasks or to conform to rigid structures in order to qualify for service provision scares them away.

This poses a dilemma for helpers because the need to discuss safety planning and health concerns cannot be compromised. The key is to cover these areas in a manner which encourages dialogue and does not compromise patient–doctor communication. In situations where the problems are many and it is difficult to know where to begin, slowing down and listening may be two of the most crucial steps.

At-risk adolescents may trigger in us confused feelings from our own adolescence or our children's, making it difficult to develop a rapport. But if physicians can move beyond these feelings and attempt to suspend their preconceived ideas, there is a real chance for making a difference. If youth can connect in a positive manner and participate in services which do not mirror their previous negative experiences, their chances for emotional and physical survival and for working toward a more promising future will be increased. In Jessie's situation, the physician's patient-centered approach helped build a rapport, ensuring that Jessie returned to subsequent treatment sessions.

Homeless and at-risk youth have typically avoided consistent medical care for a number of reasons. Doctors must attempt to bridge the distance between medicine and the streets. Services need to recognize and accept that deviant behaviors are a direct result of past experiences which have shaped young people's view of the world and of themselves. Along with their basic need for shelter, food and clothing, being heard may be another of their most fundamental needs.

13

Problems in the extended family

Judith Belle Brown, Mary Pat Tillmann and W Wayne Weston

Knowing about the lifecycle transitions experienced by patients and the social context in which they live helps doctors to understand the meaning of their illnesses.

Maria, a 24-year-old married woman with a three-year-old son, presented to the emergency department with a two-month history of episodes of palpitations, shortness of breath and sweating. After respiratory, cardiac and endocrine causes were ruled out, she was diagnosed with an anxiety disorder and prescribed benzodiazepines. Using a simplistic biological approach, which focused solely on a biomedical diagnosis, the doctor's goal was to provide the patient with relief from her symptoms. The patient's life circumstances were not considered or explored. Maria was instructed to return to her family physician if the symptoms were not relieved by the medication.

Over the next few weeks Maria's symptoms persisted and she became concerned about her ability to care adequately for her three-year-old son, Gus. On a few occasions she tried the medication prescribed by the emergency physician. But it left her feeling groggy and even more incapable of attending to Gus' many needs. She was reluctant to share her worries with her husband and tried to hide her symptoms from him. Finally, exasperated and overwhelmed, Maria made an appointment to see her family doctor.

Maria arrived at Dr McIntyre's office feeling anxious and embarrassed. The doctor began by exploring Maria's personal experience of her illness in greater depth. Among the questions he asked were: 'What do you think is causing these symptoms? How are these episodes affecting your daily life? Who else lives at

Note: This case description first appeared in the June 1993 issue of the *Ontario Medical Review* and is reprinted with the permission of the Ontario Medical Association.

home with you? Are you worried about not being able to care for your son?' From these questions he discovered that Maria's past history and current life were complex and punctuated by multiple losses.

During subsequent visits, Dr McIntyre learned that Maria's parents were both killed in a car accident when she was 18. She lived with an aunt until she married her husband, Tino, six years ago. Tino's father died suddenly from a massive coronary thrombosis eight months ago, an event which devastated the family. Unable to cope with his death, Tino's mother Angelica, aged 64, moved in with them two months ago. Since then, Maria found it increasingly difficult to cope with the behavior of her son. Gus was an active child who demanded Maria's time and attention.

With the physician's encouragement, Maria began to acknowledge the connection between the onset of her symptoms and her mother-in-law's move to their home. Dr McIntyre's questions helped Maria understand her frustration with her mother-in-law's intrusive behavior with Gus. She also saw that her feelings of inadequacy as a mother were reinforced by Angelica's constant criticism. Throughout, the physician encouraged Maria to express her feelings. They agreed on a plan that provided alternative means of emotional support for Maria and ways to enhance her coping skills.

Other concerns surfaced as Dr McIntyre explored Maria's life experience. For example, Maria feared she would lose her temper and hurt her son. She also described how she found it difficult to share her feelings with her husband, particularly about her conflict with his mother. Finally, the tragic death of her parents continued to be a deep loss for Maria and the death of Tino's father had reinforced her feelings about the fragility of life.

Through sensitive questioning, the physician identified stressors in the environment that had contributed to the patient's symptoms. The patient and physician actively collaborated to develop a more complete understanding of the situation and to consider solutions. Through extended visits the doctor accumulated the information about his patient's illness experience that went beyond a catalogue of diseases and treatments. He began to know her as a person with a complex history.

In this case, the physician's exploration of Maria's social and developmental context transported the problem from the purely biomedical domain to a broader, more comprehensive perspective. By understanding the patient's background, both past and current, the doctor helped the patient discover the meaning of her experience.

When the physician understands the whole person, he or she can work with the patient to develop more creative and helpful responses to their problems and thus avoid inappropriate and expensive treatments or investigations (Stewart *et al.*, 2000).

14

Loss

Susan M McNair and Judith Belle Brown

Homosexual patients may present to the doctor's office with symptoms compatible with HIV. However, many other organic and psychological conditions have similar presentations. A full exploration of the patient's physical, psychological and social well-being is imperative to avoid misleading assumptions and to determine the true meaning of the patient's concerns.

Thirty-six year old Marcus appeared pale and thin as Dr Loaring entered the examination room. 'You look tired', noted the doctor as he pulled up a chair. 'What brings you in?'

'I feel exhausted. I'm worried there is something wrong,' Marcus replied.

Marcus had shared the details of his homosexuality with Dr Loaring in the past and the doctor quickly responded, 'What are you worried about, Marcus? Is the HIV a concern again?'

Marcus explained that his partner of eight years was dying of AIDS. He had assumed the primary responsibility for his partner's palliative care. He described, with despair, his partner's increasing weakness, muscle wasting and progressive respiratory distress. Marcus admitted that he hoped his friend's death might come quickly and yet was afraid of what life would be like without his partner's companionship.

Dr Loaring listened for some time. He remembered Marcus' previous visits to the office during which he had expressed anxiety about contracting HIV and asked for HIV testing. Again the doctor offered, 'You must be worried about HIV yourself, Marcus? Is it testing that you want?'.

Marcus looked down, his eyes welling with tears. 'I've been tested. I know I'm okay. I'm just not myself.'

Dr Loaring sat back, silent, and waited. 'I'm going to miss him,' exclaimed Marcus. 'We've been together a long time.' Marcus had shared a number of

Note: This case description first appeared in the March 1995 issue of the *Ontario Medical Review* and is reprinted with the permission of the Ontario Medical Association.

important life events with this partner and his sense of loss was profound. He wanted his partner to live and yet prayed that his suffering might end. Marcus had been eating poorly and his sleeping had become fragmented as an outcome of his caretaking role. He feared that his partner's pain would become unbearable and that he would find himself unable to minister to his needs. Marcus was extremely worried that his partner would die when he was alone with him. He had no idea what to do nor how he would cope with the actual death. Marcus had few supports and up until this time had only shared his fears and sadness with the visiting nurse. Now, he had come to the doctor's office to talk, to express his fears and to be reassured that his feelings were normal.

Given his previous knowledge of Marcus' homosexuality, and the symptoms of exhaustion and fatigue, the doctor assumed that Marcus was presenting for HIV testing and for further reassurance of his negative status. In exploring Marcus' concerns the doctor learned that the fear of HIV was not his reason for coming to the office. During this interaction, the doctor had made an assumption which could have possibly resulted in missing the real reasons underlying the patient's current presentation.

While the doctor was understandably concerned about ruling out an organic basis for Marcus' fatigue, it was through acknowledgment of the patient's stressful personal and social situation that the greatest healing occurred. The doctor listened. Marcus was able to normalize his feelings and to understand that his partner's death meant the loss of a part of his own life.

The doctor visited Marcus regularly during this difficult time and helped him search out support groups for caregivers of people dying of AIDS. The patient–physician relationship provided an environment in which Marcus could begin to understand his own symptoms, as well as the fears and anxieties underlying these symptoms.

McWhinney (1972) has developed a taxonomy of patient behavior which is useful in understanding why patients present to our offices. In this taxonomy, patient behavior is divided into five categories of human illness responses.

- *Limit of tolerance.* The patient visits the physician because the symptoms have become intolerable.
- *Limit of anxiety.* The patient presents not because the symptoms are causing distress but because of their implications.
- *Heterothetic symptoms.* The patient complains of symptoms that are caused by problems of living. The symptoms conceal an underlying problem and the clinical diagnosis is often secondary to understanding the patient's problems.
- *Administrative encounters.* The sole purpose of the doctor–patient contact is administrative
- *No illness.* The final category includes all attendances for preventive purposes.

In this case, the physician immediately assumed that Marcus was presenting because he had reached his limit of anxiety – his fears about HIV had become too great. Instead, Marcus' symptoms concealed an underlying problem of living which needed to be defined and explained. It was only through the recognition of Marcus' reasons for presentation, free from misleading assumptions, that the doctor could provide the greatest care.

15

Child sexual abuse

Dorothy E Haswell and Judith Belle Brown

Sadly, childhood sexual abuse is not uncommon and not restricted to any one socio-economic group. When a patient tells a doctor of an experience of abuse, her revelations must be met with acceptance, belief and hope for healing. In particular, the patient must be convinced that she is not to blame.

Janice, a 26-year-old employed by a major manufacturing company, was distraught when she arrived for her appointment with Dr Graham, her long-time family doctor.

'I'm glad you were able to see me,' she said, her voice breaking. 'I've been having a terrible time with nightmares since I saw a program on television about incest a few months ago. The program brought back dreadful memories of what it was like in my family. From the time I was eight until I left home my father came to my bedroom almost every night. He threatened that if I ever told on him I would be sent away because it was my fault, that I had seduced him. He also told me that no one would believe me anyway. I was so glad to move into my own place. I thought that everything would be all right when it stopped happening, but the memories keep coming back. I can't eat and I can't sleep without tranquilizers. What can I do?'

Dr Graham was astonished. He had known Janice's family as patients for many years and had never suspected anything like this. He wondered if she was exaggerating or imagining that this had happened. On the other hand, he didn't want to disregard it if it were true. Could this be the cause of her symptoms, he wondered. What do I say? What do I do?

The doctor learned that Janice had presented to a variety of physicians in the last several years with complaints of nervousness, sleeplessness and nightmares. Previous physicians had given her benzodiazepines to help her with the symptoms. The medications helped the sleeplessness but had not reduced her feelings of nervousness or stopped her nightmares.

Note: This case description first appeared in the February 1992 issue of the *Ontario Medical Review* and is reprinted with the permission of the Ontario Medical Association.

The daughter of a couple well known in the community, Janice had one younger sister and an older brother. She completed high school with no apparent difficulty and was able to leave home to attend community college in a nearby city. Janice lived alone and dated frequently although she had no long-term relationships.

Sexual activity between adults and children within the same family has been taboo throughout the world and throughout time. Unfortunately, this taboo has not been enough to protect children from the great harm that such activity causes them. Current changes in the social environment have brought incest out into the open. Exposure through the media and the increasing knowledge of available resources have encouraged more victims to bring their personal experiences to their physicians.

Incest should not be assumed to be a rare aberration found only in situations of extreme poverty, deprivation and chaos. It is, in fact, a common experience of many children in families of all kinds, wealthy as often as poor, educated as often as not, professional as often as unemployed. Although we know it is more common than ever thought, we can never determine the exact prevalence because of the secrecy and denial that our society still tolerates around this issue.

For the same reasons, these children have been left to suffer from and cope with the effects of these experiences. Both within the family and in society at large, the child has been thought culpable of dishonesty and worthy of blame in the situations where disclosure has been attempted. During childhood these children suffer greatly both emotionally and physically. Because they are completely helpless in this situation they may use psychological defences of dissociation and amnesia to protect themselves from the devastation. The victim may deny, discount, minimize or suppress reactions and memories.

Amnesia may be so complete that the victims do not remember the abuse at all. The amnesia may be interrupted by memories which are stimulated by environmental triggers such as sights, sounds or smells or by hearing about the experiences of other victims through books, plays or TV programs. The memories may return first in dreams or nightmares. The victim may be unwilling to realize what these nightmares mean. Fragments of memories, known as 'flashbacks', may be particularly frightening and disturbing. If amnesia is complete the victim may fear she is going crazy when the memories first begin.

Symptoms experienced by adults who were victims of childhood sexual abuse are those of a chronic or delayed post-traumatic stress disorder, as described by Courtois (1988). The severity of the symptoms depends on the type of abuse experienced, who did it, how long it continued, the genetic make-up of the individual, the stage of development at which the abuse was experienced and the availability of supports within the family. If the victim remains untreated, the symptoms may include depression, anxiety, substance abuse, eating disorders and somatization disorders. The shame and guilt they feel about the problem will result in poor self-esteem and reduced ability to take care of themselves. This may lead to repeated experiences of abuse or victimization in later life.

It is vitally important that victims who disclose the abuse are met with acceptance, belief and hope for healing from their physicians. These patients need to be convinced that they were innocent victims whose lives have been damaged by the abuse. They need to understand that their dreams, nightmares and symptoms are a natural response to the trauma that they have suffered. They need to be assured that 'flashbacks' are common in victims and not a sign of being crazy.

It helps if the victim is allowed to tell her story in her own way and at her own pace. Once the incest has been exposed, the patient may feel guilty and vulnerable (Bass and Davis, 1988). It is important that the physician remain available to the patient and assist them in establishing a therapeutic plan suitable for them.

In Janice's case, the doctor responded like this: 'Janice, I'm glad that you were able to tell me this. It must have been difficult to gather enough courage. I'm sorry this happened to you. The things that your father did and said were wrong, he is entirely to blame for the abuse and for the problems you have developed as a result. Your symptoms are undoubtedly due to the sexual abuse. The TV program has broken through your defences and allowed you to remember the abuse. You may find more and more memories coming back and these may cause you increased emotional pain for a while. Could you tell me any more about these experiences today? If not, then we will meet again regularly to talk until you are established with a therapist who is an expert in helping people recover from the effects of sexual abuse. Even then I will be available to help in any way that I can.'

16

Abuse and palliative care

Susan M McNair and Judith Belle Brown

Signals of abuse in families and among caregivers represent a unique challenge in palliative care. The physician must be able to recognize the signs of abuse, be available to the patient and let the patient determine how the physician can help best.

Mrs Patrick, aged 59, always talked in whispered tones as she sat with Dr Kanuff in her front sitting room. The doctor had visited Mrs Patrick twice weekly after the diagnosis of her renal cell carcinoma. The whispering quality of her voice initially perplexed the doctor but she soon realized it represented Mrs Patrick's attempts to distance their conversation from the ears of her husband, who was always hovering just outside the sitting room door.

Mrs Patrick became a patient of the practice because she heard that Dr Kanuff did house calls. With time the doctor discovered that Mrs Patrick had been seen by three different family physicians in 18 months, all of them competent and caring professionals by the patient's standards. Yet all of them had been dismissed by Mrs Patrick's husband for what he considered to be a lack of attention to his wife's complaints. Although perplexed by this 'doctor shopping' behavior, Dr Kanuff thought no more of it.

Mrs Patrick decided against any form of therapy after the diagnosis of her metastatic renal cell carcinoma. Her only wish was to remain at home and 'let nature take its course'. When Dr Kanuff began seeing her, she was having some flank pain but she refused any analgesia, saying, 'I want a little pain, it makes me feel alive'.

As days passed and Mrs Patrick began to weaken, she developed a number of small decubitus ulcers. Dr Kanuff felt certain that Mrs Patrick would agree to hospitalization, but this was clearly not the case. Mrs Patrick's only explanation was, 'This is as good as it gets'.

Note: This case description first appeared in the May 1994 issue of the *Ontario Medical Review* and is reprinted with the permission of the Ontario Medical Association.

One evening, after a visit at Mrs Patrick's, the doctor drove home feeling uneasy and frustrated. The whispering words, the husband's decision that Mrs Patrick change family physicians, her denial of pain medication, and her persistence in staying home despite her obvious discomfort – it just didn't seem to add up. Or did it?

For her next visit to the home Dr Kanuff arranged a time when she knew Mr Patrick would be absent. She sat with Mrs Patrick, simply offering an opportunity for her to reflect on her terminal illness and on her life. Mrs Patrick talked about the house, being unable to have a child and caring for their two dogs. There was no mention of her husband. When Dr Kanuff inquired about her marriage, Mrs Patrick's eyes filled with tears.

'You look sad, Mrs Patrick,' said the doctor. 'Is this difficult for you to talk about?' Mrs Patrick said nothing. 'Can I help you?' the doctor asked.

'No one can help . . . no one ever could . . . my lot in life . . . I have tried my best . . . nothing can change now.'

Dr Kanuff gently probed a little further. Mrs Patrick confirmed the doctor's worst suspicions: she had lived a life of physical and emotional abuse for over 30 years. She told the doctor that she and her husband had run a family business together. Her husband was functionally illiterate and without her help he couldn't have made it. His abuse effectively silenced the reality of his disability.

'So what about now?' asked Dr Kanuff. 'I'm concerned about you. Are you safe here?'

'I'm fine, dear,' said Mrs Patrick, as if to make the doctor feel better. 'He hasn't touched me for months, not since the cancer thing. I guess he knows he'll get rid of me soon.'

As the doctor left the patient's home that evening, again feeling uneasy and frustrated, she wondered, 'What should I do? What can I do?'.

As time went on, Dr Kanuff and Mrs Patrick spoke further about her concerns. It was very clear to the doctor that she, herself, was the one most uneasy with the situation. She realized that her role was to ensure safety, to listen and to provide care and support for her patient. Ultimately, it was the patient who would, and should, make decisions about her own future.

This case raises several important issues. In caring for palliative care patients physicians need to be aware of signs of abuse within families and among caregivers. Abusive relationships endure, and can escalate, during these difficult times of dependence and stress. When faced with an obviously abusive relationship in the palliative care situation, the doctor must ensure the safety of her patient. Abuse, whether physical or emotional, denies choice and freedom through the misuse of power and control. Providing patients with alternatives and finally respecting their decisions about ongoing care is essential (Herbert, 1991). Ultimately, the patient must provide us with direction on how we can best help during this difficult time. As David Loxterkamp (1991, p. 354) eloquently observed: 'In listening to the stories of illness over countless sittings or at the moment of truth, we become attuned to the whispered qualities of a person's life, the essence at risk in the throes of illness. And in so doing, with human presence and the comfort of words, we can help bridge a gulley where the road washed out.'

17

Concerns of the elderly

Susan M McNair and Judith Belle Brown

The worries of the elderly may often prompt a visit to the doctor's office. While these concerns and worries may be clearly articulated by some patients, in others they are hidden behind physical complaints. Physicians must remain alert to this possibility and be prepared to explore and discuss various contributors to the patient's current presentation.

Mrs Shorten, an 83-year-old woman, walked the five blocks from her home to her doctor's office in the wind and rain. Arriving at the office she exclaimed to the receptionist, 'I don't know what's wrong with me . . . I'm afraid I'm having a heart attack!'.

When the doctor reached the patient, she found Mrs Shorten short of breath, perspiring heavily and complaining of palpitations. Gasping for breath, Mrs Shorten explained that for the last few days she had been dizzy, weak, not sleeping well and 'just not herself'. Her tearful and desperate presentation was in sharp contrast to the independent woman who had always prided herself on her problem-solving skills and ability for self-care. Now, she was clearly frightened by her inability to make sense of her multiple symptoms.

Dr Tam examined Mrs Shorten but found no obvious organic basis for her distress. The doctor wondered if her presentation was related to anxiety. Although Mrs Shorten had been widowed for several years, she had managed to maintain her modest home without any assistance. Living alone had taken its toll. As she had become increasingly more frail, she constantly fretted about the maintenance of the house and her prized garden. Her sources of support were very limited as she had few friends in a position to offer her assistance. Indeed, over the years, she had served in the role of caretaker for many of them, driving them to doctors' appointments, getting groceries, attending during times of sickness. Her only living relative was a niece who lived 500 miles away and Mrs Shorten was reluctant to ask her for help. Now she was in need of care and had nowhere to turn.

Note: This case description first appeared in the August 1994 issue of the *Ontario Medical Review* and is reprinted with the permission of the Ontario Medical Association.

After much thought, the doctor decided, given Mrs Shorten's limited social supports coupled with her complex and multiple complaints, that a short admission to hospital should be arranged. The patient agreed, with relief. A full cardiac work-up failed to reveal an organic basis for her complaints, but a new dilemma became apparent. Within only a few days, Mrs Shorten would be discharged from hospital: she was neither sick enough to remain in hospital nor well enough to return home.

Given the patient's longstanding independence and her previous ability to make clear and wise decisions about her well-being, Dr Tam chose to take time to discuss with Mrs Shorten her current dilemma. In exploring the problem with the patient, the doctor learned that she had two key fears. Her short-term fear was of becoming ill and being alone in her home. She was afraid that she might faint or fall and not be found for days. The image of lying on the floor in the darkness, unable to call for help, haunted her. As Mrs Shorten explained: 'I'm not afraid of dying. I've made my peace. I'm just so worried about being helpless and being alone.'

Her long-term fear related to who would care for her should she become seriously ill and debilitated. 'What will happen to my home, where will I live?' she asked. Mrs Shorten had been extremely proud of her self-sufficiency and her ability to remain in her own home. Although her garden had been a major source of accomplishment and joy, the responsibilities of her home and garden now felt overwhelming. For some time Mrs Shorten had managed to deny her frailty, but now it was a stark reality for her. 'Perhaps what I fear most is having to depend on others,' she explained. 'Who will care for my garden as I have done?'

The doctor rapidly responded to the patient's physical concerns. But the most significant intervention was understanding her social situation and the worries which fuelled her anxiety. Prior to discussing discharge arrangements or recommending placement in a home for the aged or a nursing home, the doctor explored what, and who, was available to the patient.

In this interaction between the patient and doctor it was important to consider not only Mrs Shorten's physical presentation but also her advancing age, her fragility and her associated worries and concerns (Connidis, 1989). At the same time, it was critical that the doctor not deny the patient's agile mind and emotional fortitude. While Mrs Shorten's frailty might prevent her from harvesting her garden, it did not lessen her capacity to make informed choices (McWilliam *et al.*, 1994). The doctor listened to her concerns, helped her examine the available options and translated them into a plan of action which promoted the most appropriate care for her. Awareness of her unique strengths and past accomplishments was balanced with her current limitations.

At times of 'medical crises' we must look beyond a patient's physical presentation and understand all dimensions of the person.

18

Communication and family roles

*Judith Belle Brown, W Wayne Weston,
Moira Stewart and Lynn Brown*

We must understand the impact of illness on the whole family. Illness can cause a major disruption, resulting in the alteration of established rules and expectations of family members, transformation of methods of communication and significant changes in the family structure.

Sam and Regina had been married for 10 years when Regina was first diagnosed with breast cancer at age 38. At the time, their two children were four and six years of age. Regina, a computer analyst, had assumed the majority of the childcare responsibilities as Sam's work demanded a great deal of overnight travel. This arrangement had been mutually agreed upon by the couple and both were comfortable with their roles. During the initial phase of her illness, including her radical mastectomy, radiation and remission, Regina was able to continue to care for the children with some help from their extended family. For over two years Regina and Sam managed to maintain their previous lifestyle with minimal change. Then the crisis struck: Regina experienced a recurrence of her cancer and her illness rapidly worsened. Despite repeated medical interventions, including several hospital admissions, her cancer continued to grow and spread.

The family was in upheaval. Sam's numerous cancellations of business meetings to care for Regina had put his job in jeopardy. Regina could no longer work, resulting in a significant loss in the family income. The care of the children had become disorganized, with multiple caregivers, leaving the children despondent and confused.

Note: This case description first appeared in the October 1994 issue of the *Ontario Medical Review* and is reprinted with the permission of the Ontario Medical Association.

Regina struggled to retain her role as the children's primary caregiver but as she became weaker she could no longer cope. Her inability to care for her children, to fulfill her maternal role, was her greatest loss. With resignation, Regina transferred the responsibilities for the care of her children to her husband. But her guilt and sense of failure were pervasive, contributing to a deterioration in the couple's communication.

Only through repeated discussions with their doctor were Sam and Regina able to resolve the tensions between them, including Regina's doubts about Sam's ability to care for the children and her own feelings of remorse. Finally, convinced that everything was in order, she died peacefully, knowing the children would be well cared for and her past roles as a wife and mother remembered.

In this case, Regina and Sam had established a mutually acceptable living arrangement, but the diagnosis of terminal cancer devastated their plan. In the end, the doctor's most important function was to listen and to understand the impact of the illness on this family. The doctor helped the couple by keeping the lines of communication open and by encouraging the active participation of the patient's husband.

Family members often play a central role in the care of the patient, particularly in the case of children, the elderly and chronically ill. The burden of illness, either acute or chronic, may cause severe disruption in the family and serve as a powerful agent of change. The impact of illness on the family ranges from the sudden loss of the breadwinner caused by a myocardial infarction to the often overwhelming challenges of a child diagnosed with a developmental disability. In other instances, the illness may initially appear superficial and benign yet family circumstances, such as a recent divorce or unemployment, may make coping with the current health problem an onerous task.

Illness in the family can cause a significant change in the way that family members relate, making it more difficult for them to deal with the consequences of the illness. Illness may demand a change in the family role structure and task allocation. Simple changes in routine may be required: other family members may have to assume food preparation and homemaking duties and frequent visits to the doctor may disrupt family schedules. In some situations, the family may have to make bigger changes: substantial home renovations to accommodate a wheelchair-bound family member, for example, or a return to work to provide for the financial needs of the family.

The disequilibrium in the family resulting from illness can also alter the established rules and expectations of family members, transform their methods of communication and substantially alter the family structure. How families respond to these changes has a major influence on the patient's quality of life. Therefore, physicians must routinely ask about the family, especially when they see patients with serious illness. The following key questions can guide the doctor's inquiry. At what point is the family in the family lifecycle: do they have young children, are they in midlife or are they at the empty nest stage? Where is each member in their own lifecycle? What illnesses have the family already experienced and how did they deal with these illnesses? What kinds of support did they mobilize to help them cope with illness? Is there currently an established support network? Have they responded with adaptive or maladaptive patterns of behavior? For example, has the family demonstrated dysfunctional responses, such as rejecting the sick person or overprotecting the patient, thus denying his or her ability to participate in decisions and make choices? These latter questions are important because they show how families may be contributing to or perpetuating illness behavior in their members. The family may represent a safe refuge for the ill person but it may also aggravate the illness through maladaptive responses.

As this case illustrates, patients cannot be cared for in isolation: they need to be understood in the context of their family system (Doherty and Baird, 1986; McDaniel *et al.*, 1990).

19

Hopelessness

Stephen J Wetmore, Leslie Rourke
and Judith Belle Brown

Families of terminally ill patients will often appear angry because of fear and loss of hope. The doctor must take care not to stifle the small hope remaining and to redirect it towards palliative care goals.

'Why do doctors have to be so blunt sometimes?' asked Mr Deepak's son suddenly during the family meeting. The question surprised Dr Abrams because of the urgent tone and depth of feeling behind it.

The family meeting had been convened to discuss Mr Deepak's prognosis and future management. In addition to Dr Abrams, the patient's son and daughter were present, as well as Mr Deepak's nurse, the unit social worker and the clinical clerk. The initial plan was to include Mr Deepak in the meeting, but he was asleep. As a result his son and daughter eagerly seized the occasion to talk with the doctor in their father's absence.

Mr Deepak was a 75-year-old widower of Arabic origin with Ménière's disease. He had been recently admitted to the palliative care service under Dr Abrams' care. The admission was precipitated by weakness and diarrhea that developed during a course of palliative radiation for metastatic carcinoma. Mr Deepak's weakness and diarrhea resolved shortly after admission with rest and improved nutrition. Unfortunately, he had fallen while in hospital and sustained an impacted fracture of his right hip. Mr Deepak had refused to consider surgery for the hip fracture and had chosen to receive only bedrest and physiotherapy. Since his fall Mr Deepak had begun to deteriorate, experiencing increasing pain and nausea.

Mr Deepak was a proud man who valued his independence. He disliked strong medication and often refused the nurses' offer of pain medication, saying, 'The pain isn't that bad. I can manage'. Dr Abrams had discussed the cancer with

Note: This case description first appeared in the August 1996 issue of the *Ontario Medical Review* and is reprinted with the permission of the Ontario Medical Association.

Mr Deepak several times. Although Mr Deepak understood that the radiation was only for palliation, he was anxious to resume treatment in order to delay the progression of his cancer. When Mr Deepak had asked, 'How long do I have to live?', Dr Abrams had cautiously advised him that it was perhaps a matter of weeks. There was hope that further radiation would prolong his life and increase his level of comfort.

During the family meeting Mr Deepak's son and daughter were startled to hear Dr Abrams' estimate that their father would live for only a few more weeks.

'Don't tell him that!' exclaimed the daughter.

His son added, 'Why do doctors have to be so blunt sometimes?' He related how upset the family had been with the internist who had initially diagnosed Mr Deepak's cancer. 'He was so blunt! It was terrible! Can't you talk to him in a vague fashion without giving him the bad news?'

Delivering bad news sometimes stimulates an angry response from family members. Dr Abrams and the medical team were sensitive to the reasons behind the anger expressed by the family. They recognized that the anger was a manifestation of the family's feelings of fear and guilt. Dr Abrams did not respond with anger or resort to defensive arguments; instead he allowed the family to vent their feelings in an accepting atmosphere.

Once the family had an opportunity to express their feelings, Dr Abrams explained that his usual policy was to be open and honest with patients about their illnesses. Dr Abrams asked Mr Deepak's daughter what she would want to know if she had a terminal disease.

'I wouldn't want to know all the bad news,' she said. 'Is there any hope?'

Dr Abrams then asked the family what their father would want to know if he were at the meeting. The son responded, 'Why, he would want to know everything!'

Dr Abrams recognized that the family's fear of their father's death was now very real and close at hand. It was important for them to have some sense of hope to cling to. They also needed to know that their father held on to some hope. Consequently, they were afraid that the doctor's discussions with their father would stamp out that flickering flame for them all.

The doctor was sensitive to the family's feeling of hopelessness. Dr Abrams made an effort to replace this hopelessness with a different goal that they could hope for: that of comfort and dignity for their father for the remainder of his life. He gently suggested that there were good reasons to maintain hope but not for a prolonged life for their father. They should remain hopeful for a comfortable pain-free decline to death. They should remain hopeful for understanding and honest communication within the family in the remaining days. They should remain hopeful for many fond memories of their father's life.

When discussing terminal illness with families it is important to remain sensitive to families' fears and to recognize and acknowledge the sense of hope, however small (Herth, 1993). As this case illustrates, the family's hope can often be directed towards comfort aspects of care for their loved one, helping them to deal with their sense of loss.

The family meeting can be valuable for allowing the family to express their feelings and to redirect their hope towards palliative care goals, based on a realistic evaluation and discussion of the issues (Davies *et al.*, 1994).

The Deepak family's story continues.

20

Cultural differences

Stephen J Wetmore, Leslie Rourke
and Judith Belle Brown

Families of terminally ill patients may feel isolated and alone without the usual familiarity and understanding of their own culture. The doctor's awareness and sensitivity to cultural differences and his or her comfort in dealing with these differences will facilitate communication and ease the family's discomfort.

Dr Abrams had quickly recognized that the Deepak family's anger was a result of their feelings of hopelessness and had been able to redirect the family's hope towards palliative care goals. Near the end of the family meeting the doctor became aware of cultural issues that were influencing communication within the family and with the medical team.

Neither Mr Deepak's son nor daughter felt comfortable asking their father who should make decisions about his future care if he was unable to do so himself. In order to better understand the family's position the doctor asked, 'How are these issues dealt with in your own culture?'.

Their response was illuminating. Families in their culture, they explained, generally avoided these discussions. They described a culture in which issues around death were dealt with by elders of the family or the elders of the community. The family identified that, for them, the cultural bridge of 'an elder' was not available in this current community. It was extremely important for the family members to not give their father the impression they were giving up hope. Without another acceptable person to bridge this gap the family felt isolated, afraid and without support.

Dr Abrams responded by offering to raise the issue with Mr Deepak. This would permit the patient to initiate the discussions with his son and daughter if he wished. Both the son and daughter were in support of this plan. Mr Deepak's daughter expressed her appreciation: 'I feel much better now that we have discussed this. I was so worried about what to do'. The family felt that a

Note: This case description first appeared in the August 1996 issue of the *Ontario Medical Review* and is reprinted with the permission of the Ontario Medical Association.

respected outsider, such as the doctor, was acceptable to introduce these issues with their father. Emotionally and culturally they were unable to do so.

The family meeting concluded with both the family and the medical team having a clearer understanding of each other's role in the care of Mr Deepak. A decision was made to meet again soon with Mr Deepak and his family.

This case demonstrates the importance of physician attributes, such as self-awareness, sensitivity and comfort when dealing with cultural issues. In order to be sensitive to cultural aspects of healthcare, it is essential that a doctor first be aware of his or her own cultural background and be sensitive to how it might differ from that of the patient. Understanding the context of the patient's illness, including family attitudes and cultural factors, is crucial to fostering effective communication.

Dr Abrams was aware of his own cultural background in which honest discussion of issues around terminal illness and consent were usually readily accepted by families. Such discussions with Mr Deepak's family had produced anger and concern. Dr Abrams did not force his beliefs or ideas on the family; instead he endeavored to understand the family's position.

'How are these things dealt with in your own culture?' was a key question in reaching a deeper awareness and understanding of the cultural barrier that existed for this family. They were paralysed by the lack of a 'respected elder' who could discuss issues of death and dying with the patient and thus allow the family to maintain their caring role.

Not only was this family fearful for their father's death but they were also afraid to address the important practical concerns that they knew needed to be addressed. They were unprepared to do this for reasons related to their cultural background. Dr Abrams was sensitive to this cultural difference. His willingness to act as a facilitator for the family discussions immediately relieved the family of a major worry and allowed them to concentrate on providing loving support for their father.

Doctors who are aware of their own cultural background and accepting of the differences that may exist between cultures will be comfortable in asking the right questions (Hall, 1986). Ignoring the cultural aspect in this case would only have increased the family's feeling of isolation and made communication about the management plan much more difficult.

When working with families from different cultures, cultural issues may be potential barriers to effective communication and finding common ground (McNeil, 1991). Common ground in this case was an understanding of the roles of physician and family with respect to consent for future treatment and discussion of these issues with the patient. The doctor's awareness of cultural differences and comfort in dealing with these differences can be helpful in relieving families' sense of isolation and fear (Tong and Spicer, 1994). In this case improved communication resulted in a more satisfactory management plan for all involved.

Component III: Finding Common Ground

Moira Stewart, Judith Belle Brown and W Wayne Weston

The third component of the patient-centered clinical method is finding common ground. To reach a mutual understanding or find common ground often requires that two potentially divergent viewpoints be brought together in a reasonable management plan. Once agreement is reached on the nature of the problems, the goals and priorities of treatment must be determined. What will be the patient's involvement in the treatment plan? How realistic is the plan in terms of the patient's perceptions of their illnesses? What are the patient's wishes and their ability to cope? Finally, how do each of the parties, patients and doctors, define their roles in this interaction and in carrying out the management plan?

Many authors describe the clinical encounter as a process in which doctor and patient negotiate to define what is important and what should be done (Anstett, 1981; Heaton, 1981; Quill, 1983; Rubin and Brown, 1975). Quill and Brody (1996) describe an 'enhanced autonomy' model in which patients can autonomously make choices using both medical information and the physician's opinion. We prefer to describe this process as a mutual effort of finding common ground between doctor and patient in three key areas: defining the problem; establishing the goals of treatment; and identifying the roles to be assumed by doctor and patient.

Defining the problem

It is a universal human characteristic to try to explain personal experiences in order to give people a sense of having some control by labelling those

Note: Parts of this chapter were published previously in *Canadian Family Physician* 1989; **35**: 147–51 and in *Patient-Centered Medicine: transforming the clinical method*, Sage Publications (1995).

experiences. Most patients want a 'name' for their illness or at least an explanation of their problem that makes sense to them (Cassell, 1991; Kleinman, 1988; McWhinney, 1997; Wood, 1991). Without some agreement about the nature of what is wrong, it is difficult for a doctor and patient to agree on a plan of management that is acceptable to both of them. It is not essential that the physician actually believe that the nature of the problem is as the patient sees it, but the doctor's explanation and recommended treatment must at least be consistent with the patient's point of view and make sense in the patient's world. People may develop quite magical notions of what is happening to them when they become ill. It seems better to them to have an irrational explanation of the problem than no explanation at all. Thus the quack who offers help will be preferred to the cryptic physician who offers little. Some patients will even blame themselves for the problem rather than see the illness as simply random or impersonal. As well, physicians may have a tendency to mislabel common problems of living using conventional medical labels.

Problems develop when patient and doctor have different ideas of the cause of the problems. For example:

- the patient says she is disabled by a repetitive strain injury and the doctor thinks she is malingering
- the doctor has diagnosed hypertension but the patient insists that his blood pressure is probably only elevated because he is nervous in the doctor's office and refuses to see it as a problem
- the parent of a seven-year-old child thinks there is something seriously wrong because the child has frequent colds: six a year. The doctor thinks this number is within normal limits and that the parent is overly protective of the child.

Defining the goals

When a doctor and patient meet, each has expectations and feelings about the encounter. If these are at odds or inappropriate, there may be difficulties. For example:

- the patient has a sore throat and expects to receive penicillin but instead is urged to gargle with salt water
- the patient is concerned about innocent palpitations but is found to have high blood pressure. The doctor launches into a treatment of the hypertension without explaining to the patient the benign nature of the cardiac symptoms
- the patient demands muscle relaxants for chronic muscular pains, but the doctor wants to use 'talking' therapy to resolve the 'underlying' problems.

If doctors ignore their patients' expectations, they risk not understanding their patients, who in turn will be angry or hurt by this perceived lack of interest or concern. Some patients will become more demanding in a desperate attempt to be heard; others will become sullen and unco-operative. Patients may be unwilling to listen to their doctors unless they believe that they have first been listened to themselves.

Some physicians find asking patients about their expectations to be awkward. Timing is important. If the physician asks for a patient's expectations too early in the interview, the patient may think that the doctor is evading making a diagnosis and may therefore be reluctant to say much. On the other hand, if the doctor waits until the end of the interview, time may be wasted on issues unimportant to the patient. The physician may even make suggestions which will have to be retracted. Doctors need to express their questions clearly and sincerely. For example, a physician might say, 'Can you help me to understand what you hope I might do for you today?'. It is important that neither the physician's words nor tone of voice suggest any accusation that the patient is wasting the doctor's time on something trivial or silly. Often, it is helpful to pick up on a patient's comments that suggest, or hint at, their ideas, expectations or feelings. For example: 'I have had this chest cold for three weeks now and none of those cough medicines you recommended has helped!' In response, the doctor should avoid becoming defensive and instead pick up on the patient's frustration: 'You sound fed up with the length of time this illness has dragged on. Are you wondering if it is something serious? Are you wanting a particular means to clear it up?'.

Thus, the goals of treatment must take into account the expectations and feelings of both physicians and patients. If the hidden agendas are not recognized, it may be difficult to reach agreement. What physicians call 'non-compliance' may be the patient's expressions of disagreement about treatment goals; in this sense the patient always has the last word.

The physician and patient need to work together to find a treatment plan that is acceptable to both. This requires that the goals and priorities of each be re-examined. It is often helpful for the doctor to explain the nature of the problem clearly and to outline the pros and cons of different approaches. It is important to acknowledge the patient's concerns first so that the patient is aware that the physician is taking these into account.

Defining the roles of patient and doctor

Sometimes there is profound disagreement about the nature of the problem or the goals and priorities for treatment. When such an impasse occurs, it is important to look at the relationship between the patient and the doctor, and at their perception of each other's roles.

One aspect of defining roles has to do with decision making. Doctors, when treating a cancer patient for example, may see themselves wanting to bring about remission and may expect the patient to assume the role of a passive recipient of treatment. Patients, however, may be seeking a physician who expresses concern and interest in their well-being and who is prepared to treat them in the least invasive manner, viewing them as autonomous individuals with a right to have a voice in deciding among various forms of treatment. This is not such a dilemma for doctors when the various forms of treatment are equally effective, but physicians are understandably concerned when the patient chooses a treatment that they consider to be not efficacious or even harmful. Another example is when a patient is looking for an authority who will tell him what is wrong and what he should do; the physician, on the other hand, wants a more egalitarian relationship in which doctor and patient share decision making.

Another important need is for the patient and doctor to define their respective roles in carrying out the management plan. Patients and doctors need to be clear about who is to arrange follow-up and referral as well as what each person's tasks are. For example, a patient might well assume that it is not her role but the doctor's to arrange for her mammogram test, if she has just moved from a town where that was the convention.

Evolution of the patient–doctor relationship over time allows the doctor to see the same patient with different problems in different settings over a number of years and also to see the patient through the eyes of other family members. The physician's commitment is to 'hang in' with the patient to the end. Patients need to know that they can count on their doctors to be there when they need them. This ongoing relationship colours everything that happens between them. If there are difficulties in their relationship or differing expectations of their roles, they will have problems in working together effectively. For example:

- the patient longs for a deep and meaningful relationship with a parental figure who will make up for everything the patient's own parent never gave; the doctor wants to be a biomedical scientist who can apply the discoveries of modern medicine to patients' problems
- the physician enjoys a holistic approach to medicine and wants to get to know patients as people; the patient seeks only technical assistance from the doctor.

The process of finding common ground

We believe that the process of finding common ground begins with the physician clearly describing his or her definition of the problem, management goals and potential roles in the ensuing care. There is considerable literature which attests to the prime importance of giving information in medical encounters (Riccardi and Kurtz, 1983) and to patients' dissatisfaction with the information and explanation they receive (Consumer Reports, 1995). Such information is more beneficial in a context of emotional support (Haezen-Klemens and Lapinska, 1984).

Subsequent discussion should include ample opportunity for patients to ask questions and raise concerns. Such active participation by patients has been shown to benefit patient outcomes (Kaplan *et al.*, 1989a, b). Engaging in a mutual discussion about the patient's questions and concerns serves to clarify issues, as well as supporting and motivating the patient. The goal is an explicit agreement between patient and physician about the definition of the problem, the management and their respective roles. It has been shown that patient–physician agreement is key to positive outcomes (Bass *et al.*, 1986; Starfield *et al.*, 1979, 1981). In the event of a lack of agreement between the physician and patient, a flexible response by the doctor would enhance the finding of common ground.

Preview of the cases

The first two cases describe instances in which the patient and doctor define the problem in different ways. The first patient is not convinced that her symptoms are panic attacks. The second patient's physical problems are an unconscious ticket of admission to the doctor's office and impede a deeper understanding. In these two cases, the physicians required patience and active listening to appreciate the patients' perspectives, especially their feelings, and the patients' life contexts before common ground could be reached.

The next two cases illustrate challenges in coming to agreement about the goals of management. They underscore the importance of discussions about patients' feelings, especially fears, before agreement on management can be reached and patient adherence can be enhanced. One patient feared that if she came to the doctor too often she would have to change her lifestyle dramatically and these feelings explained her seeming lack of adherence. Another patient assumed that her menopausal problems were the same as her mother's and the deep feelings thus engendered had important implications for her acceptance of certain management options.

The next three cases illustrate the need for explicit discussion of the doctor and patient roles during the management of health problems. A middle-aged male patient and his physician failed to have an explicit discussion and come to an agreement about their respective roles, thereby leading the physician to wonder about the patient's willingness to adhere. An elderly male patient was astonished to find himself chastised for acquiescing to another doctor's wishes, underscoring the need for professionals to respect the role the patient feels comfortable adopting in his relationship with providers. The third patient in this set expressed dissatisfaction with his previous physician because he was not as involved in his care as he wished. The current doctor, picking up on this cue, was more diligent in discussing with the patient the role he wished the doctor to play at each stage of his increasingly complex case. This case illustrates not only finding common ground but also components described later, i.e. the patient–doctor relationship and being realistic.

The final set concerns difficult relationships and angry patients or family members. The first is a case of an elderly woman who wanted a cure for a condition for which there was no cure and illustrates issues of control and physician discomfort. Next is a two-part case about a doctor and the family of a dying patient. The physician's struggle in dealing with the family's anger and the issue of power and control had implications for finding common ground and also for establishing a relationship of trust with the family.

Cases Illustrating Component III: Finding Common Ground

21

The diagnostic label

Judith Belle Brown, Marie-Claude Raymond and
W Wayne Weston

Patients and doctors use diagnostic labels for patients' problems. These 'code words' are rich in meaning and symbolism, reflecting world views which may be quite different from one person to another. It is important for doctors to understand their patients' 'code' so that they can find common ground about health management.

Rebecca, 46, complained to her doctor of 'horrible leg pain'. She described how leg cramps grew into a 'chain reaction', culminating in shortness of breath and numbness in all her limbs. Rebecca anxiously explained that these episodes were happening several times a week and were severely restricting her activities. She had been withdrawing more and more from work and social activities with friends, for fear that the symptoms would occur and embarrass her. On several occasions the 'episodes' were so unbearable that she was forced to leave work feeling humiliated and out of control. After ruling out physiological causes, the doctor proposed that the root of the problem might be panic attacks.

Shocked by this suggestion, Rebecca responded with anger. 'My legs are bothering me terribly!' she said. 'Panic attacks be damned, I don't believe it. I can just go for a walk and it happens! Why should it happen when I'm having a good time? I honestly and truly believe that I have a problem of circulation in my legs and something has to be done!'

'What does it mean to you,' the doctor asked, 'when I say panic attacks?'

'It makes me angry,' replied Rebecca forcefully. 'It suggests that you don't believe me! The cramps are very real, they stay there and they can last for hours.'

Although both Rebecca and her doctor acknowledged the existence of her symptoms, there was a vast difference in their explanations about the cause and their ideas about treatment. For Rebecca, her leg pain was purely physical: she wanted a biomedical diagnosis to explain her pain and a medication to cure

Note: This case description first appeared in the July 1993 issue of the *Ontario Medical Review* and is reprinted with permission of the Ontario Medical Association.

the problem. From the physician's perspective, the patient's symptoms were psychological. As a result, the recommended plan of management was very different from what the patient expected.

This case illustrates the central importance of the diagnostic label for both patient and doctor (Kleinman, 1988). Doctors use the diagnosis as a 'shorthand' for the problem: it explains what all patients with this label have in common and informs the doctor about what treatment is likely to be beneficial based on empirical evidence.

For the patient, the label may help make sense of the experience and may provide some degree of control over what is often a disturbing ordeal. How the patient chooses the label is often rooted in her belief system, which is influenced by age, gender, family, culture and socioeconomic status (Weston and Brown, 1989).

This case illustrates how the doctor's definition of the problem may be radically different from that of the patient (Toombs, 1992). In fact, the medical diagnosis may actually minimize the patient's continuing experience of the problem. When there is such disagreement about the nature of the problem, it is difficult to agree on management. What can be done when the patient and physician disagree about the label? Who has the responsibility to seek a solution to this dilemma?

First, it is futile for the patient and doctor to argue about whose diagnosis is correct. Ultimately it is the physician's responsibility to initiate a dialogue that will lead to mutual agreement. Common ground will only be reached by exploring how both the doctor and the patient understand the problem. Once this is achieved, doctor and patient are in a position to collaborate on a management plan.

Second, it is important to consider what the label means to the patient. Rebecca was angered by the label 'panic attacks'. Why did she respond with such intense emotion? Perhaps, when her reality was challenged, she felt even more helpless and out of control. The label did not lessen her pain but served to exacerbate it. Physicians must show respect for patients' explanatory models, even when they are at odds with their own (Weston and Brown, 1989). This does not mean acquiescing to an unscientific formulation but it does mean listening to and understanding the patient's explanation. Doctors also need to understand patients' reactions to the medical label.

When patients and doctors explore the meaning of their labels, they narrow the gap in understanding which separates them. Patients are willing to listen to their doctors only after they feel they have first been heard themselves. For example, when her symptoms were interpreted by the doctor as a panic attack, Rebecca became more adamant in her belief that they were physical. Why was it important for Rebecca to view her symptoms as having a physiological, rather than psychological, basis? Does a biomedical diagnosis provide her with greater certainty that her symptoms will be relieved? Does the label of panic attacks activate feelings of guilt or fear of insanity for this patient? Is there a history of mental illness that haunts her? The answers to these questions will help the doctor understand what 'panic attack' means to the patient. The meaning attached to the label can take many forms: fear, guilt, anxiety, denial, escape or relief.

Understanding the meaning of the diagnostic label will help clarify what the patient expects. Rebecca's expectation was that the doctor would relieve her pain. She believed that 'circulation problems' are treated with drugs, not by talking. Sometimes tests or referrals may be necessary to reassure patients that they do not have a particular dreaded disorder.

It is not always necessary to agree on the problem label as long as the explanations of patient and doctor lead to similar treatment. For example, in this case if the doctor recognized the patient's need to see her problem as biological, then he might focus on the physiological aspects and pharmacological approach to panic disorder.

A cluster of symptoms may accurately fit a specific diagnosis or label for the doctor. But for the patient, the label may be threatening or alien to her belief system. Only by understanding the meaning of the label, and the patient's expectations, can we move toward establishing a diagnosis and treatment plan that is mutually acceptable to both the doctor and the patient.

22

Resistant patients

Judith Belle Brown and W Wayne Weston

Patients frequently present with problems or complaints that appear resistant to change. Before labelling a patient as unco-operative or difficult it is important for the doctor to understand the reasons for the 'resistance'.

Mrs McIntosh, aged 39, frequently visited her doctor with physical complaints such as back pain, vague gastrointestinal symptoms or headaches for which no cause could ever be found. Usually, these symptoms occurred at times of family stress which she was reluctant to discuss with her doctor. On occasion she would request medication to 'make it all go away'. With each family crisis Mrs McIntosh offered her physical complaints as her ticket for entry into the health-care system and was not content until they were fully investigated. Only after she was satisfied that her problems were not physical would she consider that her symptoms might be a result of her worries about her husband's unemployment or her son's delinquency.

Despite repeated attempts by her doctor to relate her somatic symptoms to her family situation, he had not been able to alter Mrs McIntosh's preoccupation with her symptoms. Often, following a frustrating encounter with Mrs McIntosh, he would wonder: 'Why was she being so difficult? What prevented her from asking him directly for help? What was the cause of her resistance? How could he address her unco-operative behavior in a way that would be therapeutic? Was he somehow contributing to the problem?'.

'Resistant' behavior springs from both conscious and unconscious motivations that interfere with the therapeutic process. Generally, its purpose is to protect patients from overwhelming feelings which may immobilize them or threaten their coping abilities. Even though the intent is to protect patients, 'resistance' may prevent them from working through their problems or even from seeking help in the first place. It is important to recognize that asking for help means admitting to problems that patients cannot solve on their own.

Note: This case description first appeared in the November 1993 issue of the *Ontario Medical Review* and is reprinted with permission of the Ontario Medical Association.

Anxiety and embarrassment are common when patients share intimate details of their lives and reveal their hopes and fears. Such feelings may result in their not sharing concerns or worries. Admitting a problem may also require patients to examine how they have contributed to the problem. In many situations it is easier to blame someone else rather than assume responsibility for the problem.

Patients often experience ambivalence when they ask for help: on one hand, they seek the relief of sharing their burden with another, but on the other hand, they fear that they may not be understood or that they might make the situation even worse. For many patients the greatest source of resistance is fear of change. Often patients feel that the emotional pain they know is safer than the unknown possibilities or options that change presents. In addition, some patients lack the emotional, intellectual or physical resources required to effect change. Thus, their reluctance to change is not rooted in indifference or unco-operativeness but in a sheer lack of resources.

Patients may also fear that their doctor will not understand them or will think less of them if they confess they are unable to manage their problems on their own. Those who have had problems in relationships over the years may fear that their doctor will reject or abandon them if they reveal their inner feelings and concerns. Previous expression of problems or worries may have been met with disdain or dismissal, leading patients to question their own feelings. When physicians are busy or preoccupied with ruling out serious organic illness they may seem uninterested or miss subtle cues to personal distress. The result, in some instances, is that patients think their feelings are crazy or not worthy of consideration (Arborelious *et al.*, 1991).

In about 50% of cases, when a patient visits a primary care physician there is no disease to adequately explain the problem. Despite this fact, physicians and patients alike continue to seek a biomedical explanation for all their symptoms. One hazard of this approach is that unexplained symptoms may be overinvestigated and, when there is still no explanation, the patient's symptoms are labelled as imaginary or feigned. Physicians may label the patient as resistant, unco-operative or difficult. Blaming the patient may absolve the doctor of responsibility but does not help the patient and often leaves the doctor feeling dissatisfied and frustrated.

When confronted about their 'resistant' behavior, patients may respond with anger and hostility or become distant and aloof. It is important for the doctor not to personalize the patient's response but view it as a confirmation of the patient's struggles to express his or her problems. At this point it is essential that the physician, responding with empathy and concern, continues to address the patient's behavior. As in the case of Mrs McIntosh, the doctor observed: 'When I suggested that your problem might be more than your husband's unemployment, you seemed angry. I don't understand what your anger was about. Can you help me?' In this way the doctor gave the responsibility for the anger, and its possible resolution, back to the patient.

Frequently patients offer verbal cues that can alert physicians to the presence of 'resistance'. They may change the subject, appear to edit or censor their comments, be silent or, alternatively, become overly expressive and detailed in their description of their problem. When faced with silence from a patient or a remark such as 'Nothing comes to mind' or 'I have no idea what to say', the doctor could respond with, 'It seems like it's hard for you to begin' or 'It sounds like this is a tough subject for you to discuss'.

There are many non-verbal cues that can also serve to identify 'resistance'. Patients may become flushed, fidgeting or restless, lose eye contact or perspire visibly. Observing that Mrs McIntosh became quite flushed while discussing her anger with her husband, the doctor commented, 'While we were talking about your husband you became quite flushed; do you think there is any connection?'. Or when a patient appears restless or distracted, the physician could comment, 'You seem distracted, is there something else going on that you want to tell me?'. In Mrs McIntosh's case, it was useful for the doctor to ask, 'In the past, when you've had troubles at home, it's been hard for you to tell me about them. Is it possible that this is the situation today?'.

Finally, patients may demonstrate their 'resistant' behavior through specific actions such as being late for appointments, cancelling appointments or not showing for a scheduled appointment. When this type of behavior persists it is important for the doctor to address the behavior in a way that will be therapeutic and not further distance or alienate the patient. These are often attempts by patients to gain some control in a threatening situation. In helping Mrs McIntosh understand her behavior the doctor commented, 'In the last few months you have cancelled a number of our appointments. I wonder if this could be connected with how hard it has been for you to talk about your problems?'.

In dealing with 'resistance', it is imperative to begin where the patient is and to explore his or her ideas and feelings about the meaning of the 'resistance'. What ideas do they have about the source of their resistance? For example, the doctor asked Mrs McIntosh: 'Whenever we begin to talk about your son's delinquency you become restless. Why do you think that happens?'. He also inquired, 'Do you think maybe your headaches have become worse since you've been worrying about your husband being laid off?'

'Resistance' is often fuelled by strong emotions. By addressing patients' feelings with respect and empathy, we may uncover the root of their difficulties in both asking for and receiving help. For example, the physician reflected back to Mrs McIntosh, who was denying feeling angry at her son's acting out: 'You have said before that your feelings don't count, that no one in the family cares about how you feel. Is this the case now?'. The doctor's comments affirmed the patient's feelings and helped her see the connection between past experiences and her present concerns.

In closing, let us return to Mrs McIntosh and her physician. Mrs McIntosh continued to find it difficult to connect her physical symptoms with her family problems. Over the years her physical complaints had been the only legitimate means to communicate her emotional needs. To ask her doctor for help with personal problems represented failure. She felt ashamed by her husband's inability to maintain a job and her son's repetitive encounters with the law. Fearful that her doctor would view her concerns about her family as trivial and irrelevant, Mrs McIntosh persisted with her physical complaints. Already vulnerable and insecure, exposure of her inner feelings and fears felt extremely threatening to her and thus fuelled her 'resistance'.

Over time her doctor came to appreciate her concerns and to see her 'resistance' as a necessary means to protect herself from overwhelming feelings. With this improved understanding, her doctor was able to devise an intervention and management plan that acknowledged her needs.

23

Patients' fears

David Snadden and Judith Belle Brown

Taking the time to listen to a patient's experience of their illness can often lead to greater understanding and an opportunity to reach mutual agreement on treatment options. This often results in better care and improved patient recovery.

Sixty-two year old Mrs Lee sat in her doctor's office, describing a frightening experience. 'Last night I could hardly get my air. I was all closed up and gasping and had this terrible tight sensation across my chest. It went on and on and I had to sit at the edge of my bed pressing down with my hands, just to try and get some air into me.' She paused and looked a little embarrassed. 'The inhaler just didn't work,' she went on. 'I guess maybe it was because it was empty . . . again.'

Dr Swarztman's heart sank as he listened to the story. He needed time to sort out this patient's problem but he was running late, the waiting room was bulging at the seams, the nursing home was asking for him and he had a meeting due to start in an hour.

'I'd really like to spend some time talking to you about this,' he told Mrs Lee. 'What about me giving you a new inhaler now and asking you to make a half hour appointment with me in the next few days?'

Mrs Lee smiled. 'Yes, I'd really like that.'

The following day, when she returned, Dr Swarztman decided to encourage her to tell him about her asthma. How did she handle it, he wondered? Why did she put up with these infrequent, though severe and frightening, episodes? Noticing that she always let her inhalers run out, he asked, 'Why do you do it? You might harm yourself'.

'I . . . I don't know,' replied Mrs Lee.

Realizing that this type of questioning was not capturing the patient's perception of the problem, the doctor tried a new approach. 'Tell me how you feel when you need to come and ask for a new inhaler,' he said. After a few more indirect questions, a picture began to emerge of Mrs Lee's experience with this chronic condition.

Note: This case description first appeared in the May 1992 issue of the *Ontario Medical Review* and is reprinted with permission of the Ontario Medical Association.

Mrs Lee lived in the country and the family home contained several well-loved pets. She felt that she could control her symptoms with the occasional use of an inhaler, but something always stopped her from asking for a new one. It became apparent that she was terrified of losing control, should she seek help from the doctor. She feared that she would be referred for various tests which would lead to a recommendation to significantly alter her environment. Her dominant worry was that she would be told that she should get rid of her pets and move to the city. She was prepared to accept some limitations due to her condition but the potential loss of her beloved pets and cherished country home was something she could not contemplate. This deep-seated fear was great enough to prevent her seeking help in relation to her asthma, hoping it would 'just go away'.

After discussing these issues the doctor agreed that he would not refer her for further investigation at this time and would try to control her symptoms through medication, allowing her to maintain her present lifestyle (Barnes, 1990). With the doctor's help, Mrs Lee developed a greater understanding of her condition and more insight into her fears. Because of the understanding the doctor had shown, Mrs Lee developed trust in him. By establishing common ground, both doctor and patient had a better understanding of the treatment options and of their roles in addressing the problems at hand. From this grew a mutual understanding and a plan of management to which both felt committed. This helped Mrs Lee to accept that she could ask for help more quickly if she had any more frightening episodes.

This case illustrates the need to make time for certain patients in certain circumstances. By taking the time to listen, Dr Swarztman was able to understand Mrs Lee's view of her condition. They achieved a mutual understanding, through open discussion and clarification, which allowed better therapy and access to care. Both benefited from the mutual trust developed in the encounter. By encouraging the patient to participate in her care, the doctor allayed her fear of loss of control.

In addition, the doctor gained insight into some of the factors which influence the behavior of patients with chronic conditions. For example, patients with chronic health problems often feel they have lost control over their lives. They experience their need for healthcare as a sign of dependency. This can lead to a reluctance to seek assistance, with consequent denial of the need for help in the face of a potentially fatal condition. This response to chronic illness can only be altered by addressing the patient's fears and concerns. Only when the doctor and patient gain some insight into these worries can change occur.

In the story described above, the doctor was relieved to feel that Mrs Lee would not, in the future, allow her condition to become severe again without seeking help. The patient was relieved that she now had permission to ask for medication or help in the future without feeling anxiety, fear or guilt.

24

Patient expectations

Judith Belle Brown, Marie-Claude Raymond and W Wayne Weston

When people get sick, they often develop ideas about what is wrong and what should be done, based on their own health beliefs learned in their families while growing up. Unless directly questioned, they may not discuss these beliefs with their doctor. When a patient and doctor share the patient's ideas, both parties reach a deeper understanding of the patient's problems and are more likely to find common ground about management.

Mrs Carlotti, a 49-year-old woman with irregular periods and occasional hot flashes, had undergone a dilation and curettage three times in the past five years. Mrs Carlotti had agreed to a referral to a gynecologist for an opinion about management. But even before the visit, she had decided what treatment would be acceptable to her: she expected a hysterectomy.

The next time she saw Dr Wong, her family doctor, she expressed her concerns about being given a prescription for hormone replacement therapy. 'He's pushing patients out of there so fast, I couldn't believe it!' she said. 'He had his mind made up before I came in. He told me he didn't think that I needed a hysterectomy and I was very surprised. He didn't ask any questions and didn't give me a chance to talk about my concerns.'

'What do you intend to do?' asked Dr Wong.

'I was waiting to see you,' replied Mrs Carlotti. 'What do you think about it?'

'Clearly, you were not very pleased with how the visit turned out,' observed the doctor.

'I feel very disappointed,' she said. 'I just feel it didn't go the way it was supposed to. I don't think I had any say in what happened. I don't question that I am in menopause. My mother also experienced irregular periods and she ended up with a hysterectomy in her mid-50s. I just figured I was the same as her.'

Note: This case description first appeared in the August 1993 issue of the *Ontario Medical Review* and is reprinted with the permission of the Ontario Medical Association.

In our example, the doctor quickly recognized that Mrs Carlotti would be extremely reluctant to comply with the gynecologist's recommendations until they reached some degree of common ground: they needed to establish a mutual understanding of the problem and the available treatment methods. The doctor also realized that, before she embarked on this discussion, it was critically important to offer Mrs Carlotti an opportunity to express her frustration and disappointment with the consultation without colluding with her or 'taking sides' in the discussion. Although the doctor agreed with the consultant's opinion, she knew that it would serve no purpose to argue this point with her patient. First she supported her patient in talking about her feelings, then she attempted to understand what was fuelling these intense emotions (Britt *et al.*, 1992).

'You mentioned earlier that you thought you were just like your mother who ended up with a hysterectomy,' said the doctor. 'Can you help me understand your thoughts on this?'

'I assumed that I had inherited my menstrual problems and would likely end up with a hysterectomy by the time I was 50,' said Mrs Carlotti. 'If I'm going to need it anyway, I'd just as soon get it over with.'

'That's a reasonable assumption,' said the doctor. 'However, times have changed a lot since your mother faced this problem. Often hysterectomy is unnecessary now.'

'But I don't like the idea of taking drugs the rest of my life.'

'What concerns you about that?'

As the doctor extended her inquiry, Mrs Carlotti explained that her family did not believe in taking pills: their idea was, 'If you have a problem, cut it out!'. This was a widely held belief in her family and Mrs Carlotti found it difficult to run counter to this viewpoint. This information helped the doctor understand her patient's resistance to hormone replacement therapy and subsequently guided her explanations of what the treatment regimen would entail. The patient was encouraged to ask questions about the proposed treatment and to express her reluctance.

In addition, it was important to assist the patient to distinguish between her own experience and that of her mother, to see her problem as unique and specific to her. But this was not a simple matter of transmitting information: it was also important to be sensitive to the patient's strong association with her mother's experience and its possible emotional or symbolic meaning.

Rather than confronting the patient's beliefs and labelling them as foolish or, at best, misguided, the doctor used this knowledge to better understand Mrs Carlotti's concerns about the proposed treatment. Instead of engaging in a struggle with her patient, the doctor encouraged Mrs Carlotti to participate in a discussion of the problem. Once they had established a common understanding of the problem, both doctor and patient could collaborate on a treatment plan acceptable to both.

In many instances the task of finding common ground will not be as difficult as in the case of Mrs Carlotti. Yet most patients bring their own specific health beliefs, and associated expectations, to the interaction. Challenging these beliefs risks alienating patients and reinforcing their resistance. By understanding the powerful influence of the patient's belief system, the physician will be better equipped to reach a shared agreement with the patient.

25

Referrals

Martin J Bass, Diana Lemaire and Judith Belle Brown

To make a successful referral, the physician must establish common ground with the patient on the problem and the approach to managing it. The patient must understand his or her role, the role of the referring physician and the role of the health professional to whom the referral is made.

Mac, a 45-year-old self-employed electrician, calmly waited for the doctor to finish the examination. Although he perceived himself to be in relatively good health, Mac regularly visited his doctor for a 'check-up'. His only major health risk was that he smoked one package of cigarettes a day.

As the routine physical came to an end Dr Donach summarized her findings and recommendations for the patient. 'Well, you are in pretty good shape but I'd like to do some blood work, particularly your cholesterol, because of your high-risk status as a smoker. Then we'll see if there is anything else we need to do.'

Mac accepted the lab requisition form from the doctor, thanked her for her time and thought nothing more about the visit.

A week later the patient's wife visited the doctor for a recheck of a skin rash. During the visit she said that Mac had asked her to find out about the results of his cholesterol test.

Dr Donach, already one hour behind schedule due to an earlier emergency, said, 'It's high. Here's a brochure for Mac to look at and the receptionist will make an appointment for counseling for him with the dietitian at the hospital. I'd like to see Mac in three months to reassess his cholesterol. Have him call us for an appointment to repeat the blood test.'

When she got home that evening, Mac's wife relayed the information to him, observing that the doctor had seemed quite busy. Neither Mac nor his wife thought anything more about the visit.

Note: This case description first appeared in the March 1993 issue of the *Ontario Medical Review* and is reprinted with permission of the Ontario Medical Association.

Three months later, Mac returned to the doctor's office as instructed, having completed the required blood work. Reviewing the laboratory results, the doctor was surprised to learn that the patient's cholesterol was even higher.

'I don't understand these results,' she said, frowning. 'How did the counseling with the dietitian go?'

'I never got around to it,' Mac replied. 'I got very busy at work and I didn't think it was a big deal. I could figure it out for myself.'

Dr Donach persisted: 'I'm sure you were busy at work but why didn't you go to see the dietitian? Meeting with the dietitian is important in getting your cholesterol under control!'

Why wasn't this a successful referral? Had work demands distracted the patient or did he lack the motivation to follow through with the appointment? Had the patient and his wife colluded in denying the results of the blood work? Why didn't they understand the importance of meeting with the dietitian? Where did the communication break down between the patient and the doctor?

The success of a referral is often dependent on the doctor's ability to facilitate the referral process. The doctor serves as a bridge between the patient and the health professional. To act in this capacity the doctor must reach a mutual understanding and agreement with the patient concerning the problem and the action to be taken (Brown *et al.*, 1995). This will assist the patient in accepting and engaging in the referral. The physician can also clarify the reason for the referral, what is expected of both the patient and the health professional and the potential outcome of the referral. Such a clear explanation is a prelude to a mutual discussion about the referral process.

In this case the doctor needed to determine if the patient understood that his elevated cholesterol was a problem. Secondly, she had to ascertain if her patient perceived the problem as requiring attention. Thirdly, the doctor needed to discuss what management plans would be acceptable and feasible for this patient. For example, was he prepared to participate in a program to alter his cholesterol status? This might include exploring the logistics of attending counseling appointments during work hours or helping Mac understand what the counseling sessions would involve. In this case Mac's lack of knowledge about nutrition counseling may have interfered with acceptance of the referral or he may have been reluctant to seek help for his problem. Also, the patient may have been unclear about what his role would be in the counseling process, thus reinforcing his reluctance to participate. Because many male patients don't have an investment in food decisions, such as selection and preparation, they may view referral to the dietitian as a low priority. Finally, the process of finding common ground must occur with the patient and not be communicated through a relative if the referral is to have a successful outcome. This is not to dismiss the important role that relatives or significant others may play in the referral process. Rather, it emphasizes the importance of communicating directly with patients whenever possible.

In summary, to make a successful referral, the doctor must establish a mutual understanding and agreement with the patient of:

- the problem
- the approach to management
- the roles that each of the participants – the patient, the physician and the health professional – will assume in the referral process.

26

Collaboration

Carol L McWilliam, Judith Belle Brown and Brian K E Hennen

When a hospitalized patient is under the care of several different health professionals, one physician should be appointed to communicate with him or her. If differences of opinion arise, the attending physician should decide if and when they will be shared with the patient. The attending physician's role is to ensure that the patient plays an active part in any decisions about his or her care.

Mr Williams had been through a great deal during his four-week hospitalization. Initially admitted for repair of an abdominal aortic aneurysm, he had also had an elective cholecystectomy and subsequently, a transurethral prostatectomy. Finally severe diarrhea had complicated his post-operative recovery. While physically weakened by these events, he looked forward to returning home to his garden and to the company of his good friends. 'Yes', he thought to himself, 'it has been quite an ordeal, but at 73 years of age, that's what you expect. It will be nice to go home and to be my old independent self again.'

This moment of quiet reflection was broken by the arrival of Dr Kahn, a resident on the third surgical team to have responsibility for his care during this hospitalization. Mr Williams had not spoken with Dr Kahn for several days and was greatly perplexed by the abrupt exchange which followed.

Without introduction, Dr Kahn began: 'Why did you agree to have your gallbladder out?'

'Well, I trusted the surgeon,' replied Mr Williams. 'I thought he was good. If I take my car to the garage and they tell me it needs fixing, I get it fixed!'

'Well, I think gallbladders are very important and should never be removed,' the doctor retorted. 'You realize that the bile is formed in the gallbladder and controls your bowel system?'

Note: This case description first appeared in the May 1993 issue of the *Ontario Medical Review* and is reprinted with permission of the Ontario Medical Association.

Somewhat taken aback by the doctor's comments, Mr Williams responded, 'I'm sorry. I didn't know this, and at this point, I haven't got my gallbladder any more, so I'm not particularly interested. I do know a lot of people who don't have their gallbladders, and they are living normal lives.'

'Yes, and some of them have chronic diarrhea for the rest of their lives!' replied the doctor as he departed from Mr Williams' room, seemingly exasperated with this patient.

Mr Williams perceived the doctor's comments as a direct criticism of his having consented to a cholecystectomy and he felt blamed for his diarrhea. He had placed his trust, and subsequent care, in the hands of the surgeon who had done the cholecystectomy. Relying on the surgeon's knowledge and skill, Mr Williams had felt confident and satisfied. Now he doubted his decision and wondered, 'Who knows best?'.

Deference to professional authority is not unusual, especially for older people, who place high value upon their doctor's recommendations (McWilliam *et al.*, 1994). Patients, often overwhelmed by the severity of their problems, depend on their physicians to direct the decision-making process (Ende *et al.*, 1989). Such behavior presents challenges for professionals, as it raises questions about how to involve patients in decision making about their care. Who will be involved in the decision-making process? How will it be communicated? In what ways can the patient be supported and encouraged to participate in decisions about his or her care? Is there a shared understanding of both the doctor's and the patient's roles in the decision-making process? Does the therapeutic outcome appear consistent with the patient's long-term goals and interests? The challenge does not end once the decision is taken. Understanding and dealing with the consequences of interventions are also a part of the shared decision-making responsibilities. For example, Mr Williams clearly needed support and guidance in dealing with his post-surgical complications, not chastisement.

The challenge increases when several physicians with differing views about interventions are involved in providing care. At the outset all the medical personnel involved should decide who will assume responsibility for keeping the patient informed. Ideally, the physician with whom the patient has established the most comfortable relationship should take this role. Practically speaking, the attending physician often undertakes this communicator role for the patient's entire hospitalization. In a community hospital this is frequently the patient's family doctor. Increasingly, however, in larger tertiary care hospitals, when the focal problem area of the patient changes, so does the attending physician. To complicate matters further, in teaching hospitals such communicating responsibilities frequently get delegated to house staff.

If patients are to be appropriately informed and involved, communicating responsibilities should rest with one person, known to the patient and the health-care team. The physician who assumes this task must keep colleagues informed, so that the patient is not forced to judge the competence of one physician against that of another. Other physicians and health professionals involved should also ensure their communication with the patient is consistent with that of the physician directing care. Differences of opinion should be presented to the patient only after thoughtful discussion and agreement about how and when it should be done. The patient should not become the debating platform for differences of opinion, as in Mr Williams' situation.

Brody (1992, p. 65) notes that: '... a good medical outcome should be designed not merely to resolve the problem of the moment but also to cement and reinforce a mode of relating to the patient that encourages his full and active participation over time.' This can only be achieved if the physician communicates an understanding and respect for the patient's chosen role in the decision-making process. For some patients this will include extensive involvement while others, like Mr Williams, may choose to defer to the physician. It is the physician's responsibility to secure and promote the patient's position by clearly communicating his choice to the other healthcare professionals involved in his care. Only through a consistent and timely use of this approach can physicians expect to do more good than harm in their efforts to involve patients in decision making about their own care.

27

Successful referrals

*Carol L McWilliam, Judith Belle Brown
and W Wayne Weston*

Complications of chronic illness frequently erode the coping abilities of elderly patients. Fear of the unknown and loss of control often escalate when patients feel they are at the mercy of the healthcare system. Explicit discussion of the roles of the patient and the doctor can reduce patient frustration and dissatisfaction.

Mr Ribera was a 75 year old widower who had managed to live independently in his own home, despite advanced congestive heart failure. Recently, he had developed severe dependent edema and, following yet another frustrating experience with his doctor, had decided to change physicians, seeking the services of Dr Donaldson.

As Mr Ribera waited for the new doctor to see him in the examining room, he cautiously confided in the office nurse. 'You know, Dr Green looked after my family for 37 years,' said Mr Ribera. 'He delivered my three children, and even made house calls to my wife when she was dying of cancer. I never had to see him myself, until I had my first heart attack five years ago. Since that time, he has always seen me when I called for an appointment. But he doesn't seem to pay any attention to me. Perhaps it's because he told me right off I should quit smoking, and I never did. Perhaps he more or less gave up on me right from that point. What's worse, though, he doesn't seem to want to really get to know me. When I had the heart attack, he sent me to Dr Yip, the cardiologist. When I had trouble with my prostate, he sent me to Dr Zimmer. This time, he wanted me to go see Dr Axworth, about this swelling. Like, he never did anything! He just always sent me to see somebody else and every time, I'd end up waiting for weeks to get seen, and longer to get anything done. So I told him I didn't want to go see Dr Axworth, and I decided I'm not going to bother going back to him again. Either he doesn't care or maybe he's going to quit work. He is getting on. So it's just time for a new doctor, I guess!'

Note: This case description first appeared in the April 1995 issue of the *Ontario Medical Review* and is reprinted with permission of the Ontario Medical Association.

Dr Donaldson had entered the examining room as Mr Ribera began this story and made careful mental notes. He automatically explored with Mr Ribera what role he wanted his new family physician to play in his care, confirming for Mr Ribera that he had heard that Dr Green was retiring. Additionally, however, he explored Mr Ribera's needs and expectations for referral, explaining to him that he had signs and symptoms suggesting some kidney problems. The doctor explained that these could potentially become very serious, even with a family doctor's care. Together, patient and doctor identified what specific roles and routines might work for them, deciding that regular blood work, medication and weekly office visits would allow them to find out whether the symptoms could be managed conservatively. While Mr Ribera was reluctant to accept a referral to a nephrologist, he did agree that early attention to any serious signs of renal failure was important to him. He advised Dr Donaldson that he would think about it and 'check it out'. At the next visit, Mr Ribera told the doctor that he would consider going to the nephrologist if and when necessary, provided that he didn't have to wait a long time to be seen.

Several months later, when renal failure and the need for dialysis became apparent, Dr Donaldson and Mr Ribera had come to know one another. Dr Donaldson, in response to his knowledge that Mr Ribera expected him to play an active role in hospital care, had made certain that he gave Mr Ribera his schedule for visiting hospitalized patients and reassured him that he and Dr Moss, the nephrologist, would together manage his care.

Dr Donaldson had paved the road to successful referral, creating a positive patient–doctor relationship by consistently finding common ground with his patient on this potentially difficult issue. He had listened carefully to Mr Ribera's past experiences and incorporated his ideas, feelings and expectations into treatment planning. He understood that all patients exhibit ambivalence about wanting to know the truth about their illness, often needing to deny the possibility that anything is wrong when symptoms first appear. He also knew that at 75 years of age, Mr Ribera experienced these new symptoms as yet another threat to remaining independent. Furthermore, he surmised from Mr Ribera's story that he did have a need to feel personally cared for and taken care of.

Dr Donaldson managed the process of responding to the crisis of illness exceedingly well. He built in time for doctor and patient to get to know each other, so that Mr Ribera could develop some feeling of trust in him. He approached the referral process gingerly, allowing Mr Ribera to retain some sense of control over his own life and helping minimize the sense that his independence was threatened. He also recognized that Mr Ribera's sense of time would be constricted and fears of the unknown heightened while awaiting his appointment with the nephrologist. Finally, he ensured that Mr Ribera would experience some sense of continuity in his care, by arranging, in advance, his own regular ongoing involvement in managing the patient's care.

A year later in the office, Dr Donaldson fully appreciated the value of his efforts to be patient-centered when Mr Ribera said to him, 'Well, my life's a bit of a rocky road these days, but I want to thank you for standing by me, and making the ride as smooth as possible'.

28

Angry patient

Sharon Graham and Judith Belle Brown

It isn't always easy to find common ground with an angry patient. Doctors must recognize their feelings of frustration and futility and ensure that they do not interfere with the patient–doctor relationship.

Dr Monterey had just been told that his patient, Alma, had suddenly died. The doctor felt immediate relief, followed quickly by guilt.

Alma was 75 when she died. Life had not been kind to her. She had worked hard to make a living from a very young age. She married late to a man who was very dependent on her and not her intellectual equal. She also battled several health problems: breast cancer with metastasis to the mediastinum, glaucoma, cataracts, hypertension and a swallowing disorder for oesophageal dysmotility.

Alma's need to have the world on her own terms led to many conflicts with healthcare professionals and the healthcare system. At times she refused treatment that would help her and at others, she insisted on treatment that would be risky. Her way of dealing with her vision problems is a good example of the conflicts that arose.

Alma had suffered from glaucoma for many years and several ophthalmologists had given her excellent advice and treatment. Late in life, she developed dense bilateral cataracts and her vision deteriorated to the point where she could no longer drive a car. Several ophthalmologists advised her that surgery for her cataracts was too risky. Suspecting that one eye was totally blind due to the glaucoma, they felt the risk of total blindness was too great. Alma didn't agree and eventually found an ophthalmologist who would take the risk. Her vision was significantly improved by the surgery and she immediately began insisting on the same surgery for the other eye.

Eventually the ophthalmologist returned her to Dr Monterey's care with a note that she didn't need to see him again and that no further surgery was warranted. Alma was bitter and held Dr Monterey responsible for what she saw as the shortcomings of his profession.

'You doctors are all in cahoots,' she would say angrily. 'You don't really care what happens to an old woman like me.'

On good days, Dr Monterey understood that this was simply Alma's way of getting along: her anger was not directed at him personally but at life in general. On bad days, he felt quiet desperation and anger. They were still at an impasse when she died.

Alma was a difficult and complex patient. Finding common ground with a patient like this can be a daunting task. Usually doctors and patients can come to agreement about the nature of the problem and its solution. Even if they fail to come to complete agreement, they will likely develop some mutual understanding.

In this case, the doctor had developed some understanding of Alma's situation but she was oblivious to his. When conflict is inevitable, the doctor must understand his own need for power and control (Brody, 1987). His understanding of himself, the patient and the context of the problem will go a long way to preventing difficult situations from disintegrating into power struggles.

Time is also an important factor. Doctors who have the luxury of developing a long-term relationship with a patient, in which understanding and trust are developed gradually over time, are more likely to be able to find common ground.

Dr Monterey's feelings of frustration and futility were natural. Such feelings must be recognized and dealt with, so that they do not interfere with the patient–doctor relationship. Alma's struggle reflected her need to have some element of control over a difficult life. Dr Monterey was correct in assuming that her anger was not levelled at him personally but at her untreatable condition.

Doctors tend to feel guilty when they cannot cure their patients. This is the result of a medical culture that is increasingly based on technology and intolerant of failure. It is often difficult to care for a patient who is incurable and to accept that further referrals are futile. Dr Monterey's guilt was probably greater because he couldn't convince Alma that her condition was untreatable. But the fact that Alma kept returning suggests that she found his care helpful.

Doctors should not feel guilty when the only help they can offer is support and understanding. Nor should they feel guilty when they react with anger to a patient's anger. Recognizing these feelings and dealing with them constructively will lead to relief and resolution. Dr Monterey's consideration of the problems presented by Alma as a patient will help him work difficult relationships in future.

29

Family anger: 1

John Jordan and Judith Belle Brown

When a family is faced with a serious diagnosis of a relative, one response may be anger directed at the physician. Responding therapeutically to the family's anger is critical in ensuring the patient's future care.

Mrs Barber, an 85-year-old widow, living independently in her own apartment, was not in the habit of visiting the doctor's office. Over the years Mrs Barber had taken pride in her health, particularly in being a non-smoker and taking no medications. In fact, it had been several years since her last visit to Dr Keith's office when she had a malignant lesion removed from her right cheek.

Consequently, it was rather unusual when Mrs Barber was ushered into the family doctor's office by her daughter Jana, who urgently explained: 'My mom has a lump on her neck that has gotten bigger in the past month and we are quite worried about it'. The doctor learned that Mrs Barber had first noticed the lump about four months ago but, as it hadn't caused her any discomfort, she had dismissed any sinister problem. Indeed, Mrs Barber felt her daughter was over-reacting and expressed embarrassment over 'all the fuss'.

When Dr Keith examined the growth he was alarmed by the fact that it was quite hard and fixed to the underlying tissue. He clearly explained the problem to Mrs Barber and her daughter. Mrs Barber readily agreed to see the consultant who, a few weeks later, performed a fine needle aspiration biopsy. The diagnosis was a metastatic cancer from an unknown primary site. Subsequently, Dr Keith reviewed the treatment options with Mrs Barber and her daughter, explaining that the options would be for palliation not cure. At that time, Mrs Barber and her daughter opted not to have any treatment.

Several months passed before Mrs Barber returned to Dr Keith's office, this time accompanied by both of her daughters. Mrs Barber was complaining of a sore throat and once again expressed her embarrassment about bothering the doctor. Dr Keith's examination revealed large axillary and infraclavicular

Note: This case description first appeared in the December 1995 issue of the *Ontario Medical Review* and is reprinted with permission of the Ontario Medical Association.

masses, leading him to conclude that the tumor had gradually increased in size. Once again the doctor explained that Mrs Barber was not a surgical candidate because of her axillary metastases and advanced age, nor was she a candidate for radiation because of previous radiotherapy to the region. In addition, chemotherapy was dubious without certainty of the primary malignancy.

It was apparent that her health was beginning to decline and this news was devastating to the family. As Dr Keith related his concerns to Mrs Barber and her family, the eldest daughter, Rita, interrupted in an angry tone, 'Why didn't you pick it up sooner when there was still a chance to do something about it. If you really cared about our mother you would have detected this problem and taken care of it when it first started. You should have done something about it before now!'

The doctor was initially stunned by this angry response and wondered how to respond to this apparent attack on his integrity without escalating the hostilities further. Mrs Barber was going to require medical care as she was clearly entering the terminal stage of her illness. How could he provide care that would be accepted by the family, who were now extremely angry?

Dr Keith gently responded to Mrs Barber's daughter Rita: 'I sense that you are very concerned for your mother's welfare. Over the years she has always been pretty healthy. It must be frightening for you to see how much she has declined lately.'

Both daughters looked deeply saddened, but remained defensive. Dr Keith went on to explain: 'I'm afraid she will continue to decline and at some point you will need more help in caring for your mother. It will be important for a doctor to supervise her ongoing care. If you aren't comfortable with me providing that care I will help you find another doctor.'

Rita rapidly responded, 'Jana will move in with mother and I will come over to spell her off for a few hours most days. We don't need any more help and we don't plan to put her away in a home somewhere.' They promptly left the office, with the silent Mrs Barber in tow, failing to commit to any follow-up plan with Dr Keith.

Dr Keith was confident that Mrs Barber had understood and agreed with him during the investigation and decision making about her management. However, he realized that he had failed to establish trust and mutual agreement with her family. He was not sure how to remedy this difficult situation.

A few weeks later, Mrs Barber and her daughters returned. Characteristically, Mrs Barber did not express any concerns and denied she was experiencing pain. In contrast, her daughters were extremely apprehensive about their mother's health, reporting increased weakness, declining appetite and difficulty in swallowing some foods. Their greatest concern was satisfactory pain control. Dr Keith listened carefully to their concerns and attempted to address their worries about their mother. He offered to make house calls in the future, which the family readily accepted.

Now acutely attuned to the family's tendency to respond with anger, Dr Keith actively engaged both the patient and family in the management plan. During subsequent house calls, which extended over the next two months, the doctor consistently reviewed the options for future care either in the patient's home, at the hospital or in the palliative care unit. Eventually, Mrs Barber's daughters requested that their mother be transferred to the palliative care unit as they no longer felt capable of caring for her at home. This was a major step for the family who were now able to entrust their mother's care to the doctor and his team. Acknowledging the family's worries and, more importantly, their anger was central in establishing trust.

When families are faced with the serious diagnosis of a family member, their response may include denial or anger. Anger is often the most difficult emotion to respond to, because it is often directed against the physician (Longhurst, 1980). When confronted by a family's anger, doctors respond in several ways. They may assume the blame, respond with equal hostility, reject the patient and family or, as illustrated in this case, use the anger to help the family come to terms with their significant loss (Brody, 1992; Letchky, 1992; Schwenk and Romano, 1992). Anger is an extremely difficult emotion to deal with. It takes self-awareness and sensitivity to respond to a patient's or family's hostile attack. The physician must avoid personalizing the anger and assuming a defensive stance.

Mrs Barber's story continues in the next case.

30

Family anger: 2

John Jordan and Judith Belle Brown

Assisting in the resolution of a family's anger in response to a relative's terminal illness, and subsequent death, can be both challenging and satisfying.

The first night after admission to the palliative care unit, Mrs Barber appeared quite uncomfortable. She was clutching at her right shoulder and moaning in pain when attempts were made by the nurses to reposition her. The nurse telephoned Mrs Barber's daughter, Jana, and they discussed her past methods of pain control. Jana explained that her mother had been using Tylenol Extra strength 500 mg q4h and 1000 mg at bedtime for the past few weeks. However, she noted that it had been difficult to get her mother to accept pain medication for several reasons. First, Mrs Barber was a woman who viewed medication as unnecessary, priding herself on never having taken more than aspirin. Second, to accept medication would mean acknowledging her pain and Jana speculated that her mother had denied her pain in order to stay home. A decision was made to continue with the previous course of management.

Several hours later, after a warm flannel and additional Tylenol had failed to relieve Mrs Barber's discomfort, an order for morphine 2.5 mg q4h was requested from the family doctor. Sensitive to both Mrs Barber's views on medication use and the family's struggles with her decline, the doctor conferred with Jana about the use of morphine for pain control before proceeding with the medication order. With three doses of morphine Mrs Barber was significantly more comfortable.

The next day, when both daughters, Jana and Rita, appeared at their mother's bedside, it was rapidly apparent that Rita was against her mother receiving morphine. Rita angrily stated to the nurse attending her mother, 'My mother hasn't been bothered by pain up until now. Tylenol seemed to work just fine at home and I don't think she needs to be on morphine. You had no right to give her medication without my permission!'

Note: This case description first appeared in the January 1996 issue of the *Ontario Medical Review* and is reprinted with permission of the Ontario Medical Association.

Clearly, Mrs Barber's two daughters didn't agree about the existence of her pain and its management. Once again, the family's anger about their mother's care had surfaced. Their divergent opinions and accompanying anger were of concern to Dr Keith who feared that Mrs Barber's care might be jeopardized by the family conflict.

Later the same day, the nurse spoke alone with Jana who revealed more about the family's struggles. 'I am fine with the care my mother is receiving,' she said. 'I know my mother has been uncomfortable, but Rita refuses to believe that Mom could be in pain.' Jana's trust in Dr Keith was evident when she confided to the nurse, 'Our doctor knows what is best for Mom'. As the day progressed, Mrs Barber appeared much brighter, reassuring the nurses that she wasn't having any pain. Although she dozed for long periods throughout the day, she chatted amicably with nursing staff while awake. Her mobility was less impaired and her pain was under control.

Rita returned to see her mother that evening and was still upset and angry about the care plan developed for her mother, exclaiming, 'I just don't understand why my mother has to be on morphine. She's not complaining of any pain. She is fine now!'.

The nurse tried to reassure Rita that her concerns were being respected. She explained, 'You're right, your mother is not experiencing any pain now and she's had a relatively good day. But the reason for her present comfort is the morphine. The best we can offer her now is comfort.' Suddenly, Rita became tearful. As the nurse encouraged her to talk about her feelings, it became clear that Rita's grief was being fueled by her guilt about not being able to care for her dying mother at home (Charlton and Dolman, 1995). The nurse encouraged Rita to share her feelings with the doctor the next day.

The following morning Dr Keith met with Rita and discussed her concerns. Rita said that she was angry about the decision to place her mother on morphine without her knowledge or approval and that she thought her mother's deteriorating status was a result of the use of morphine. Dr Keith listened to Rita's anger and addressed her feelings of ambivalence and guilt about admitting her mother to the hospital. Reluctantly Rita acknowledged her deep guilt in not being able to care for her mother at home and her need to blame someone for her mother's decline. When the doctor offered Rita the choice whether or not to control her mother's pain with morphine, Rita decided that morphine was the best way to keep her mother comfortable.

A few days later Mrs Barber slipped into a coma and died. The morning before she died the doctor told both daughters that her death was imminent. He reassured them that the nurses would continue to keep their mother as comfortable as possible. They thanked him for talking to them and for not rejecting them when they had been angry and distraught about their mother's care. The daughters were at their mother's bedside when she died peacefully in her sleep the following day.

Throughout this case the pervasive anger experienced by the family could have easily destroyed the patient–doctor relationship. From the time of the diagnosis of terminal cancer to the patient's death, the family's anger constantly challenged the doctor's ability to care for both the patient and her family (Longhurst, 1980). The doctor could not avoid the anger, nor accept it as blame. For him, the challenge was to catch the anger, rather than being hit by it. A direct hit would have struck a severe blow, not only to the doctor but also to his relationship with both the patient and her family.

We are uncomfortable with anger and often shy away from it. Yet failure to address anger leaves the doctor, the patient and the family with unresolved feelings, which may fester. If the doctor hadn't addressed the anger directly, he would have been powerless to help the family through this difficult time. Nor would he have been able to help the family resolve their conflicted emotions surrounding the patient's illness and death. By not personalizing the anger or accepting the blame projected on him by the family, the doctor remained available to the family and his patient. This enabled him to work with the family in understanding, and ultimately addressing, their feelings of anger, guilt and loss.

The second issue central to this case is the role of power in the patient–doctor relationship. When physicians exert their authority, it can often result in the escalation of tension and a decline in communication. Had the physician in this case exerted his authority, for instance in the use of morphine for pain control, the result might have been further alienation of the family and more anger and mistrust. Heightened hostility could have dissolved the doctor's relationship with his dying patient.

If the doctor's position of authority is challenged, it should usually be sacrificed without a fight. To do this, the doctor must be self-aware and have a strong sense of professional integrity (Brody, 1992). In this case the doctor's willingness to acquiesce to an apparent power imbalance in the patient–doctor relationship led to improved trust and communication.

Component IV: Incorporating Prevention and Health Promotion

W Wayne Weston, Carol L McWilliam and Thomas R Freeman

Every encounter with a patient is an opportunity to promote health as well as to prevent disease (McWilliam, 1993). Helping patients change unhealthy practices or develop new health-promoting behaviors is one of the most difficult but potentially most rewarding challenges in medicine. A patient-centered approach is essential for two reasons. First, health, like disease and illness, requires an integrated understanding of the whole person. Second, disease prevention and health promotion require a collaborative effort on the part of patient and physician, who must find common ground in order for these activities to be pursued.

The foundations of health promotion and disease prevention

In 1984, the World Health Organization (WHO, 1986a) redefined health as 'a resource for everyday life, not the objective of living. This concept of health emphasizes social and personal resources as well as physical capacities'. Thus, the notion of health is moving away from its former abstract focus on complete physical, mental and social well-being toward 'an ecological understanding of the interaction between individuals and their social and physical environment' (de Leeuw, 1989; Hurowitz, 1993; Stachtchenko and Jenicek, 1990). How patients and practitioners think about and experience health continues

Note: Parts of this chapter were published previously in *Patient-Centered Medicine: transforming the clinical method*, Sage Publications (1995).

to evolve. These partners in healthcare may have unique and differing understandings of health and, in turn, different understandings of health promotion and disease prevention.

The process of care also has been altered and continues to evolve in light of new definitions. Health promotion most recently has been defined as 'the process of enabling people to take control over and to improve their health' (WHO, 1986b). The intervention strategy for promoting health has been labelled 'health enhancement' – increasing the level of good health, vitality and resilience in all people. This includes discussions with patients about nutrition, physical activity and adjustment to life stages.

Risk avoidance aims at ensuring that people at low risk for health problems remain at low risk by finding ways to avoid disease. Immunization, breast feeding and bicycle helmets are good examples. *Risk reduction* addresses moderate- or high-risk characteristics among individuals or segments of the population, by encouraging people to reduce risky behavior or by treating risk factors such as high blood pressure or elevated serum cholesterol. Early *identification* aims at increasing the awareness of early signs of health problems and screening people at risk in order to detect the early onset of health problems. Two examples are Papanicolaou smears and mammograms. *Complication reduction* comes into play after disease has developed; there are many ways to ameliorate the effects of disease even at this stage. For example, warfarin is used for atrial fibrillation to prevent stroke.

Health promotion and disease prevention require patient-centered care

Preventive care and health promotion depend upon the patient's commitment to the pursuit of health. Thus, the patient-centered approach is essential to the process of promoting health, preventing disease or reducing its impact. As described in the preceding chapters, effective patient care requires attending to the patient's personal experience of health, illness and disease; understanding patients in the context of their lives; and finding mutually acceptable approaches to preventive care and health promotion.

Most of the earlier efforts in the field of prevention and health promotion have used a population-based approach and have ignored the role of the individual physician working with individual patients. Yet achieving new directions clearly hinges on individual, as well as collective, effort. The patient-centered clinical method provides a clear framework for the practitioner to apply in health promotion and disease prevention efforts by using the patient's world as the starting point.

Understanding the patient's world

Health promotion and disease prevention begin with an understanding of the patient as a whole person. To achieve such an understanding, the physician must assess five components of the patient's world:

- present and potential disease
- the patient's experience of health and illness
- the patient's potential for health
- the patient's context
- and the patient–doctor relationship.

Present and potential disease

Comprehensive patient care is not limited to a focus only on the presenting complaint; it is necessary also to consider the patient's other present or potential problems. For example, when a 42-year-old male appears in the office with an acute respiratory infection it is important to check his blood pressure. High blood pressure is common in this age group and male patients tend not to visit doctors until they have symptoms, thus missing the opportunity for risk reduction. Another example is a patient who does not follow up on care of her diabetes. When she presents with another problem it is wise to discuss her diabetes too. Good medical records will include problem lists or other reminder systems to draw the physician's attention to these ongoing problems. Much of the literature in primary care pertaining to prevention deals with appropriate screening maneuvers (Canadian Task Force, 1994; US Task Force, 1996) and establishing a practice infrastructure to bring these about (Audunsson, 1986; Battista and Lawrence, 1988; Goldbloom and Lawrence, 1990; Woolf *et al.*, 1996).

The patient's experience of health and illness

To understand the perspective of the patient, the practitioner needs to explore the patient's beliefs in relation to health and illness and what each means to that person (Calnan, 1988). The practitioner needs to discover the value and priority of health as one of many competing values in order to assess the patient's commitment to its pursuit. Fundamental to determining common ground regarding preventive behavior is the extent to which the individual feels responsible for and in control of his or her own health. Beliefs about health risks and the degree of control that a patient has over these risks will affect his or her actions. Several studies have identified that potential strategies for promoting health are adopted only if they are perceived to be beneficial. Others have found that the greater the individual's perceptions of barriers to health, the lower that person's health status (Gillis, 1993).

The patient's potential for health

The patient's potential for health is determined by age, gender, genetic potential for disease, socioeconomic status and personal goals and values. Although it is perhaps the most important element, the patient's valuing of health cannot be assumed. Yet, holding this value is logically fundamental to a health-promoting lifestyle and a positive correlation between the two has been demonstrated in many studies (Gillis, 1993).

Self-efficacy – the power to produce one's own desired ends – is fundamental to the patient's potential for health. Bandura (1986) suggests that self-efficacy behavior is a function of the person's perception of their ability to perform a behavior and beliefs that the behavior in question will lead to the specific outcomes desired. Numerous studies document the positive correlation between these two factors and actual decision making regarding health behavior (Brod and Hall, 1984; Ewart *et al.*, 1983; Jeffrey *et al.*, 1984; Jenkins, 1987; Kaplan *et al.*, 1984; McIntyre *et al.*, 1983; Nicki *et al.*, 1984).

Physicians will have more success in discussing health promotion and risk avoidance with patients who have a strong sense of self-efficacy. Patients with lower self-efficacy may respond better to the physician's more traditional role of risk reduction and early identification.

The patient's context

The patient's context – the physical and interpersonal environment of the person – includes family, friends, job, community and culture (Epp, 1986; Watson, 1984). Mass media can influence health attitudes and beliefs in both subtle and obvious ways and may either enhance the patient's potential for health or detract from it (National Research Council, 1989). Similarly, the availability or absence of resources such as social support groups may enhance or detract from the individual's potential for health.

Likewise, the doctor's office setting is an important part of the patient's context. The 'personal' element and emphasis on continuity of care may make the family physician's office setting more conducive than other medical settings to the type of patient–doctor relationship necessary for the practice of health education (Calnan, 1988). Yet, family doctors have found that lack of time, space and necessary staff are barriers to preventive activities (Becker and Janz, 1990; Bruce and Burnett, 1991; Pommerenke and Dietrich, 1992). Office hours, location and physical structure have the potential to represent real barriers from the patient's perspective. Ease of access, proximity to screening resources such as mammography sites and the privacy and comfort of the doctor's office all constitute contextual factors which influence the patient's receptivity to using the family physician as a resource for health promotion and disease prevention (Carter *et al.*, 1981; Godkin and Catlin, 1984). Furthermore, the skills, perceptions and attitudes of office staff, particularly the office nurse, affect patients. Staff need to be supportive of the doctor's health promotion and disease prevention efforts by providing positive reinforcement to patients, especially reinforcing patient perceptions that changing health-related behavior is possible.

The patient–doctor relationship

Very much a part of the patient's context and potential for health is the nature of the patient's relationship with the doctor and personal experience of care. Built up over time, the physician's approach determines how much and what kind of trust the patient places in the physician, what the patient's expectations of the roles of doctor and patient are and what kind of power relationship exists between them (Brody, 1992). The patient's approach to assuming or relinquishing power to the physician shapes the physician's approach to patient care and, ultimately, the patient–doctor relationship. Thus, the doctor's power to intervene both shapes and is shaped by the patient's world. Several authors (Pommerenke and Dietrich, 1992; Quill, 1989; Sanson-Fisher and Maguire, 1980) note that poor physician communication skills may be one of the most important and overlooked barriers to preventive care.

Patient education using a patient-centered approach

Physicians must adopt current thinking about adult learning in their approach to health promotion with adult patients. The patient-centered educational approach is a learner-centered process. The doctor precipitates the patient-learner's critical reflection about health through dialogue that makes the patient aware of the potential threats to health inherent in the individual's current life. The physician guides the patient to explore the personal meaning of current practices and the personal values, needs, motives, expectations and understanding which underlie them. Over time, the process of guiding the patient-learner also includes exploring alternative ways of looking at current practices and finding and trying new ways of fulfilling personal values, needs, motives and expectations. A supportive role is also part of this process – listening, empathizing, validating changed perspectives through rational discourse and working out new relationships with the patient-learner, consistent with changes in perspective. This approach shares many similarities with motivational interviewing strategies (Miller and Rollnick, 1991).

The learning is self-discovered and often cannot be directly communicated (Rogers, 1961) by the physician. The commonly known strategies of health education, most of which emphasize information giving and behavior modification, comprise only a small part of the process of health promotion. True personal growth and change require a very different approach.

Patient and doctor together must find common ground regarding decisions about the goals and priorities of care and their respective roles in it. Physicians must be particularly alert to the sense of powerlessness which patients often experience, supporting and encouraging the patient's own exercise of power 'so long as it is consistent with a good therapeutic outcome and with the patient's long-term goals and interests' (Brody, 1992, p. 65). This illustrates the ethical aspects of preventive care (Doxiadis, 1987; Hoffmaster, 1992). Through this process, the physician and patient together decide the health promotion and/or prevention strategies to be pursued.

The patient's world is understood as a dynamic situation that varies with each patient at different points in time and with each healthcare issue. The doctor's aim is to find the best fit with the patient's world. Sometimes, for some issues, the patient requires a health enhancement strategy. At other times, for other reasons, the patient requires prevention strategies.

Conclusion

Evidence is compelling that health promotion and prevention efforts can be applied effectively by physicians. Yet both physician education and attitudes (McPhee and Schroeder, 1987; McPhee et al., 1986)), and patient education, expectations, motivations and attitudes (McGinnis and Hamburg, 1988) can undermine such interventions. Overcoming such barriers to achieve success in health promotion and disease prevention efforts can be helped by using a patient-centered approach.

Preview of the cases

The first case describes a patient with multiple cardiac risk factors and little motivation to change. This case illustrates the importance of patience and focusing on small gains over time. The second case describes the role of the physician in helping patients with important lifecycle transitions. The importance of early identification of substance abuse and the use of motivational interviewing strategies is illustrated in the third case, while the next case poses the challenge of incorporating prevention in everyday practice without offending patients by appearing to be more interested in forcing behavior change rather than addressing the reason they sought medical help. The fifth case demonstrates how the use of simple screening questions can assist patients in disclosing difficult and painful problems such as woman abuse.

Genograms can serve as an important visual aid in educating patients about generational patterns that influence their illness experience. The sixth case demonstrates how understanding these patterns can stimulate health-promoting behaviors throughout the family system. Enacting prevention and health promotion strategies can be a challenge when patient and doctor do not share a common view on the problem. The seventh case describes how a patient perceived her menopausal symptoms in a very biomedical manner compared to her physician who perceived the broader implications for the patient's whole life context.

The next case, a patient with chronic pain and drug-seeking behavior, reflects on how motivating patients to change can be a daunting task. Furthermore, it illustrates the importance of setting limits with patients and recognizing our emotional reactions to patients. The ninth case discusses how health promotion necessitates finding common ground on multiple levels in assisting an elderly patient to overcome years of learned helplessness– and to regain control over her life and health.

The final case illustrates the importance of clear communication. Communicating risk in everyday language is a key skill for helping patients make decisions about preventive care. Another important skill is explaining the implications of a positive test result in a manner that informs patients without causing undue alarm.

Cases Illustrating Component IV: Incorporating Prevention and Health Promotion

31

Illness prevention in the patient's life context

*Leslie Rourke, Stephen J Wetmore
and Judith Belle Brown*

Patients' and doctors' perceptions of illness prevention may differ. Also, patients' potential for change may be limited by the reality of their life context, including personal, economic or social factors. Thus, reaching mutual agreement on prevention strategies can be a challenge for both patients and physicians.

Dr Harris re-read the internist's consultation letter about Jack. 'This gentleman is a cardiovascular time bomb. He is his own worst enemy and he freely admits this.'

Dr Harris ruefully nodded his head in agreement. Jack was a 40-year-old plumber with many risk factors: long-standing hypertension with variable control; symptomatic gout currently controlled with allopurinol; hyperlipidemia; obesity; a positive family history for cardiovascular disease; and smoking one pack of cigarettes daily. In addition, Jack's history included chronic renal insufficiency. His renal function had slowly and steadily declined over the past few years. Surprisingly, he had no obvious heart complications . . . yet.

Despite these threatening medical problems, Jack viewed his most significant health problem as his arthritis, involving especially his hips. He had tried various treatments over the years including physiotherapy but was unable to manage without daily NSAID medication, which was likely aggravating his renal failure.

Jack and his family had been Dr Harris's patients for 20 years, yet most of Jack's visits were for acute illness. Appointments to check his blood pressure and review other risk factors were often rescheduled by Jack because of

---

Note: This case description first appeared in the March 1996 issue of the *Ontario Medical Review* and is reprinted with the permission of the Ontario Medical Association.

his erratic work schedule. On more than one occasion, Dr Harris or his staff had unlocked the office door as they were preparing to leave when Jack arrived late for his appointment.

Jack maintained a fatalistic attitude about life, saying 'If I'm going to die young, I'd like to die happy'. Over the years he had been adamant that he was not willing to lose weight, see a dietitian, quit smoking or pay for any 'expensive medications' even though he did have a drug plan. The internist, exasperated, had predicted that Jack would be on dialysis in the next few years, if he lived that long.

As he reviewed the internist's letter, Dr Harris reflected on Jack's life. Jack had a strong work ethic, putting his job as the number one priority above all other issues, including his own health. Jack's wife, Andrea, had expressed her frustration to Dr Harris about Jack not looking after himself. She was afraid he would suffer an early death and she was angry that he didn't appear to care about the future. Andrea had acquiesced to his wishes and had stopped trying to push him to make changes. Dr Harris understood Andrea's feelings; he experienced the same frustrations in caring for Jack.

How could Dr Harris find common ground with Jack when his concerns for Jack's future did not match those of the patient? How could he help Jack prevent or delay what appeared to be a future of early death or disability? Dr Harris had tried prescribing small quantities of medications to encourage more frequent office visits, but it hadn't worked. Jack merely waited until he had a break from work to see the doctor, often going without medication for a considerable time.

Despite their conflicts on this issue, Dr Harris found Jack to be a likable person. Jack was very appreciative and apologetic when the doctor saw him at the end of a long day. He didn't expect the doctor to cure him of his problems but he trusted his judgment and was willing to try his suggestions, within limits. He was also candid about his poor adherence to certain treatments.

The doctor felt that he had achieved a good relationship with Jack over the years. Yet he still felt pressure to prevent illness, something that did not appear to be on Jack's agenda. By avoiding discussion of Jack's risk factors, was the doctor diminishing their importance and silently validating Jack's avoidance? On the other hand, by repeatedly emphasizing the many risk factors, was Dr Harris harming the patient–doctor relationship and inducing guilt that could hinder Jack from mentioning early warning signs of impending heart trouble?

With many patients like Jack, disease prevention may only be possible when the doctor understands the patient's illness experience and finds common ground based on a realistic appraisal of lifestyle issues. This case illustrates how important it is for the doctor to explore the patient's understanding of illness, disability and death. Often patients do not consider the possibility of prolonged illness, such as a stroke, and its potential effect on themselves and their families. Exploring the patient's ideas about illness helps the doctor understand the patient's motivation, or lack of motivation, for change. The doctor needs to explore the patient's feelings about disease and the doctor's role. This information helps the doctor to understand the patient's ideas about illness and prevention and will aid the doctor in finding common ground around issues of prevention.

Understanding the patient's life context, including personal, economic and social factors, will give the doctor a more realistic view of what lifestyle changes are possible. Over the course of time, the cumulative effects of small gains can be significant. Doctors must take a long-term view of management; the family doctor, who cares for the patient continuously over the course of many years, is often in a better position to help the patient with gradual change than is the consultant, who sees the patient on one or two occasions.

Reaching common ground with patients may mean no more than acknowledging and encouraging small changes in lifestyle. When viewed in this way, the doctor may feel less frustrated and more satisfied with the therapeutic plan. Patients, for their part, may feel empowered by goals that are realistic and achievable and consequently be more receptive to change. With these simple changes in expectations on both the part of the patient and the doctor, the patient–doctor relationship is enhanced.

Dr Harris decided to acknowledge the small yet positive lifestyle changes that Jack had made, rather than emphasizing the ones he had not. This allowed him to talk to Jack about his difficulties in adhering to a therapeutic regimen and to explore alternative methods of risk reduction in his life. This will provide more satisfaction for the doctor and may even result in improvements in the patient's health.

32

Fatherhood

Neil R Campbell, Judith Belle Brown and Thomas R Freeman

The transition to fatherhood is an unsettling and uncertain time for men. Physicians need to engage fathers-to-be in discussions about their relationships with the baby and their spouse, as well as feelings about themselves and their work. In encouraging a balance among the responsibilities of family, work and play, doctors may assist men in the transition to fatherhood.

As the nurse gently laid the baby in her mother's arms, the doctor placed his arm on Alex's shoulders. 'Congratulations, Dad,' he said. Alex leaned forward to touch his daughter and asked to hold her. As his wife gave the baby to Alex, both the nurse and doctor held out their arms under the baby. Unconsciously they sent a message to the new father: 'Be careful, you might drop her'.

A few minutes later as Alex carried his daughter to the nursing station his feelings of excitement and pride conflicted with fear and anxiety about his competence. 'How prepared am I?' wondered Alex. Memories of his own father flashed before him. Was he ready for the responsibility of fatherhood? Yes, he wanted this baby and he had learned a great deal during the prenatal classes. But now the moment of truth had arrived — he was a father. What was expected of him? What should he say, what should he do?

Alex's reactions are not uncommon but are rarely verbalized. For many men the transition to fatherhood is an experience that leaves them feeling unsettled and uncertain. Rarely do they have an arena to express their feelings or concerns and consequently, fatherhood can be a lonely experience. Men often feel on the periphery of the parenting experience and frequently lack adequate role models to guide the way.

The prenatal period is often viewed as a time for tasks to be accomplished. There is furniture to be bought, the baby's room to be decorated, a wife's hormones

Note: This case description first appeared in the October 1993 issue of the *Ontario Medical Review* and is reprinted with the permission of the Ontario Medical Association.

to be considered. The pregnancy is a time-limited experience. But being a father is a lifetime commitment with little direction.

Prenatal classes address many concerns and issues but the actual adaptation to fatherhood, with all the inherent responsibilities, is often left unattended. In many instances the focus is on the mother-to-be and the care of the baby, with only passing mention made of the father's role.

Research has shown that attendance at psychoeducational groups, specifically designed to address the transition to fatherhood, can help men become more nurturing and supportive in their role as fathers (Giefer and Nelson, 1981; Miller and Bowen, 1982). It can also help them learn how to balance their needs for work, home and recreation.

So what are the responsibilities and goals of medicine in this process? First, physicians need to be aware of the challenges, reactions and responses that men experience as they become fathers. In addition, doctors need to be familiar with the various resources available to assist men during this period of transition and they should be sensitive to the demands and responsibilities faced by fathers today. Men want to assume a nurturing, caretaking role in their families but are buffeted by competing demands and responsibilities. The physician can help fathers to establish priorities and become more comfortable in their transition to fatherhood.

To achieve these goals doctors can engage fathers-to-be in discussions about bonding, security and the attachment that may develop between a father and his baby. This may be an area of discussion never before presented to the emergent father. Concerns about the marital relationship, such as communication, sexuality, stress and level of satisfaction during the transition to parenthood, can also be examined. How does the man feel about himself and what role models has he observed that will guide him in his parenting? For many men in the midst of establishing their careers, the birth of a child may present conflicting priorities. For many couples in dual-career marriages, conflicts may arise around issues of work demands and childcare responsibilities. Finally, the physician can assist the father-to-be in establishing his priorities and finding a comfortable balance among home, work and play.

While many of these discussions can take place during the prenatal period it is essential that the doctor monitors the father postnatally. Most of the excitement and support will be directed towards the mother and the newborn. It is during this time that many men become disillusioned and lost. Time and consideration should be extended to the emergent father, as well as to his new family.

33

The hidden alcoholic

W Wayne Weston, Judith Belle Brown and Moira Stewart

Physicians should be aware of cues to alcohol problems in their patients. Simple screening tools may be used to identify the problem and open the way to offers of help. Motivational interviewing strategies help prepare patients to change.

Mr Quin was a 43-year-old executive who, along with his wife and two adolescent sons, had been a patient of Dr Wright's for five years. He presented at the doctor's office, complaining of vague indigestion and occasional heartburn. In addition, he requested that Dr Wright remove the sutures above his right eye. He explained that he had an accident while up north 'fishing with the boys' and had six stitches inserted by an emergency physician.

As Dr Wright inquired further about his gastrointestinal symptoms, Mr Quin described irregular eating habits but denied any excessive alcohol intake. He tended to minimize his symptoms, although he did indicate he had been having some trouble sleeping lately. When Dr Wright asked him for more information about the accident, Mr Quin seemed embarrassed and unwilling to tell him much about it.

This case illustrates several cues of an alcohol problem: GI symptoms, accidents and sleep disturbance. Other important cues of problem drinking are: mild depression; appetite loss; heavy smoking; slightly elevated blood pressure (or hypertension which is difficult to control); and sexual or marital problems (Skinner *et al.*, 1981). It has been estimated that 10–20% of patients seen in family practice have a problem with alcohol (Rush, 1989). Early recognition and intervention may improve the outcome for these patients (Cyr and Wartman, 1988).

Several approaches have been suggested for screening. Ewing and Mayfield's (1974) CAGE questionnaire is an effective general screening tool consisting of four questions.

Note: This case description first appeared in the February 1990 issue of the *Ontario Medical Review* and is reprinted with the permission of the Ontario Medical Association.

C Have you ever felt you ought to **cut** down on your drinking?
A Have people **annoyed** you by criticizing your drinking?
G Have you ever felt bad or **guilty** about your drinking?
E Have you ever had a drink first thing in the morning (**eye opener**)
   to steady your nerves or to get rid of a hangover?

Another, even briefer, screen is to use two simple questions: 'How much do you drink in an average week?' and 'Have you ever had a problem with alcohol?'. Patients with problem drinking, especially if it is picked up early before the problem is compounded by loss of job or marital discord, are often very open about their drinking and prepared to reduce or eliminate alcohol consumption.

Many physicians wonder what to do next when patients minimize or deny the possibility of an alcohol problem. It is important to avoid moralizing or attempting to frighten the patient into quitting. According to Miller and Rollnick (1991), patients are often ambivalent about their use of an addictive substance: on the one hand they recognize some of the potential or actual problems associated with its use but on the other hand enjoy the pleasures it brings. Pushing patients too hard to quit may backfire by producing greater resistance to change. It is as if they had a need to maintain their ambivalence by countering the doctor's arguments for quitting with their own arguments for continuing. This is particularly problematic in the early stages of change when the patient is just beginning to contemplate a life without the offending substance.

If the physician suspects an alcohol problem, he or she might suggest that a blood test to assess liver or bone marrow function (serum gamma GT or MCV) might be helpful to determine whether the patient is drinking more alcohol than their system can tolerate (Holt *et al.*, 1981). This avoids arguing over how much is too much and helps physicians to clearly identify alcohol as a problem (Barnes *et al.*, 1987). This in turn opens the door to discuss whether or not the patient wants help and what help is available, and to arrange for follow-up.

The five principles of motivational interviewing provide valuable guidelines for helping patients to change their behavior (Miller, 1983; Miller and Rollnick, 1991).

1 *Express empathy.* Understand patients' feelings and perspective without judging, criticizing or blaming. 'Paradoxically, this kind of acceptance of people, *as they are* seems to free them to change, whereas insistent non-acceptance . . . can have the effect of keeping people as they are' (Miller and Rollnick, 1991, p. 56).
2 *Develop discrepancy.* Help the patient recognize discrepancies between their current behavior and important personal goals. It is important for the patient to verbalize the reasons for change rather than the doctor doing so.
3 *Avoid argument.* The doctor may need to help the patient to gently confront unwanted consequences of their behavior but should avoid badgering the

patient to accept the label 'alcoholic'. This may provoke defensiveness. All that is needed is for the patient to verbalize concern about some aspect of their behavior.

4   *Roll with resistance.* Acknowledge that reluctance and ambivalence are to be expected – they are natural and understandable. Invite the patient to consider new information or to consider their situation from a different perspective but do not impose new views or goals. Avoid offering solutions but turn problems and questions back to the patient.

5   *Support self-efficacy.* Motivational interviewing is 'more than a set of techniques for doing counseling. It is a way of *being* with clients, which is probably quite different from how others may have treated them in the past' (Miller and Rollnick, 1991, p. 62). Demonstrate respect for the patient's abilities to find solutions to their own problems.

34

Health promotion

Joseph Morrissy, Moira Stewart and Judith Belle Brown

Although physicians are encouraged to use unrelated visits to introduce health promotion issues to their patients, it must be done with sensitivity and care. Patients will not be open to the health promotion discussion until their own agenda has been met.

Mandy, a 16-year-old female patient, accompanied by her mother, was seen by Dr Roti's younger colleague in an 'on-call' situation one weekend. Mandy was usually well and rarely visited her physician, though the family had been long-time patients of Dr Roti.

On this occasion, the 16-year-old patient presented with paroxysms of coughing, according to the clinical note. The cough was worse at night and Mandy occasionally had difficulty drawing her breath during coughing spells. The cough was intermittently productive of small amounts of yellow sputum. There was no fever, earache, sore throat, nasal congestion or wheezing. The symptoms had been present for one week.

On examination, the ears and eyes were normal and the nose was clear. The throat appeared slightly erythematous with no exudate. There was no cervical lymphadenopathy. The patient was well hydrated and the chest was clear. The clinical impression was 'post-viral cough'.

The patient was advised to try one of the cough suppressant syrups, together with sleeping in a propped-up position at night and removal of potential irritants. The note continued with the comment that health maintenance was discussed when the patient's mother was out of the room.

Two days later, Dr Roti was confronted in his office by an obviously upset daughter and mother. When asked what the problem was, Mandy's mother said

Note: This case description first appeared in the September 1992 issue of the *Ontario Medical Review* and is reprinted with the permission of the Ontario Medical Association.

to him, 'We came to find out what was wrong with Mandy and what we got was a lecture on sex and smoking'. Both mother and daughter agreed that their concerns were not met and were able to identify without prompting that they needed to know what was causing the cough. Further, the young patient was really afraid that the cough was so severe that she might die from lack of breath. She also felt 'lectured at' not to smoke and not to get pregnant. Her mother commented that these issues were openly discussed in their family and had already been addressed. In her view they did not need any lectures on the subject.

In some ways the young physician can hardly be criticized for attempting to put into practice what he had learned in his training, where the topic of prevention, including opportunistic prevention, had been addressed in a number of ways. He knew that when given the opportunity to interact with infrequent attenders at the practice, he ought to discuss some specific areas relevant to the age and social situation of the patient. He felt a responsibility to indicate to teenagers like this patient a willingness to discuss issues related to sexuality. He also felt he should do what he could to prevent what he saw as two major preventable problems in young women in this age group – smoking and unwanted pregnancy (Feldman *et al.*, 1986).

In this instance, his attempt backfired on him and left his senior colleague with an awkward problem. What happened? Was this the wrong time to try this prevention strategy? Was there something wrong with the physician's manner? Was the subject irrelevant to the patient and her mother?

These are not easy questions to answer. Family doctors today are frequently criticized for paying insufficient attention to prevention issues. The family physician's task is to try to meld two distinct but equally valid agendas. The question is, how do you do this effectively?

The key may be understanding more clearly what the patient's concerns and needs are. It is appropriate for a physician to have a health promotion agenda during most office contacts with patients. However, to be successful in addressing this agenda, in this case sexuality and smoking, he must first understand precisely the question the patient needs answering.

A reassurance that 'This is just a post-viral cough and you do not need penicillin' is not enough when the patient is concerned that she might die. Sometimes in practice, the doctor knows through experience what the patient's concerns are, but not always. Physicians should develop a technique which allows them to listen more acutely to their patient's fears and worries. Often this can be achieved by using open-ended questions such as, 'Can you tell me what your concerns are?' or 'Do you have any worries stemming from what has happened during this illness so far?'. Questions like these may allow the patient to open up and express her fears. Before launching into a discussion of specific prevention issues, it is important for the physician to ask the patient if they would like information about these topics.

A couple of weeks after the incidents related above, the mother was asked how this problem might have been better addressed. She said that it would have been acceptable to raise the smoking and sexuality issues in the context of the first visit, if and when the physician had first satisfied their agenda; that is, they understood the cause of the cough and had the young patient's fears assuaged.

35

Woman abuse

Judith Belle Brown, Barbara Lent and George Sas

Physicians must always be alert to the possibility of woman abuse. When a patient reveals abuse, the doctor must be supportive, non-judgmental and available to provide whatever help the patient needs. The physician should assess the safety of the patient and provide referrals to available community resources.

As Paulette sank into the chair next to the doctor's desk she looked tired and despondent. Dr Rovinelli was surprised by the appearance of this usually bright and congenial 40-year-old patient. He was equally unprepared when, without hesitation, she said, 'I've had it. I need to see a psychiatrist'.

Paulette and her 45-year-old husband had been patients of the practice for many years. Dr Rovinelli had delivered their two daughters, now aged 13 and seven. Bewildered, he began, 'A psychiatrist? I don't understand ... tell me what's happening.'

The patient explained that she wasn't herself. She was often short with the children and found it more difficult to cope with the daily demands of maintaining the home. She was also having trouble sleeping and was plagued by persistent tension headaches. Finally, she was worried that her lack of concentration at work might jeopardize her job.

'Obviously there is something wrong with me,' she concluded with downcast eyes. 'Maybe I'm depressed or nuts. At least, that's what my husband says. He thinks I need to see a shrink.'

Having cared for this family for over 15 years, the doctor had not observed any behavior that would support such a request. In fact, he had always perceived them as a close and caring family. They were active contributors to a number of volunteer programs and consequently had gained the respect of the community.

Note: This case description first appeared in the December 1992 issue of the *Ontario Medical Review* and is reprinted with the permission of the Ontario Medical Association.

However, concerned by the patient's symptoms, the doctor began to search for other signs of depression that might warrant intervention and perhaps a referral to a psychiatrist. During his inquiry about her depression, Dr Rovinelli paused and asked how things were going in her marital relationship – had there been any tension lately? With shaking hands and tear-filled eyes, Paulette began to talk. As her story unfolded, a lengthy history of emotional and physical abuse was revealed.

The doctor was not prepared for her disclosure of abuse. He felt somewhat guilty that he had not been more alert to previous warning signs. He vaguely recalled a time when Paulette had come to the office with cuts and bruises on her chest and arms. She had blamed the injuries on a careless fall while cycling. On another occasion, Paulette had presented with vague undiagnosed abdominal pain. The pain had resolved within a few days and there had been no recurrence of the symptoms to the doctor's knowledge. Perhaps, pondered Dr Rovinelli, these had been signs of abuse that he had missed.

Initially, the doctor felt unsure of how he might intervene in this situation, which had been hidden from his sight for years. He had to move quickly from a position of feeling inadequate (or, to put it another way, of having a bruised ego) because he had missed previous signs, to a position of being open to the patient's current needs. Although the patient minimized the impact of the abuse on her psychological well-being, Dr Rovinelli wisely acknowledged her emotional pain and validated her experience. He did this by being supportive and non-judgmental (Lent, 1986). In addition, he carefully assessed issues of safety for the patient and her children (Herbert, 1991). He discussed the various resources that were available and how to gain access to them. The doctor began to realize that he could be of assistance to the patient by recognizing her problem, being knowledgeable of the available resources and prepared to be of help to her in whatever way would be most useful to her and her family.

Like many of the vignettes presented in this book, this story is complex. We could travel down several avenues in understanding the interaction that transpired between the patient and the doctor. For example, why did the doctor miss the earlier cues of woman abuse? What helped the doctor make the transition from viewing the family in the context of their community stature to questioning the presence of abuse in the marital relationship? What facilitated the patient's disclosure of abuse during this encounter? How did the doctor deal with his guilt for missing earlier signs? What promoted the doctor's movement from lack of awareness to being a source of support for the patient and her family?

What was different during this visit was that the doctor began to listen to Paulette from a different perspective. Instead of just hearing the signs and symptoms of depression or attending to the bruises from a bike accident, the doctor heard the patient's real pain. He listened and asked some key questions early in the visit, such as, 'How do you resolve tension in your marriage?' and 'Has there ever been any abuse in your relationship?' (Brown et al., 1996).

The doctor was not constricted by his guilt for missing earlier cues of abuse, nor was he confined by his prior perceptions of the family. Instead he was activated to serve as a resource and support to the patient. The doctor gave the patient permission to share the pain of her experience. In response the patient took the risk to trust the doctor with her story. Finally, the doctor made it clear that he would support his patient through whatever decision she made.

Two days later the patient and her two daughters moved to a shelter for abused women and their children. It was a dramatic move for the patient, filled with fear and anxiety. Despite her apprehension and concern about the potential consequences of her actions, she was assured of one fact: her doctor would support her and remain constant in his commitment to her as she continued to make changes in her life.

36

Visual aids in patient education

Judith Belle Brown, Lynn Brown, W Wayne Weston and Moira Stewart

Genograms and other practical tools can assist physicians in communicating with patients and their families and learning about their experiences of illness.

Two years ago, Tom Clark, aged 47, injured his back in a work accident. Despite treatment he was unemployed because of ongoing pain and functional limitations. His wife Sara, 45, worked as a clerk and her income now served as the family's mainstay. The couple had two children, John, 17, and Cindy, 15, who had until this time enjoyed good health.

Since his injury Tom frequently presented at Dr Warner's office with vague complaints and recently, during a visit with Sara, the doctor had sensed some marital tension. The doctor was also concerned about Cindy's increasing complaints of abdominal pain which had no clear etiology. Her pain was so severe that she often remained home from school.

Perplexed by the situation, Dr Warner suggested a family meeting, presenting it as 'a way to learn how all of you have been coping with the changes over the last two years, so I can be as helpful as possible'. All the Clark family members agreed to meet with the doctor and after brief introductions, Dr Warner asked each member if they would agree to have their family experience drawn on the board in her office. The family, interested by this prospect, began to share their individual and collective experiences.

At the completion of the genogram Dr Warner asked about the changes in the last two years. The family acknowledged it had been a difficult time. The doctor's further questions helped to clarify this. She inquired, 'Who do each of you see as being the most worried about how things are going in the family?' The family identified Tom and Cindy as being openly concerned. John stated that his mother was also worried but didn't show it. In addition, the doctor asked

Note: This case description first appeared in the December 1994 issue of the *Ontario Medical Review* and is reprinted with the permission of the Ontario Medical Association.

about tasks, such as household, yard work and finances, adding these to the genogram. What emerged at a glance was Sara's increased load. Since Tom's injury she had been doing a 'double shift', working full time both in and outside the home. The family seemed somewhat surprised by this. Tom said they had previously shared the household responsibilities and regretted that Sara now did it all.

When Dr Warner asked 'Who gets to spend the most time together now?', Tom and Cindy were in clear agreement. Cindy and her father were confidants, with Cindy's abdominal pain often resulting in her remaining at home with her father. This too was drawn on the genogram and when the physician asked about this apparent bond, they said that 'we understand each other's pain'. Sara and John were clearly absent from this picture, with Sara at work and John devoting his time to his cadet activities which would lead to a career in the armed forces, away from home.

When the doctor asked 'Who would like to spend more time together?', Tom quickly indicated he wanted more time with his wife. Sara hesitantly agreed and this was represented in the form of a dotted line between the couple on the genogram.

The physician was getting a picture – and so was the family. Sara was clearly overwhelmed yet she rarely spoke of it unless she was very frustrated. Tom was also frustrated and described his helplessness with the statement, 'I can't do much to help now in my present state'.

An understanding of the family's situation was further deepened when the physician added the previous generation to the genogram, reflecting both Tom's and Sara's families of origin. The genogram revealed that Tom's mother had suffered a similar debilitating back injury during midlife. This led to a discussion of how Tom's family's life had changed as a result. The family began to talk about how they wanted their adjustment to the current problem to be different from the previous generation's. With a greater awareness of some of the historical meanings of the illness, particularly for Tom, the family was equipped to make changes.

The changes brought about by illness in a family can affect their beliefs about themselves, as well as their sense of future vision and purpose. The effects on family life can alter cherished roles, familiar tasks and reassuring routines which are the daily expressions of family coherence (Baird and Grant, 1994). These multiple and complex changes are difficult for families and often complicated for physicians attempting to organize and understand the information before them.

Visual tools can assist in making evident what would require many words to capture. One of these visual tools is the genogram – the construction of a family tree (Waters *et al.*, 1994). The genogram is customarily used to organize family information (i.e. membership, ages, dates of marriage, illness and deaths). The resultant family picture can also capture the nature of relationships – close, conflicted, distant. When the preceding generation is recorded in the genogram a quick glance at their health and family history provides further information about the family's health beliefs and legends.

Genograms lend themselves to the creative use of symbols representing task changes and losses for members of the family that signal changes in roles and relationships. Questions such as: 'Who are you most worried about at this time?' or 'Who gets to spend a lot of time together?' can be represented visually and woven through a genogram-based assessment with the family. Doctors can also use genograms to help family members describe how they have changed since the illness. They may ask, for example, 'How would this picture have looked before you were coping with this illness?' The genogram also offers another way to ask about the future vision of the family. 'Although you have to deal with this illness, and life has changed as a result of it, how would you like to be coping with it differently in the future?'

In the case of the Clark family, the doctor ended the family meeting with a wealth of information to draw upon. So did the family. By making use of a genogram and a series of searching questions, the doctor acknowledged the family's difficulties, identified their strengths and resources and supported their commitment to change.

37

Menopause

W Wayne Weston, Judith Belle Brown and Moira Stewart

Physicians must understand reported symptoms in the context of the patient's whole life situation. What presents as a medical problem may have other causes or contributing factors. Some patients expect and prefer a biomedical explanation and solution for their problems. When a doctor disagrees with the patient's formulation of the problem, he or she must be willing to work with the patient to find common ground.

'Doctor, these hot flashes are driving me mad! What can I do about them?'

Marlene is 49 and had her last period six months ago. She reports that she occasionally feels hot and nervous and has trouble sleeping, but is never awakened by typical hot flashes.

Through further questioning, Dr Leung learns that Marlene's last child has just left home. Her relationship with her husband of 25 years is warm and friendly but lacks intimacy and she wonders if he understands her worries. He is busier than ever with his career and she is reluctantly considering returning to work after many years. She denies feeling depressed, but does express concerns about succeeding in her job and about a lack of self-confidence. 'I just can't imagine how I'd manage these hot flashes when I'm working,' she says. 'Couldn't you put me on estrogen or something?'

Patients like this present many challenges for their doctors. First, physicians must understand patients' requests, not only in terms of their changing physiology but also in the context of their whole life situation. Change and life transitions may cause considerable stress which is often manifested as physical and emotional symptoms. Second, management for menopausal symptoms may include hormonal replacement therapy but is incomplete without addressing

Note: This case description first appeared in the March 1990 issue of the *Ontario Medical Review* and is reprinted with the permission of the Ontario Medical Association.

the other factors which are part of this patient's life, such as her ambivalence about returning to work. Third, patients and doctors may have quite different ideas about the patient's problems and priorities.

Physicians have been criticized for 'medicalizing' problems of living by translating patients' expressions of distress into disease (Illich, 1976). For example, a patient living on welfare, trying to raise four children on her own in a high-rise apartment building filled with drug pushers, may reach the end of her tether. Feeling abandoned or abused by society, she may lash out at her physician, who may label her very complex problem as 'depression' or 'personality disorder'. Although the label may be accurate, it does not capture the full extent and context of the patient's problems and does little to help solve them.

Similarly, the patient who complained of feeling hot and nervous might be labelled as 'menopausal syndrome' and be treated only with a prescription for estrogen. Attempting to understand her problems in broader terms is more difficult and time consuming. Adopting a comprehensive approach may even create tension with patients who prefer doctors to use a narrower biological approach.

The biomedical model has been remarkably successful for understanding many diseases such as infections, nutritional deficiencies and acute surgical conditions. As a result, many patients expect physicians to be able to diagnose their problems and prescribe a specific remedy. They are often disappointed that many of the problems of living do not lend themselves to easy formulations and a quick prescription. The first step in helping these patients is to establish a trusting patient–doctor relationship. The patient must know that her concerns have been heard and understood and that they will not be dismissed. But if the physician disagrees with the patient's formulation of the problem, he must be willing to explain the reasons for his disagreement and work together with the patient to find common ground.

In a fascinating and largely ignored study, Donovan (1951) found that patients labelled as having the 'menopausal syndrome' were expressing symptoms that they often had experienced for years prior to any change in menses. Also, attentive listening was often associated with a resolution of their symptoms without any pharmacological treatment.

Donovan (1951) wrote:

'Regardless of the type of somatic symptoms of which the patient had initially complained, women who were able to discuss their nervousness experienced relief from somatic symptoms. Although they spent entire interviews talking about their nervousness they stated that this too was much improved. As long as the opportunity was provided, they seemed satisfied to talk and voiced no demands for medication. In each case the nervousness or the known emotional factors which caused the nervousness antedated the menopause by decades.' (p. 1289)

Donovan is describing the healing power of an effective patient–doctor relationship; the attentive listening and concern of a physician are often as powerful as drug therapy.

This is not to say that drugs should be ignored. Many women present clear-cut symptoms of estrogen deficiency – hot flashes or dry vagina – and will respond dramatically to estrogen replacement.

It takes time and energy to sort out the multiple causes of the patient's problems, rather than leaping to a simple pharmacological answer. Physicians must listen to their patients' ideas and expectations about their problems and address them in a thoughtful and sensitive manner. Patients need to know that they have been heard and that their concerns have been taken seriously before they can be expected to listen to their physician's recommendations regarding strategies for prevention and health promotion.

38

Setting limits

W E Osmun, Judith Belle Brown and Juan Muñoz

Patients with chronic pain can be both frustrating and challenging. An integrated approach to care requires counseling and establishing a relationship based on trust and limit setting. Physicians must guard against their own anger and feelings of failure.

After losing her job in the city, Elna, age 33, moved back to the small town where she was born. Within days of her arrival, Elna presented to the local emergency department complaining of severe abdominal pain. She gave a history of frequent hospital admissions for chronic lower abdominal pain resulting in a hysterectomy six months earlier. Unfortunately, the surgery had not helped the pain.

Dr Taylor explored the past history carefully. Elna had tried many remedies to lessen her chronic pain but nothing had worked. The only thing that alleviated her pain was acetaminophen with 30 mg of codeine supplemented with intermittent demerol injections.

Elna revealed that her life was chaotic, characterized by numerous transient relationships, frequent moves and long-term unemployment. Dr Taylor became increasingly uncomfortable, feeling concerned with Elna's use of narcotics and her troubled past history.

After the examination, Dr Taylor expressed his worries about Elna's drug use. Elna rejected Dr Taylor's concerns regarding possible addiction, adamantly stating that this was not a problem. All she needed was an injection. As Dr Taylor tried to explore the various alternatives to narcotics, Elna's eyes filled with tears. 'Aren't you going to help me, Doctor?' she asked pathetically.

Before he could respond, Dr Taylor was interrupted by a nurse telling him that three seriously injured accident victims were about to arrive. He would have preferred to spend more time with Elna but as the sole physician on duty in the emergency room, he would soon be needed elsewhere. Feeling trapped, Dr Taylor ordered the demerol and exited the room with Elna thanking him.

Note: This case description first appeared in the July 1996 issue of the *Ontario Medical Review* and is reprinted with the permission of the Ontario Medical Association.

Four days later, while scanning the appointment book at his family practice office, Dr Taylor felt his heart sink. Elna was booked to see him. He went through the day dreading the appointment. It eventually came and with a sigh, Dr Taylor entered the room.

Elna explained that she had come for her prescription of acetaminophen with codeine 30 mg. Then she would be on her way as she had a job interview in 15 minutes. She was really hoping to get this job, it would mean a new start for her. Elna thanked Dr Taylor for his previous excellent care at the hospital and said that she had heard 'great things' about him around town.

Dr Taylor felt manipulated and angry. Consciously controlling his feelings, he once again expressed his concerns about Elna's use of narcotics. He openly acknowledged his frustration with their previous encounter and his unwillingness to continue without some changes. Dr Taylor explained to Elna that her problem was chronic pain, for which no cure was likely to be found.

Elna began to cry. Twisting her hands, she expressed her own concerns about her drug use but explained that nothing else seemed to help. Glancing at her watch, Elna reminded the doctor of the need to get to her job interview. Once again feeling pressured, Dr Taylor quickly outlined a plan of gradual withdrawal of the acetaminophen with codeine and no further demerol injections. Elna agreed, took the prescription and hurried from the office.

Dr Taylor sat silently for a few moments. Although he realized he had been manipulated, he felt he had set appropriate limits and that a reasonable compromise had been reached. He felt uncomfortable having to prescribe any acetaminophen with codeine, acknowledging that the real issue of Elna's underlying personal difficulties and drug use had not been addressed. But he realized time would be needed to build the trust necessary to explore all the issues contributing to Elna's problems.

Elna subsequently came to see Dr Taylor for two more appointments. She continued to focus on her abdominal pain and was unwilling to discuss any other aspects of her life. When it became apparent that Dr Taylor was not going to deviate from the original compromise, Elna left his practice and left town three weeks later.

Patients who suffer from chronic, undiagnosable pain are a challenge to the physician. Unable to verbalize their emotional pain, these patients often present with complex physical symptoms. When the presenting problem is interwoven with multiple personal issues, every encounter can feel like a power struggle. For example, the patient's frequency of attendance, demands for narcotics and attempts to manipulate may cause the physician to react with anger and rejection. Their drug-seeking behavior may make it difficult for us to see the person behind the problem.

Various labels have been used to describe patients who demand narcotics for their chronic pain, such as the 'hateful patient', the 'heartsink patient' or the 'difficult patient' (Mathers and Gask, 1995; Norton and Smith, 1994). These labels reveal as much about the reactions they engender in the profession as they do about the patient's symptoms and behaviors. Negative emotions in the physician are a cue to step back, recognize what is happening and re-enter the encounter with a new perspective.

Many 'difficult' patients have difficult pasts. Exploring the patient's past will promote a fuller understanding of the patient's need to use bodily pain to present their psychic distress. Encouraging patients to discuss their difficult life experiences may help them gain some insight into their struggles. Understanding the patient's past enables the physician to react with compassion, not anger.

While limits must be set, flexibility is important. The physician may agree to prescribe a limited amount of pain medication as part of a carefully monitored program. Limit setting must be done in the context of a caring relationship, emotional support and a realistic hope for improvement (Green *et al.*, 1988). Providing the patient with alternatives such as pain management clinics and support groups may be helpful. The opportunity to meet with others who are in recovery from similar problems is invaluable.

The physician needs to be prepared for the patient to relapse and to respond with a firm yet empathetic approach. Substance misuse disorders are chronic relapsing illnesses, just like diabetes and COPD, and we should not be surprised or react with indignation when patients have a setback. It is essential for physicians to view problems of substance misuse as illnesses, not moral faults. In addition, these patients often have significant problems establishing trust and will test the physician. While the initial reaction to this behavior may be one of anger, it is more effective to respond with understanding.

It is important for the physician to remain realistic and not allow the patient's frequent attempts at manipulation to be experienced as a personal failure. Rather we must see the behavior as a manifestation of a very difficult chronic illness requiring care which is patient-centered.

The physician must also be prepared for failures. Setting limits will mean the inevitable loss of some patients. Still, a long-term supportive relationship is often the most therapeutic tool for these patients and may result in promoting their future health and well-being.

39

Learned helplessness

Carol L McWilliam, Judith Belle Brown and W Wayne Weston

Some elderly patients who appear unable to care for themselves may be suffering from 'learned helplessness', having relinquished the power to make decisions for themselves to efficient caregivers. In these complex situations, the role of the physician is to help patients regain control over their lives.

Mrs Victor was a 76-year-old widow with chronic obstructive lung disease. She had had a hard life, bearing and raising nine children. Because her husband died young, she struggled for many years supporting the family by working as a cleaner. After her children left home, Mrs Victor remarried and was widowed for a second time within a few years but expressed little grief over this loss. Both of Mrs Victor's husbands had been blue collar workers and she had never been well off financially. However, she had learned to live frugally and managed on her old age pension, living alone in a senior's apartment, just a few blocks away from one of her daughters.

Mrs Victor's breathing difficulties were not serious enough to necessitate regular respiratory therapy or use of oxygen. However, her physical activity was severely curbed and this made life even more bleak. She was worn down by years of struggle and hardship and her lung disease was the last straw. It was no surprise to the health professionals involved in her care that Mrs Victor would 'use' the label of chronic obstructive lung disease to both explain and legitimize many vague complaints of chest pain. These obscure pains served as her excuse for not doing household chores, not attending to her personal care and not socializing with family and friends. As well, the chest pain and minor breathing difficulties solicited concern from her family, friends and physicians and served as the 'ticket of entry' for frequent hospitalizations.

Note: This case description first appeared in the February 1993 issue of the *Ontario Medical Review* and is reprinted with the permission of the Ontario Medical Association.

Mrs Victor's 52-year-old daughter, understandably concerned about her mother's health, quickly assumed responsibility for her care. Grocery shopping, making meals, doing laundry and regularly supervising her mother's personal hygiene were added to her own household duties and full-time job in a clothing factory. Not surprisingly, over the years her daughter began to resent the added burden of 'parenting' her own mother. Thus, when yet another admission to hospital occurred, she enlisted the help of Dr Aaron, the family's physician, to arrange her mother's placement in a nursing home.

Dr Aaron knew that Mrs Victor was strongly opposed to entering a nursing home. He also recognized that Mrs Victor was mentally and physically capable of living at home and capable of making her own decisions. Nevertheless, feeling caught in the middle, he agreed to at least discuss the matter with her daughter. Meanwhile Mrs Victor waited passively in hospital, resigned to having her future decided by others. Yet she was alert and aware of what was going on around her. Mrs Victor despondently related her view of the situation to the nurse attending to her care:

'My daughter and Dr Aaron have a meeting tonight,' she said. 'I don't know what they are going to do. So I'll just sit and wait for their conclusions. I'm all jittery and I don't know what to do. It will be the doctor's orders, so I've got to do what he says. I guess they know what's best.'

This was a dangerous liaison. Dr Aaron could have been swayed by his desire to relieve Mrs Victor's daughter of her distress. He was tempted to support the idea of nursing home placement on the grounds that Mrs Victor was not safe alone at home and seemed uninterested in pursuing alternative solutions. The very fact that the doctor was meeting with Mrs Victor's daughter in Mrs Victor's absence spoke volumes. It reinforced everyone's impression that Mrs Victor was helpless to do anything for herself.

Clearly, it was time to engage the patient in the decision-making process. Mrs Victor's helplessness and child-like compliance were fuelled by depression and apathy associated with a lack of role and meaning in her life. Her helplessness had been unwittingly reinforced by her daughter and belied the many coping skills and other personal strengths which her earlier life experience had cultivated. She had no need to be institutionalized; rather, she needed help to mobilize her own personal resources and to unlearn learned helplessness.

A sense of meaning or purpose in life is essential; without it, people have little feeling of self-worth and no energy to identify goals and mobilize resources to achieve them. Helping older persons to unlearn learned helplessness begins with an assessment of the individual's life goals and expectations. This begins with an understanding of the patient's perception of the problem. In this case it was important to encourage both the patient and her caregivers to discuss their mutual concerns and different perceptions of the problem.

Similarly, goals for change or management of the problem needed to be considered. Different solutions needed to be examined, particularly those that would help the patient to regain control and direction of her life (Waters and Goodman, 1990). Finally, the patient needed to be helped to resume more responsibility for her own care.

In Mrs Victor's case, this effort included counseling, medication to treat her chronic depression and an examination of ways to help her overcome apathy and boredom. Only when these underlying symptoms were addressed and Mrs Victor regained some sense of purpose in life could empowerment strategies become helpful (Dunst *et al.*, 1988). It was important to work with the patient as a partner in her care rather than to treat her as a dependent individual who could not make sensible decisions for herself. The doctor needed to make himself available for prolonged time to talk and time to listen in such a complicated case. But weighed against the cost of years of unnecessary institutionalization and lost human potential, the cost did not seem too high.

40

Screening tests

Thomas R Freeman, Judith Belle Brown
and Moira Stewart

Patients should be involved in the decision to perform screening tests that may involve risks or lead to controversial results. The physician should explain the purpose of the test, the meaning of a positive result and treatment options in the case of a positive result, before performing the test.

Erica, aged 28, attended her third prenatal visit with excitement. It was a planned first pregnancy and she was eager to learn how the baby was developing and what to expect. During the visit Dr Teves, her physician, informed her that he would be drawing blood for some tests and asked her to check back with him in a week for the results. The doctor reassured Erica, indicating that things were going well. Content with this information, she left the visit and had no further thoughts about the blood tests.

When she returned to the office a week later, Erica's physician indicated all the blood tests were normal, except that alpha-fetoprotein (AFP) had not been detected in her blood. The doctor explained that, 'This could mean that the fetus is either dead or suffering from Down's syndrome'. He explained that this specific test was also used to determine the presence of congenital defects, such as spina bifida. 'Under most circumstances, further testing such as amniocentesis and ultrasound are recommended,' he said. 'Depending on the results of these tests, termination of the pregnancy may be something to consider.'

The patient stared at him in disbelief. Numbed by the shock of this information, it took her a few moments to reply. Why hadn't the doctor informed her of the intent of this test at the outset? Abortion was not an option for her. This information was very upsetting to Erica and she wondered aloud how she would cope with waiting three weeks to learn whether or not her baby was normal. Undaunted by her anger and distress, Dr Teves indicated that while he

Note: This case description first appeared in the October 1990 issue of the *Ontario Medical Review* and is reprinted with the permission of the Ontario Medical Association.

appreciated her concerns, she would have to live with the uncertainty for a few more weeks.

This case raises several important issues with respect to patient–doctor communication and screening tests. Some screening tests carry little or no risk and the treatment of identified cases is effective and non-controversial. These tests are generally performed with little or no patient involvement (e.g. hemoglobin in pregnancy, PKU in newborn infants). Other screening tests may carry a risk or the indicated treatment may be controversial. Screening for AFP falls into the latter category; confirmation of a positive result requires amniocentesis, which carries the risk of spontaneous abortion, and a major intervention for neural tube defects is termination of the pregnancy (Carroll *et al.*, 1997; Evans, 1997).

This type of screening test requires that the physician involve the patient as early as possible. Any test must be understood in the context of a decision-making process. This entails communicating relevant information about the sensitivity and specificity of the test and about the proposed management, should the test prove to be positive.

A study in Great Britain (Marteau *et al.*, 1990) found that when obstetrical patients were presented with the need for AFP screening, 4.4% were told that the test was for spina bifida but only 16.4% were informed that screening included Down's syndrome. In addition, the meaning of a positive result was discussed only 1.9% of the time and the treatment procedures available following a positive result were reviewed 33.3% of the time.

Adequate information is necessary for fully informed consent. It may also be useful in reducing the patient's anxiety about the screening procedure, as well as reducing the kind of anger that gives rise to complaints against doctors (Wall, 1989).

This case carries the added ethical weight that the treatment may involve a recommendation for abortion (Marshall, 1996). If the patient is opposed to abortion, the impetus for doing the test diminishes.

Several steps have been recommended to avoid these problems (Marteau, 1990). First, when inviting the patient to participate in screening, the physician should explain:

- why the patient is being invited to have the test
- the condition(s) being screened for
- how participation in the screening may reduce the risk.

Next, if the patient agrees to be screened, the physician should discuss:

- the test procedure
- when and how test results are available
- the likelihood of a positive result
- the meaning of both negative and positive results
- alternatives for action for those with a positive result.

Component V:
Enhancing the
Patient–Doctor Relationship

Moira Stewart, Judith Belle Brown and Ian R McWhinney

The relationship is the bedrock or the basis for all interchanges between two people and could be described as a primal exchange between the two individuals. Relationships in general involve caring, feeling, trust, power and a sense of purpose. In a patient–doctor relationship the purpose is to help the patient, i.e. to be a therapeutic relationship and frequently to foster healing.

We have chosen to divide the component into six sections, each covering some well-known conceptualizations of helping relationships. The sections deal with: power; attributes of the therapeutic relationship; caring; healing; self-awareness and transference.

Power in the patient–doctor relationship

Much has been made of power and control in the patient–doctor relationship in the literature in the past 20 years. There is no doubt that the relationship which is the foundation for patient-centered care, compared to the traditional relationship, demands a sharing of power and control between the doctor and the patient (Brody, 1992). Other models of patient–doctor relationships have variously described the state of high patient control of decision making as: mutuality (Szasz and Hollender, 1956); the contractual relationship (Veatch, 1972); the consumerist approach (Haug and Lavin, 1983; Roter and Hall, 1992; Stewart and Roter, 1989). Patient–doctor encounters have been described as meetings between experts (Tuckett *et al.*, 1985).

Note: Parts of this chapter were published previously in *Patient-Centered Medicine: transforming the clinical method*, Sage Publications (1995).

The resulting therapeutic alliance is related in complex ways to enhancing patients' sense of self-efficacy, i.e. sense of control over themselves and their world or, to put it another way, a sense of omnipotence (Cassell, 1991).

Attributes of a therapeutic relationship

Many authors, representing various disciplines, have described specific facilitative attributes of the clinician that promote the development and maintenance of the helping relationship. These include empathy, congruence, genuineness, respect, positive regard and caring and concern for the other (Carkhuff, 1987; Cournoyer, 1991; Dubovsky, 1981; Perlman, 1979; Rogers, 1961). In addition to these core therapeutic qualities are the appreciation of the importance of mutual trust, a readiness to share power and accept difference (Brody, 1992; Kleinman, 1988; Perlman, 1979; Sherwin, 1992).

Trust lays the groundwork for the possibility of reciprocity. Cassell (1991) highlights the role of trust and reciprocity in the patient–doctor relationship.

'Doctors are people who, because of their special knowledge, are empowered to act by virtue of the trust given by patients, and who acquire responsibility thereby. In their actions on behalf of the sick person, endangered by the possibility of failing their responsibility, doctors become threatened by what threatens the patient. *Doctor and patient are bound in a reciprocal relationship* – failure to understand that is failure to comprehend clinical medicine.' (p. 76)

On the other hand, the relationship is not always reciprocal. In spite of this it remains the doctor's responsibility to be constant in his or her commitment to the well-being of the patient. As Stephens (1982) explains: '... physicians do not have the luxury of limiting their involvement to those patients who can make and keep promises' (p. 164). The required commitment is not easily achieved because the doctor may experience feelings of failure and has to encounter a patient's anger or other expressions of mistrust. Nonetheless, 'Constancy to the patient is necessary' (Cassell, 1991).

Caring

Caring implies that the doctor is fully present and engaged with the patient. The notion of the detached clinician who keeps a safe emotional distance is replaced by the notion that doctor and patient are interconnected in such a deep way that the doctor can fully immerse him or herself in the concerns of the patient (Montgomery, 1993). Intense caring moments in relationships involve mutual recognition on the part of patient and practitioner and a reciprocal learning of both individuals (Frank, 1991a; Suchman & Matthews, 1988; Watson, 1985). Boundaries may be much more blurred than in the traditional, distanced, one-way relationship. However, the closeness restores the patient's sense of connectedness (Belenky *et al.* 1986; Candib, 1988; Cassell, 1991) to the human race, a connectedness which may have been broken by their physical or emotional suffering.

Arthur Frank (1991b) says that care is a matter of recognizing that every patient is different: 'The common diagnostic categories into which medicine places its patients are relevant to disease, not to illness. They are useful for treatment, but they only get in the way of care' (p. 45). The problem is, says Frank, that most people who deal with ill persons do not want to recognize differences and particularities because to do so takes time and involvement.

For generations, medical students have been taught: 'Don't get involved'. In the conventional clinical method, the doctor is assumed to be a detached observer and prescriber of treatment. Remaining uninvolved may protect doctors from some very disturbing things, especially in the encounter with suffering, but it also has a personal price. To remain uninvolved, physicians have to build up protective shells to suppress their feelings. This lack of openness makes difficulties for relationships, not only with patients but also with colleagues. To suggest that one can remain uninvolved is also a fallacy. One cannot help being affected in some way by the encounter with suffering, even if the result is avoidance and denial.

Candib (1987) has spoken about not only the inherent intimacy of patient–doctor relationships but also their reciprocity. She noted that doctors' sharing their own story with a patient can go awry but also can be healing for the doctor as well as the patient. The question then becomes one of what it means to be involved. Perhaps what the conventional teaching intended to say was: 'Don't get involved at the level of your egoistic emotions'.

Becoming involved in the right way is crucial to the care of patients, but very difficult in practice. The problem is that none of us is very good at recognizing the ways in which our egoistic emotions can intrude into our actions. There are so many ways in which our unrecognized self-absorption can interfere with care: our helplessness in the face of suffering; our career commitment to a certain point of view or procedure; our anger when a patient challenges our self-worth; or even when the patient becomes an instrument in our crusade for a worthy cause. Sometimes our difficulty is a failure to understand that what the patient wants is something very simple: a recognition of their suffering or perhaps only our presence at a time of need.

Healing

The attributes of the doctor and the characteristics of the relationship are what make the patient–doctor relationship therapeutic. Like many other helping professionals, doctors are experienced as instruments (agents) of healing. This image of the doctor is contained in numerous stories of patients (Stephens, 1993). In particular, Arthur Frank wrote in his book *At the Will of the Body: reflections on illness* (1991b), about his own experience as a patient:

> 'Medicine has done well with my body and I am grateful. But doing *with* the body is only part of what needs to be done *for* the person. What happens when my body breaks down happens not just to that body but also to my life, which is lived in that body. When the body breaks down, so does the life. Even when medicine can fix the body, that doesn't always put the life back together again.' (p. 8)

Healing the body and healing the person are not identical and do not even necessarily go hand in hand. The healing of a patient involves a process of restoring the patient's lost sense of connectedness, indestructibility and control. The healing process is 'no more than allowing, causing or bringing to bear those things or forces for getting better that already exist in the patient' (Cassell, 1991, p. 234).

Physicians for the most part see themselves as curers of patients' physical ills. They are less conscious of the need to restore patients to wellness by embracing the mandate to care and to heal. The words *heal, health* and *whole* all come from the same linguistic root in old English. To heal is to restore a sense of coherence and wholeness after the disruption in a person's life that is caused by a serious illness. After a heart attack at the age of 39 and cancer at 40, Arthur Frank wrote about his experience in a healthcare system which was technically proficient but essentially uncaring. It was a system that seemed to have lost the capacity to heal the patient as well as treating his body.

Examples of the work of a doctor who recognized the use of the drug 'doctor' (Balint, 1964), in a much deeper way than in the previous example, are contained in Berger and Mohr's (1967) story of a country doctor, *A Fortunate Man*. Because illness and crises separate people from the ordinariness of the rest of humanity, one requirement of the doctor is to recognize accurately the pain of the patient in order to help restore the patient's lost sense of connectedness and therefore promote healing (Stephens, 1982). This is not only difficult to do but it also takes courage, a fact that often goes unacknowledged.

> '... (the country doctor) is acknowledged as a good doctor because he meets the deep but unformulated expectation of the sick for a sense of fraternity.

He recognizes them. Sometimes he fails – often because he has missed a critical opportunity and the patient's suppressed resentment becomes too hard to break through – but there is about him the constant will of man trying to recognize. 'The door opens,' he says, 'and sometimes I feel I'm in the valley of death. It's all right when once I'm working. I try to overcome this shyness because for the patient the first contact is extremely important ... All diffidence in my position is a fault. A form of negligence.' (Berger and Mohr, 1967, pp. 76–77)

Self-awareness

Whatever use doctors make of themselves and the relationship, in caring for patients, it affects them as well as their patients. The use of self, and attending to the impact on self, both require a depth of self-knowledge.

Self-awareness can be a natural outgrowth of reflection on experience and sharing these reflections with colleagues, friends and family. It can be further enhanced by supervision or consultation, professional and personal development. Epstein *et al.* (1993) proposed three possible venues for developing self-awareness: Balint groups; family of origin groups; and personal awareness groups which have evolved from the contributions of Carl Rogers (1961). Other authors endorse the important knowledge and understanding imparted in the classical literature or the insights offered by narratives of illness (Brody, 1992; Kleinman, 1988; McWhinney, 1997).

The development of self-awareness requires doctors to know their strengths and weaknesses. What are potential blindspots or emotional triggers that elicit a negative response to certain patients? As Longhurst (1989) notes, self-awareness means confronting one's emotional baggage but also has positive value in that it promotes and nurtures the qualities of empathy, sensitivity, honesty and caring in the physician. Because acquiring self-knowledge is often a painful process, this form of knowledge is the most difficult of all to acquire. It is perhaps best seen as a lifelong journey, a process which is never complete.

Transference and countertransference

All human relationships, and in particular therapeutic relationships, are influenced by the phenomena of transference and countertransference. Thus any discussion of the patient–doctor relationship that excluded these important psychological processes would be lacking. We do not intend to provide the reader with a detailed examination of transference and countertransference but rather with a brief description.

Transference is a process whereby the patient unconsciously projects, onto individuals in his or her current life, thoughts, behaviors and emotional reactions that originate with other significant relationships from childhood onwards (Dubovsky, 1981; Hepworth and Larsen, 1990; Woods and Hollis, 1990). This can include feelings of love, hate, ambivalence and dependency. The greater the current attachment, such as a significant patient–doctor relationship, the more likely that transference will occur. Transference, while often perceived as a negative phenomenon, actually helps build the connection between patient and doctor. Frequently, doctors are intimidated by the concept of transference, which has its roots in psychoanalytic theory, viewing it as something mysterious and to be avoided. However, knowledge of the patient's transference reaction assists the doctor in understanding how the patient experiences his or her world and how past relationships influence current behavior.

Stein (1985) has noted 'how rarely the issue of physician countertransference was addressed in medical school, residency training, or continuing education'. He believes that '... most of the problems in clinician–patient relationships did not have to do with technical or procedural issues in patient management but with those unconscious agendas which physicians and patients brought to the encounter' (p. xii). Like transference, countertransference is an unconscious process which occurs when the doctor responds to patients in a manner similar to significant past relationships (Dubovsky, 1981; Hepworth and Larsen, 1990; Woods and Hollis, 1990). Doctors need to be alert to what triggers certain reactions, i.e. unresolved personal issues, stress or value conflicts. It is here that self-awareness, coupled with the ability for self-observation during the consultation, are paramount.

Preview of the cases

The cases which illustrate the fifth component cover the areas just described, including: power issues, trust, constancy, confidentiality, caring, healing, self-awareness and transference.

The first case involves an elderly female patient and illustrates many important aspects of patient–physician relationships, but most prominently the issue of sharing power. The next two cases demonstrate the contribution of constancy and continuity of care to the development of the patients' trust.

Confidentiality, and its implications for therapeutic relationships, is explored in the fourth case. A relationship gone wrong illustrates the themes of a perceived lack of caring and the misunderstanding of preferred roles in the fifth case. In contrast, a caring relationship is demonstrated in the case of breaking bad news to a breast cancer patient.

Two cases illustrate the importance of physician self-awareness to the healing relationship. The first case tells of a physician's struggle to overcome his own negative reaction to a patient's behavior in order to create a therapeutic relationship with the patient. The next case recounts a story of a physician's confrontation with his own homophobia.

The final case has two parts which weave together most of the issues raised in this component. The case deals with a medical emergency during childbirth and describes the family doctor's crisis in finding a role for himself during the resuscitation of the postpartum mother. The second part of the story illustrates the extraordinary role of the doctor in facilitating the husband's role in the difficult delivery and in caring for the whole family during the ensuing medical crisis by ensuring clear communication and emotional support.

Cases Illustrating Component V: Enhancing the Patient–Doctor Relationship

41

The embittered patient

*Carol L McWilliam, Judith Belle Brown
and W Wayne Weston*

When doctor and patient meet, each has expectations and feelings about the encounter. Understanding those expectations in the larger context of the patient's experience with the healthcare system is crucial to building a constructive patient–doctor relationship. Where experiences have been particularly negative, extra time and effort are required to demonstrate commitment and caring in order to insure a positive outcome.

Dr Gilly sat at his desk, pondering the events of another long day. Many things had gone well, but he had some trepidation about his commitment to Ralph Dunn.

Ralph, a bachelor aged 52, lived with his 84-year-old mother. He had come to the office today for a 'check-up', but had used the visit to explore his concerns about his aging mother. Ralph described his mother as a 'holy terror', who frequently had 'panic attacks' for which she demanded to be taken to hospital. Although she suffered from congestive heart failure, most often the emergency department staff sent Mrs Dunn back home, explaining to Ralph that there was nothing unusually wrong and little they could do for her.

Twice during the past year, the exasperated physicians had responded by admitting Mrs Dunn to hospital. These occasions had been equally frustrating for Ralph. His mother's demanding, controlling behavior had even led the nurses to take away her call bell. Her frequent tongue lashing of professionals added to her reputation as a 'difficult patient' and resulted in the doctors and nurses avoiding her as much as possible.

In the last six months she had dismissed two internists and her family doctor of 20 years. Ralph didn't know what to do for his mother and didn't feel he could continue to care for her without a physician to monitor her medical needs. 'She

Note: This case description first appeared in the January 1995 issue of the *Ontario Medical Review* and is reprinted with the permission of the Ontario Medical Association.

is 84, after all.' he explained. 'She suffers from heart trouble, needs oxygen and has to use a walker to get around.'

Ralph therefore asked Dr Gilly to assume the role of his mother's physician and the doctor, somewhat reluctantly, agreed. Having arranged to begin with a home visit a few days hence, Dr Gilly now wondered what challenges he faced.

The visit to Mrs Dunn went ahead as scheduled. Dr Gilly intentionally arranged this initial assessment to occur at Mrs Dunn's home, where she could feel as unthreatened as possible and on a more equal footing with him as 'the professional expert'. He purposely let Mrs Dunn take the initiative in telling him how he could help her. He quickly learned that she perceived healthcare professionals as 'the enemy' who were threatening to put her in a nursing home against her wishes. He learned that her expectation of him was that he provide the medical care and advice she needed to keep managing at home. He also learned, over the next few visits, that she was a very strong-willed woman, with every intention of doing anything necessary to keep healthy and avoid institutionalization. Mrs Dunn appeared to have a high need to be in control of her life and all decisions about it.

During subsequent conversations Dr Gilly came to understand this better as he listened to her embittered tales of having had her life controlled by her father and, in later years, by her mother-in-law.

Dr Gilly decided that the most effective way to decrease Mrs Dunn's inappropriate use of healthcare services was to work with her to achieve her goal of staying out of a nursing home. He arranged a brief weekly visit to her apartment and advised her to call his office, at any hour, if she had an 'attack'. This provided Mrs Dunn with the assurance that she would receive medical attention and monitoring without going to the emergency department. Her previous illness behavior had been to handle most problems on her own: Dr Gilly was confident that she would be unlikely to call after hours if she knew that help was available when needed. With this approach, Mrs Dunn's 'panic attacks' immediately disappeared. While Mrs Dunn initially greeted Dr Gilly's 'Good morning' with a crusty 'What's good about it?', over the months she mellowed. In time, she made an effort to impress him with her progress in walking and eventually shared personal life stories with him. Ultimately, Dr Gilly established a positive relationship with her, where many others had failed.

The secret of Dr Gilly's success was revealed to a visiting nurse in a conversation some months later.

'Dr Gilly comes over every Tuesday,' said Mrs Dunn. 'He'll be here tomorrow.'

'Are he and you getting along better now?' asked the nurse.

'I think so,' replied Mrs Dunn. 'We know each other now. He's always got a story. He's a good man. He has taken the time to get to know me.'

Dr Gilly has succeeded because he knew the importance of caring and, equally important, of showing that he cared. Mayeroff (1971) says: 'to care for someone, I must *know* many things. I must know ... who the other is, what his powers and limitations are, what his needs are, what is conducive to his growth ...'

When doctor and patient meet, each has expectations and feelings about the encounter. Taking on a new but elderly patient, whose reputation for being 'difficult' precedes her, challenges the most skilled practitioner. The relationship is further taxed if the patient's perceptions of past experiences with physicians have rendered her disillusioned, embittered and ready to do battle with any physician, just on general principle. Given such circumstances, extra attention has to be paid to setting the stage for a positive patient–doctor relationship.

42

Continuity of care in chronic illness

*Judith Belle Brown, Bridget L Ryan
and W Wayne Weston*

Continuity of care is important for patients with chronic illness. Emphasis should be placed on the continuity of the caregiver, as opposed to continuity of the care plan, thus highlighting the central role of the patient–doctor relationship.

Signy Barnes, aged 43, had a busy and productive life, combining her roles as a wife, mother of a five-year-old son and manager of a clothing store. Four years ago, shortly after her son's birth, Signy developed Crohn's disease. The diagnosis of this chronic condition came as a shock to Signy, who saw herself as healthy and vital. Her gastroenterologist, Dr Engel, was a key person in her acceptance and management of the disease.

Signy's relationship with Dr Engel was positive. She trusted his judgment and appreciated his willingness to listen and respond to her concerns. Apart from a severe initial presentation, Signy's disease activity had been mild; typically, she experienced a flare-up every 12–18 months. In the past, this mild activity caused her to delay visiting her physician, as she tended to discount her symptoms. At her last visit, Dr Engel had suggested that next time Signy should seek attention sooner.

In the last few weeks, Signy had begun to experience some symptoms of Crohn's disease. Remembering Dr Engel's advice, she tried to make an appointment to see him but was told she would have to wait a month. When Signy explained that her Crohn's disease was acting up, she was told to come in one week to a special clinic. Signy assumed that this was a new program instituted under Dr Engel's care.

When Signy arrived for her appointment, the nurse at the clinic told her that she would be seeing Dr Reis. Signy recalled meeting Dr Reis when Dr Engel was on holidays and the experience had been positive, but she was disappointed that she wouldn't be seeing Dr Engel.

After a discussion with Dr Reis, a course of treatment was prescribed. He told her not to wait so long before checking in with the clinic in future. Signy explained that she and Dr Engel had agreed that she need only come in when she was experiencing difficulties. Dr Reis said she should be seen yearly regardless of her current health status. While Signy recognized this was simply two different approaches to patient care, she was annoyed that the arrangements previously made with Dr Engel were set aside so easily.

When Dr Reis left the examining room Signy noticed that her chart recorded Dr Reis as her physician. When the nurse returned and began discussing follow-up with Dr Reis, Signy asked if Dr Engel was no longer her physician. The nurse explained that Dr Engel had taken on an increased administrative workload at the hospital; if she wanted to see him, she should arrange an appointment at his office. Signy did so, setting up an appointment with Dr Engel in six weeks' time.

In the past when Signy had needed to see a specialist, she was not as concerned about continuity of care. She recognized that in a teaching centre, you often deal with 'the team'. This had not been a problem before when her health issues were acute and resolvable. However, Signy valued her relationship with Dr Engel, as she knew that ongoing care was essential for her Crohn's.

As a result, Signy was concerned about a possible change and bothered that Dr Engel had not told her himself. She wondered if, had she not spoken with the nurse, she would have been assigned to Dr Reis without consultation. She resolved to clarify with Dr Engel at her next appointment whether he was still her physician and to express her concerns.

Six weeks passed and Signy was still experiencing discomfort when she arrived for her appointment. After inquiring how Signy was doing, Dr Engel examined her and together they discussed her treatment. Signy was beginning to think that she had misread the situation. Everything seemed as usual and knowing how busy Dr Engel was, Signy was reluctant to express her concerns.

After they had agreed on a course of action, Signy hesitated and asked if she could discuss something else. She described her last visit to the clinic and asked if Dr Engel was still her physician.

Dr Engel explained that he had been getting more heavily involved in administration. 'You know, I think I'm a good doctor but I also think I'm a good administrator . . .'

Signy interjected, 'But it's hard to do both.'

'Well, if you were a new patient, then probably I would refer you to someone else. But I want to be faithful to my patients who have been faithful to me. So if it's all right with you, I would prefer to remain as your physician,' said Dr Engel.

'That would be my preference as well,' said Signy.

'I'm honored you feel that way,' said Dr Engel. 'You should just set up your appointments here at my office. However, if you get into any trouble and need help immediately, there is always someone who can see you.'

Signy left the office feeling that she had been heard and respected. She was proud of herself for speaking her concerns and pleased with the kind and professional nature of Dr Engel's response. Her mind was at ease regarding her future care.

As this case illustrates, patients with chronic illness are concerned with both continuity of care *and* continuity of the caregiver. The significance of the ongoing relationship between patient and doctor in the primary care context is well established (Gabel *et al.*, 1993). However, the patient–doctor relationship is also important in specialist care, particularly in the care of patients with chronic illnesses.

Continuity promotes two important elements in the patient–doctor relationship: trust and communication. Trust is often based on the shared experience of past events. Continuity also allows the physician and patient to quickly address key issues without the preliminaries required in testing out a new relationship. The physician has a tacit knowledge of the patient, information that can never be reflected in the medical chart. Trust and communication result in increased patient confidence, in both the doctor and the patient's own ability to manage his or her chronic condition.

Sometimes we assume that the experience of continuity can be replaced by a comprehensive and thorough care plan. But the 'system' can create problems, such as the automatic reassignment of patients to another doctor when a senior physician becomes too busy with administrative, teaching or research responsibilities. We must always take into consideration the patient's feelings and wishes, never viewing the transfer of care as 'automatic' or 'routine'.

The essence of continuity is the strength of the relationship forged between the patient and the doctor. That relationship is based on a concrete demonstration of concern, a commitment to future care and mutual enjoyment of the relationship.

43

The reluctant patient

Stephen J Wetmore and Judith Belle Brown

In certain circumstances drastic measures must be undertaken to ensure a patient's well-being. Such actions may threaten the patient–doctor relationship but they can also serve to forge a therapeutic bond that guides the way to better care and improved health.

'I don't know where to turn,' said Sophia. 'My mother is in awful shape and my father just can't cope with her any longer. Can you help us?'

Sophia, aged 38, was desperate to obtain help for her mother and father. For two weeks her 60-year-old mother, Mrs Enio, had been lying on the living room couch, eating very little and drinking several beers per day. She was frequently incontinent of both urine and stool. Mrs Enio's husband, aged 70, was finding it increasingly difficult to respond to her many needs. Despite encouragement, Mrs Enio flatly refused to see a doctor.

Earlier that day, Mr Enio had called the ambulance service, hoping the ambulance attendants could convince his wife to go to the hospital. But Mrs Enio had been quite indignant and refused. Both Sophia and her father were exasperated and did not know where to turn. Because her parents did not have a personal physician, Sophia called her own family doctor, Dr Yu, to request his help.

Dr Yu decided to make a house call, recognizing that a personal visit was perhaps the only means to adequately assess the family's dilemma. There he found an elderly couple in a foul-smelling and extremely untidy apartment. Mrs Enio was lying on the couch, partially clothed and unable to get up. There was evidence of dried fecal material on her lower legs and numerous cigarette burns were scattered on the furniture and rug around her. The doctor confirmed Mrs Enio's history of not being able to get up for approximately two weeks, eating very poorly, drinking 6–8 beers per day and smoking heavily.

Note: This case description first appeared in the July 1995 issue of the *Ontario Medical Review* and is reprinted with the permission of the Ontario Medical Association.

It was all Mr Enio could do to keep her reasonably clean and to care for her basic needs. At night she would cry out for a doctor or ambulance, yet she refused to accept any care when these services were offered again during the day. Neither her husband nor her daughter had been successful in convincing her to accept any medical attention.

The doctor talked with Mrs Enio for over an hour. She appeared to be oriented to time, place and person but denied that there was anything wrong with her. She did not acknowledge the severity of her weakness or her inability to care for herself.

Mrs Enio reluctantly consented to a limited physical exam. It revealed that she had normal lung fields but she was tachycardic and had an elevated blood pressure. While her abdominal examination was unremarkable, the examination of the central nervous system revealed decreased muscle power generalized over the lower extremities, particularly with hypoactive reflexes. The left plantar response was equivocal. Despite these findings Mrs Enio adamantly rejected all suggestions of admission to hospital.

The doctor attempted to reach a compromise with Mrs Enio. He explained that admission to hospital would help her regain her strength, reassuring her that she would be able to return home as soon as possible. Her husband and daughter pleaded with her to accept the doctor's suggestions, but Mrs Enio steadfastly refused. She became increasingly agitated, yelling and cursing at the doctor and her family, demanding to be left alone.

Perplexed by this situation but determined to find some solution for this family, the doctor returned to his office. He wanted to commit Mrs Enio to hospital for treatment but was unsure where he stood legally. He conferred with the psychiatrist on call. The psychiatrist recommended Mrs Enio be certified on the basis of danger to her own health and the safety of all others in the apartment building. With reservation, the doctor followed the psychiatrist's suggestion and certified Mrs Enio for admission to the family medicine floor with a consult to psychiatry.

Later that evening at the hospital, Mrs Enio was reasonably calm, yet determined to return home. As the doctor talked to her, valuable information became available. She had a history of alcohol abuse with frequent hospital admissions over the last 10 years. Although she had attended Alcoholics Anonymous in the past, she did not find the meetings helpful. Her most recent admission to hospital had occurred three months earlier, when she was admitted with nausea, vomiting and anorexia of one week's duration. She was discharged after four days but, similar to past admissions, had not kept a follow-up appointment with an internist. Mrs Enio had not established a relationship with a primary care physician since her family doctor retired 15 years earlier. It was evident that previous interventions had been unsuccessful and her care remained sporadic, lacking any continuity.

For the first few days in hospital Mrs Enio complained about everything and told everyone, 'I'll be getting a new doctor as soon as I get out of this wretched place'. However, despite her multiple complaints, she never directly asked to change physicians.

As time went on she began to eat and, with increased strength, was up and walking. The doctor continued to provide regular supportive visits and on each occasion, gently reinforced that Mrs Enio's weakness and difficulty caring for herself stemmed directly from abuse of alcohol.

After four weeks in hospital Mrs Enio's condition was considerably improved and she was ready for discharge. The doctor held a family meeting with Mrs Enio, her husband and her daughter. They discussed at length the importance of reducing alcohol intake in order to maintain Mrs Enio's self-sufficiency. Reluctantly, Mrs Enio acknowledged that her alcohol consumption was a serious problem and agreed to make an appointment with the local addiction treatment center to receive help.

Following discharge from hospital, Mrs Enio did not make an appointment with the treatment center but continued to visit the doctor on a regular basis. At each encounter alcohol intake and lifestyle factors were addressed. Mrs Enio reduced her intake to approximately two beers per day but showed no intention of stopping or attending an alcohol rehabilitation program, including Alcoholics Anonymous.

This case illustrates how, in certain circumstances, there is a need for drastic action, such as committal to hospital against a patient's wishes, to bring about a therapeutic relationship. With patients who are alcoholic, many doctors are reluctant to become involved when relatives request help. This reaction is based on the premise that nothing can be done until the patient chooses to change his or her behavior.

However, as this case demonstrates, the willingness of the family doctor to take action under dire circumstances, coupled with a willingness to persist with treatment and support, can be a turning point (Gupta, 1993). The doctor's actions ultimately lead to the development of a therapeutic relationship. Despite Mrs Enio's initial negative response, the doctor demonstrated his commitment to her and by his persistent actions gradually earned her respect (Gearhart *et al.*, 1991). The patient–doctor relationship gave the patient a foothold by which she could climb out of her despair.

Mrs Enio continues to drink, albeit much less. However, she is now able to manage her self-care, comes for regular doctor's visits and has a much better appreciation of how a frank and open relationship with her family doctor can promote her well-being. Hopefully, over time, this therapeutic relationship will lead to a reduction in her alcohol intake and continue to enhance her health and that of her family.

44

Confidentiality

Sharon Graham and Judith Belle Brown

Although patient confidentiality is a serious responsibility, there are situations in which it may be appropriate to breach it. There are times when the concept of 'family' should be extended from the traditional unit to include a group of close, concerned friends.

Rounds were complete and patients admitted the previous night were improving or at least stable. Dr Chevron decided a walk in the cold air, with a stop for lunch at the local restaurant, would refresh him for the afternoon in the office.

The restaurant was a local gathering spot for the small community. Dr Chevron exchanged hellos with several people and slipped into a booth.

Shortly after his meal arrived, he was joined by Tim, a member of the local police force. The doctor immediately wondered if there was a coroner's case and began mentally reshuffling his afternoon schedule. But Tim had something else on his mind.

'How is old Sam, doc?' he asked anxiously. 'Is he going to pull through?' Dr Chevron sighed to himself and thought, 'How do I answer this?'.

Old Sam was a bachelor who had lived in the town most of his life. He had contributed greatly to the community by leadership in local politics, service clubs, organizations and sports teams. He was best known and loved for the enthusiasm with which he had coached youth baseball and basketball teams. There were few families in the town who had not been touched by Sam's kindness.

The night before, Sam had suffered a CVA while at a basketball game. He was hemiplegic, dysarthric and slightly stuporous.

There had been an attempt to notify Sam's family, but without success. Old charts indicated that he had a sister in a town 300 miles away but the number was no longer in service and no new listing was available. Dr Chevron recalled the comment of the nurse on duty: 'We're all his family'.

Tim asked again, 'Well, how is he? Can I help him?'

'He's holding his own,' said the doctor vaguely. 'Time will tell, we'll just have to see how things go.'

Tim looked as if he was going to speak again.

'Oh look, it's nearly one!' exclaimed Dr Chevron quickly. 'I've got a patient scheduled. Excuse me, Tim.'

As he walked the final block to his office, the doctor thought about what he had said to Tim. He trusted and respected the young man, who was obviously deeply concerned for Sam. If Sam was going to recover, he would need the help and support of friends like Tim. It was the doctor's duty to respect patient confidentiality – but who were Sam's family, anyway?

By chance, Tim was Dr Chevron's last patient of the day and had been booked for a re-check of a previous throat infection. He said he had been to see Sam.

'I could see he was in real bad shape,' he said, visibly shaken. 'What's going to happen to him?'

Sam had helped Tim through some tough times in his younger years and was probably his most important role model. The two men were closer than many family members.

The doctor explored Tim's relationship with Sam, asked him how he had handled sad and difficult events in his life before now and what it would mean to him if something dreadful happened to Sam. It was clear that Sam's death would be a serious blow to Tim.

In the end, the doctor told him Sam was indeed gravely ill. If Sam became able to communicate, the doctor would ask him who he would like to know about his condition. In the meantime, he would need the care and concern of his friends. With this information, Tim was able to prepare himself to help Sam or to deal with his death. He could also communicate with and gather support from the rest of the community.

In this situation, the doctor had three patients with needs: Sam, Tim and the community. As Sam's doctor, he had an obligation to protect him and provide an atmosphere conducive to recovery. Tim was also his patient; he needed to know how his friend was doing and how he could help. The community as a whole was a patient, too, dealing with the grief caused by Sam's illness.

From their first days in medical school, doctors are made aware of the moral and legal responsibility of patient confidentiality. But in small isolated communities, patient confidentiality can be difficult to maintain. In some situations, the strict definition of 'family' is inadequate: there are times when a close group of concerned friends have stronger and more significant bonds than family.

In a case like Sam's, not disclosing information about a patient might be doing the community and the patient a disservice (Needleman, 1985). However, any breach of confidentiality must be based on thorough knowledge of the patients, their circumstances and, if possible, their expressed preferences in similar situations in the past.

In the strictest sense, Dr Chevron breached Sam's patient confidentiality. But he did so in the interests of Sam, Tim and the community – all of whom were his patients.

45

Presuming to know

John Biehn and Judith Belle Brown

As the relationship between the patient and doctor extends over many years it is easy to take the relationship for granted, assuming that it is complementary and mutually agreeable to both patient and doctor. However, what patients experience and what doctors intend may differ. Failure to recognize and resolve this difference in perspective may bring an end to the relationship.

One evening while reviewing his mail, Dr Elliot came upon a request to transfer the medical records of one of his patients to another family physician in the area. As is often the case, the request for record transfer came as a surprise: the patient had not indicated her intent to change doctors, nor had there been any hint of dissatisfaction expressed by Mrs Lewis about her care.

Since there is usually valuable information to be gained from open and frank discussion in these situations, the doctor telephoned the patient. Mrs Lewis was not home, but the doctor spoke briefly with her husband, who was also a patient of the practice. Mr Lewis said he was aware of his wife's decision but offered no explanation. The doctor explained that he would appreciate an opportunity to talk with Mrs Lewis, to better understand her decision to seek her healthcare elsewhere. Mr Lewis agreed to relay the doctor's message to his wife.

Mrs Lewis, aged 48, had been a patient in the practice for over two decades. Dr Elliot had attended at the patient's two deliveries and cared for Mrs Lewis and her family throughout the years. In recent years the patient had become hypertensive with a 'white coat' component. In addition, Mrs Lewis had become significantly overweight, gaining some 35 kilograms in weight.

Throughout the years, Mrs Lewis had often presented with overt stress. The majority of her medical problems required consideration of her life circumstances and physical status. For example, it was difficult to ignore the relationship between her weight and hypertension. Her full-time job as a computer

Note: This case description first appeared in the September 1994 issue of the *Ontario Medical Review* and is reprinted with the permission of the Ontario Medical Association.

analyst in an organization always seeming on the brink of bankruptcy caused Mrs Lewis significant stress. As well, her elderly parents, also long-standing patients of the practice, had significant health problems. The doctor was aware of the excessive demands and expectations they placed on Mrs Lewis and the conflicted feelings she experienced about their care.

In the past, she had frequently presented with a list of written complaints. On one occasion, she had written out a detailed description of her early developmental history which described the difficulties she had experienced with her parents. This shed some light on her current struggles in caring for her parents and her accompanying anger and frustration with their constant demands. The doctor's response had been supportive and empathetic, or so he thought.

As time had gone by, Dr Elliot had become less aggressive in his approach to Mrs Lewis's problems. He had developed a more supportive approach and had learned from experience, or so he thought, that the patient was able to regroup from emotional crises and was less threatened by this type of approach. However, her weight continued to be a problem and her blood pressure remained labile. Her parents' demands on her never ceased, in spite of the involvement of numerous healthcare services arranged by the doctor. Yet, overall Dr Elliot felt positive about his relationship with Mrs Lewis and presumed she felt similarly.

A week after Dr Elliot had telephoned Mrs Lewis to discuss her decision to change physicians, he received a neatly typed letter from her. While he was not surprised by her decision to write rather than call him, he was not prepared for the content of the letter. Mrs Lewis initially apologized for not contacting the doctor in advance of the request for record transfer and for not having the 'intestinal fortitude' to call him. She then proceeded to outline the problems she had been experiencing over time in her relationship with Dr Elliot. She listed her concerns as follows.

- You perceived all my problems as being age or weight related and you were not aggressive in getting to the bottom of things.
- You didn't do any tests to determine a possible physical cause for my difficulties in controlling my blood pressure. I felt like you thought it was all in my head.
- You referred me to the social worker for counseling after I told you about my troubles with my parents years ago. I guess you were not interested in my problems.

The patient's concerns about treatment and doubts about the physician caring for her are topics of enough general interest that they have been addressed by other authors (Loxterkamp, 1991; Sensky and Catalan, 1992).

The doctor wrote back to Mrs Lewis, expressing regret that she had felt uncomfortable with him for such a long time and wished her well in the future. He had no further contact with her.

On reflection, the patient's letter raised several points for Dr Elliot to consider. Chief among them was the tendency to take the patient–doctor relationship for granted, assuming the relationship was complementary and mutually agreeable to both patient and doctor. We often fail to be aware that patients are, from their own perspective, observing and assessing the physician's attitudes and behaviors, reaching conclusions at each visit and, ultimately, over the duration of the relationship.

The doctor had assumed that his non-intrusive, supportive approach with Mrs Lewis had been acceptable and helpful. But he had not asked the patient what she wanted or needed him to do in the context of their relationship. Her expectations and perceptions of the relationship had been different from Dr Elliot's, but it was only upon her departure that she was able to articulate her needs. Mrs Lewis had not felt comfortable in expressing her dissatisfaction with the doctor's approach to her care. She had remained silent and her silence was interpreted as agreement. Dr Elliot had learned how his failure to understand and acknowledge Mrs Lewis's expectations of him had prevented both doctor and patient from developing a more mutually acceptable and helping relationship by finding common ground.

Undoubtedly, Dr Elliot will see Mrs Lewis in the future as the health of her parents deteriorates. Both are at risk of sudden death. As the doctor interacts with her parents, he will be aware of the ambivalent feelings she has for them and the difficulties she experiences in coping with their declining health and ultimate deaths. He will be attentive to Mrs Lewis's perspective and will inquire about her needs and expectations. Although the focus will be on Mrs Lewis's parents it will bring the doctor a step closer to demonstrating that he cares for this former patient.

46

Breaking bad news

Judith Belle Brown, Jo-Anne Hammond and W Wayne Weston

Conveying bad news to a patient is a complex and difficult process. First, it requires that the doctor come to terms with his or her own feelings. Secondly, the news must be presented in a manner that is flexible, attuned to patient cues and ultimately caring.

The report from the breast screening clinic arrived promptly on Dr Oliver's desk. The findings were not encouraging and would require further investigation. She knew that her patient would receive immediate notification from the screening clinic that the results of her mammogram were positive. The doctor thought about her patient's possible responses to the bad news.

In the last four years Dr Oliver had grown to admire and respect her patient's strength and resources in dealing with her personal struggles. Mrs Yuill, aged 57, had been a widow for six years. Her husband's sudden death had required that she return to work to support herself and her three children. Last year her youngest child had left for college, opening up new opportunities for Mrs Yuill to focus on her own life and interests. A healthy woman, she had practiced regular preventive healthcare, except in the area of mammography.

Dr Oliver paused and wondered whether she should have been more insistent that Mrs Yuill go for a mammogram sooner. Mrs Yuill had a positive family history. For this very reason, she had been reluctant to participate in breast cancer screening. Over 30 years ago, her mother had died of breast cancer after undergoing a radical mastectomy. Mrs Yuill remembered only her mother's mutilating surgery and protracted death and refused to subject herself and her family to a similar experience. Consequently she declined to participate in breast cancer screening procedures. Despite the doctor's thorough explanations and ongoing encouragement the patient had been firm in her decision. Only recently, after

Note: This case description first appeared in the September 1993 issue of the *Ontario Medical Review* and is reprinted with the permission of the Ontario Medical Association.

further prodding, did Mrs Yuill reluctantly agree to a mammogram. Now, her greatest fear had become a reality. The doctor wondered how she could soften the blow. What would make this painful news more bearable for Mrs Yuill? She felt badly for her patient and somewhat guilty for not being more adamant about screening.

The case of Mrs Yuill is not unusual. Many women do not participate in breast cancer detection because of a perceived lack of risk and procrastination (Brown, 1989; Kruse and Phillips, 1987). Others deny their risk of breast cancer based on prior family experience, fear of surgery and radiation, fear of pain and loss of femininity (Lantz *et al.*, 1990; Nattinger *et al.*, 1989). But their denial does not protect them from breast cancer and ultimately they may face the diagnosis and subsequent treatment options. Dr Oliver's situation is not unique, either. Physicians can educate, inform, offer and encourage but cannot force patients to participate in screening procedures against their will. Having met their moral, ethical and legal obligations doctors are frequently left with the responsibility of breaking the bad news.

Several publications outline the essential principles of communication in giving bad or sad news (Brewin, 1991; Buckman and Kason, 1992; Fallowfield, 1993). First, physicians need to come to terms with their own feelings including guilt, disappointment, apprehension or a sense of responsibility for 'missing the boat'. Every day they may face a diagnosis that they cannot cure. Over the years, physicians often form close relationships with their patients and grieve with them when they become seriously ill. Consequently, breaking bad news is a painful experience for the messenger as well as the recipient. It is important for doctors to be able to discuss these difficult times with their colleagues.

This leads to the second principle: breaking the bad news in a caring way. Brewin (1991) recommends blending reassurance and encouragement with the bad news. Almost all patients want, and need, to hear the truth but there is a limit to how much patients can bear at each encounter with the doctor. Brewin (1991) stresses that physicians must remain flexible and base all comments and suggestions on their patients' responses to the news. By attending to patients' reactions, doctors can learn about their patients' fears, concerns and hopes, as well as how they cope with the bad news. This will help physicians tailor their support and guidance in a way that is most useful for each patient.

Another important observation made by Brewin (1991, p. 1208) is: 'The first thing that is said is often remembered best; and may be the only thing retained'. Thus physicians must not only choose their words carefully but also be sensitive to the time and place the news is delivered. A quick telephone call or an interview, double booked during a busy office, will not suffice. Patients need time to digest the information, to reflect on it and to ask questions. They may need to return for a second or third visit to clarify their understanding of the significance of the diagnosis and the options available to them. It is also important to offer, with the patient's permission, opportunities for family members to participate in discussions about the illness and their own reactions to the bad news.

Dr Oliver was fortunate in that she knew her patient and was already familiar with her circumstances. On one hand she could anticipate her patient's fears, rational and irrational, and alleviate them. On the other hand she had to be cautious and not make unwarranted assumptions.

Breaking the bad news is a critical step in forming a therapeutic alliance between patient and doctor. It is the foundation for their work together in dealing with the total impact of the illness on the patient.

47

The abusing patient

John Yaphe and Judith Belle Brown

Occasionally a physician may find himself treating a patient whose actions are personally repugnant to the physician. If the physician is self-aware and caring, this need not interfere with the therapeutic relationship.

'Mr Albert is a patient that nobody wants to see after what he has done. Would you be willing to take him on as a patient?'

Dr Orin had always enjoyed the team meeting on Thursdays at noon. This was the one chance in the week for the family practice clinic staff to get together in a relaxed atmosphere, to share not only sandwiches and cakes but also ideas and updates on their ongoing work with patients. But Dr Orin knew that this question, posed by his partner Dr Tarquin, presented a particular challenge.

Dr Tarquin provided more details. A patient of his, Mr Albert, had just written him a letter that had been hand-delivered to the clinic. Mr Albert described in great detail his misfortune on being arrested and detained for assaulting his wife, his humiliation at the police station, his regret over the departure of his wife from their home and his fears for the future. Given the patient's past history of depression, Dr Tarquin suggested that Mr Albert was at increased risk now and asked if Dr Orin would be willing to see him for counseling during this difficult period.

Dr Orin recalled his past experience in treating victims of woman abuse and the memory set up a chain of negative feelings in him. Yet what intrigued him was that this patient was 71 years old. Faced with Dr Tarquin's request and some supportive suggestions from the team, Dr Orin accepted the challenge.

At his first meeting with Mr Albert the doctor was impressed with his stature: at six feet tall and weighing over 220 pounds, he was an imposing figure. His hearing aid, reading glasses and lined face completed the picture of a man in his eighth decade.

Note: This case description first appeared in the July 1992 issue of the *Ontario Medical Review* and is reprinted with the permission of the Ontario Medical Association.

Dr Orin began by expressing his willingness to listen to what had happened. Mr Albert related the events that led to the assault on his wife. He told of a trivial argument over cleanliness in the house (like one of many before), his wife's response, his violent outburst and her attempt to telephone for help from their daughter. He had struck his wife on the head with the telephone receiver, causing a laceration requiring sutures. His wife had filed a police complaint and the arrest and charges led to his present request for help.

He expressed shame over what had happened but felt that he had been provoked. He hoped that some sort of reconciliation with his wife could be reached. 'How much longer do we have together?' he asked.

Listening to Mr Albert, the doctor wondered what effect this violent act might have on his life. Dr Orin thought about the legal implications, the effect on the patient's marriage and his family and the effect on his mental and physical health. He suggested to Mr Albert that they might meet again in a week to see how he was coping. Mr Albert accepted the doctor's offer and thus began a learning process that stretched over the next eight months.

The events of the fall and winter were complex. A legal notice of separation from his wife was served to Mr Albert, followed by a recurrence of his depressive symptoms and suicidal gestures. He was hospitalized briefly and his antidepressant medication was restarted. Further legal and economic twists in the story were met with angry responses from Mr Albert, all of which he recounted to the doctor each week.

His most poignant loss following the separation from his wife was the estrangement from his daughter and grandchildren. Over time Dr Orin learned of his other losses: the death of his only son at age 23 in a car accident, his wife's mastectomy for breast cancer in her 50s, his hospital admissions for depression. It became apparent that the pattern of verbal and physical abuse stretched back over many years, as a response to his multiple losses. Together, they explored his unmet needs from these losses and he slowly began to sense the hurt he had caused others by his violent outbursts. He knew that Dr Orin was not there to condone his aggression or to agree with him that his wife had 'done him wrong' by leaving. He knew that the doctor was there to listen and perhaps work with him on understanding what had happened.

Woman abuse is a prevalent ill in our society. Although studies report its occurrence in 10% of couples, it is frequently missed or poorly treated by physicians (Burge and Espino, 1990). It has been reported that up to 47% of battered women who have visited their family physician while they are in an abusive relationship do not reveal the battering, citing shame, fear or the hurried attitude of the physicians as the reason (Hopayian *et al.*, 1983). Abuse in seniors' relationships may be more frequently missed than in younger couples.

Key principles in treatment of victims of abuse include early recognition of the signs of abuse, support for the victims and removal from the abusing environment. One approach to treatment of men who batter is referral to self-help groups for abusers. These groups help men to identify the origins and antecedents of the abusive behavior and may be potent agents for change.

A difficult issue for practitioners is their attitude toward perpetrators. Physicians need to be aware of negative responses evoked by these patients, including feelings of disapproval and rejection. The physician may also experience countertransference in the form of revulsion based on previous experiences with woman abuse, either personal or professional. These feelings may interfere with the therapeutic process and make it impossible for the doctor to provide care. Support from colleagues or an outside consultation may be helpful in identifying the physician's feelings and exploring how they may be most effectively addressed.

From a patient whom nobody wanted, Mr Albert became a man who had taken responsibility for his actions and was now making choices he could live with. For his physician, it meant taking time to listen to him, to help him make sense of what he had done.

48

Self-awareness

Judith Belle Brown, Moira Stewart and W Wayne Weston

Occasionally physicians are confronted with situations which may challenge their own beliefs and values or raise uncomfortable issues. To help their patients, physicians must be self-aware. When an interaction is troubling, reflection and consultation with colleagues can turn the experience into an opportunity for growth.

Seventeen-year-old Stephane had been instructed by his employer to receive an employment physical. A healthy adolescent, he had not attended his family doctor's office in a couple of years. As the physician began the examination he observed that Stephane was perspiring profusely and looked faint. The physician commented on the symptoms and noted that the patient seemed quite anxious. The adolescent replied quickly that he was uncomfortable about having a physical examination. The doctor, unsure of how to reply, began to ask him if he was dating or if there was a special girl in his life.

'No!' responded Stephane emphatically. The physician resumed the examination, finding him healthy and fit for employment.

Later, reflecting on the interaction, the doctor wondered about the patient's apparent anxiety. What had caused it and why had he, the doctor, so rapidly dismissed it by questioning the teenager's heterosexual activity? The doctor, a young man in his early 30s, had just begun to practice and this patient was new to him. Perhaps the dismissal of the anxiety was based on unfamiliarity, not knowing the patient. More accustomed to the concerns of the chronically ill or the acutely sick, the physician was baffled by the extent of the anxiety presented by this normal, healthy male adolescent (Weston and Lipkin, 1989).

It was not that the doctor's knowledge base was lacking or that his understanding of disease and illness was absent. He had accurately assessed the teenager as fit and healthy and had aptly observed his symptoms of anxiety. What

Note: This case description first appeared in the April 1990 issue of the *Ontario Medical Review* and is reprinted with the permission of the Ontario Medical Association.

he had failed to establish was the source and meaning of the patient's discomfort with the physical exam. Had the physician's own anxiety about what he might uncover led him to dismiss the patient's distress? Did questions of prior sexual abuse or sexual orientation feel intrusive or too far-fetched? Did some of his own personal issues, perhaps his own homophobia, prevent him from exploring the extent of the patient's response to the physical examination?

Frequently, when we are confronted by situations that are unfamiliar to us or which challenge our own value systems, we choose, consciously or unconsciously, to sidestep the issue. We are apt to see the behavior as idiosyncratic or irrelevant to the larger picture. While our knowledge base may be quite extensive regarding uncomfortable issues like sexual abuse or homosexuality, our own attitudes and beliefs may interfere with our skills in understanding such issues from our patient's perspective.

This case illustrates the importance of self-awareness (Longhurst, 1989). When physicians feel troubled by an interaction with a patient, they need to step back and reflect on what happened. By discussing the experience with his colleagues, examining his own behavior and ultimately challenging his own beliefs, this physician gained a better understanding of both the patient's anxiety and his own. In the future, he will have an opportunity to use this insight to alter the influence of his attitudes on patient interactions and thus to enhance his skills.

49

Emergency: 1

June C Carroll and Judith Belle Brown

Family doctors may question their role when faced with an obstetrical emergency in a tertiary care setting. However, as specialists take charge of the patient's medical needs, the family physician can play a critical role in facilitating communication and providing support to the patient and family.

Dr Holmes had practiced obstetrics for many years. It was an aspect of his practice which generated much pleasure and satisfaction. The following experience, however, rocked his confidence and caused him to reflect on his role as a family physician during an obstetrical emergency in a tertiary care facility.

The doctor first met 24-year-old Mrs Rodriguez when she presented for prenatal care at 20 weeks gestation. Mrs Rodriguez and her husband, recent refugees from Central America, were eager to start a family in their new homeland and consequently were very excited about the anticipated arrival of their first child.

Mrs Rodriguez' pregnancy progressed uneventfully until 37 weeks' gestation, when she was found to have an elevated blood pressure, edema and protein in her urine. The diagnosis was mild pregnancy-induced hypertension, treated with bedrest and more frequent follow-up. The mild toxemia continued throughout the rest of her pregnancy and at 40 weeks' gestation, a biophysical profile was obtained. It showed a marked decrease in the amniotic fluid, indicating chronic fetoplacental insufficiency. Induction of labour appeared advisable.

After Mrs Rodriguez was admitted, Dr Holmes requested a consultation with the obstetrician to discuss the method of induction and to inform her of the medical concerns. A decision was made to give Mrs Rodriguez intracervical prostaglandin to induce labor. After receiving three doses of prostaglandin, with only mild cramping and no cervical change, intravenous oxytocin was started.

With this management Mrs Rodriguez progressed to full cervical dilatation. After she had pushed for about 30 minutes with no descent of the head, the fetal heart tracing began to develop late decelerations. Dr Holmes again consulted with the obstetrician.

A forceps delivery of a healthy baby was performed by the obstetrician without any difficulty. Following the delivery there was some uterine atony which initially responded to oxytocin intravenously and ergotrate intramuscularly. However, hemostasis could not be maintained and Mrs Rodriguez went into shock. Resuscitation was begun. Again, uterine atony appeared to be the cause. Massage was begun along with administration of intramyometrial prostaglandin and ergotrate. The uterus did not respond. A D&C was performed with no effect. At this point the bleeding was quite brisk.

Despite all attempts at conservative measures to control the bleeding, it was necessary to carry out a hysterectomy. Mrs Rodriguez had suffered extensive blood loss and transfusion was required. She was transferred to the intensive care unit.

This account reflects the medical summary of the obstetrical emergency. But what was the subjective experience of this medical crisis for the doctor? Dr Holmes had described the progress of labor to both the patient and her family, carefully explaining the need for the forceps delivery and the essential role of the consultant obstetrician. Throughout the initial period of uterine atony and bleeding, the family doctor continued his role of explaining what was occurring. When Mrs Rodriguez went into shock, Dr Holmes quickly discussed the severity of her condition with Mr Rodriguez and promptly returned to the delivery room to participate in his patient's resuscitation.

For those who have worked in a tertiary care hospital, what follows will be very familiar but for those who have not, let us paint the picture. Tertiary care facilities are excellent at responding to emergencies of this kind. The medical team immediately assembled. It included a staff anesthetist and anesthesia resident, two obstetricians, the senior resident and chief resident in obstetrics, countless nurses and the family doctor. The obstetric staff were busily trying to stop the bleeding and eventually performed a hysterectomy. The anesthetist had the situation under control, the obstetrical resident had taken charge of checking the blood products and hanging them. Mrs Rodriguez was intubated and ventilated. She had no need of the family doctor's support at that moment.

Suddenly, Dr Holmes felt useless. It had been many years since he had actively participated in the resuscitation of a patient in shock. Dr Holmes didn't know how he could help. What should he do, what was his role? At the same time he felt extremely concerned about his patient. He was worried that Mrs Rodriguez might die and was horrified by all that had happened to his patient after giving birth to a healthy baby.

Something prompted Dr Holmes into action. Surrounded by the chaos of the emergency setting, he pulled himself together. Realizing he had an important role to play, he went to speak with the family, who by now had grown to include Mr Rodriguez' mother and several other family members. Dr Holmes briefly examined the baby, reassuring the family that the infant was healthy and alert. He continued to keep the family informed of Mrs Rodriguez' condition and supported them, offering them encouragement and hope. The family was very appreciative of the information and the doctor's concern.

This is a particularly dramatic case but it highlights the helplessness you can feel as a family physician when working in a tertiary care environment, if you see your role as only offering medical or technical expertise. At first Dr Holmes was so overwhelmed by the horror and urgency of the medical situation that he only perceived his role as a technician. Once he reconnected with his skills as a family physician and fulfilled the role of supporting and communicating with the family, he was able to help.

During a medical emergency, the patient's family members are often left on the periphery as all the energy and concern are focused on the patient. Feelings of bewilderment and uncertainty can be magnified when something goes wrong unexpectedly during a routine procedure or event such as a delivery. The anxiety and fear experienced by the family are intensified when they are unfamiliar with the healthcare system or face language barriers. As this case illustrates, the family physician's role of advocate and interpreter can help alleviate the family's worry and concern.

We continue this story in the next case.

50

Emergency: 2

June C Carroll and Judith Belle Brown

The trust developed between the patient and doctor enhances communication and support during a medical emergency. Knowledge of the patient's life context also assists the physician in understanding the patient's and the family's response to the emergency.

This case illustrates the importance of the patient–doctor relationship during medical emergencies. Having developed a trusting relationship with his patient during her pregnancy, Dr Holmes used the strength of their relationship to support Mrs Rodriguez and her family during the crisis. The respect and comfort which had grown in the relationship allowed Dr Holmes to ask sensitive and personal questions. He also served as an advocate and 'interpreter' for both patient and family during the chaos and terror of the medical emergency. In the midst of all the technology and ever-changing hospital personnel, the family doctor remained a constant presence. In brief, he offered the patient and the family continuity of care.

The family doctor continued to visit Mrs Rodriguez several times daily in the ICU throughout her hospitalization and reassured her that her baby was growing and thriving. He also told the staff in the ICU that Mrs Rodriguez had been a healthy and vital woman prior to her medical crisis. He went beyond explaining the physical needs of the patient and her family, including their emotional concerns as well. This helped the ICU staff to understand and respond to Mrs Rodriguez as a new mother, separated from her infant and fearful of her future abilities to care for her child, let alone her own chance of survival.

This case also demonstrates the importance of understanding the context of illness. Mr Rodriguez, the patient's husband, had been present in both the labour and delivery room, supporting his wife and interpreting the medical information when necessary. When the doctor had explained that because of fetal distress, the obstetrician was going to help Mrs Rodriguez deliver by using forceps, Mr Rodriguez seemed to understand and translated this for his wife.

Suddenly tears welled up in his eyes and he rushed out of the delivery room. The doctor followed him.

'Mr Rodriguez, you seem upset, can you tell me what's bothering you?' he asked.

'I had a premonition that something absolutely terrible was going to happen,' replied Mr Rodriguez. 'I am very afraid for my wife and baby!'

The doctor tried to reassure him about the obstetrician's excellent skills and expertise. 'Everything should be fine,' he said. 'There is no need to worry.' Little did he know how true Mr Rodriguez' words would turn out to be.

As the medical situation became more complicated, Dr Holmes realized that Mrs Rodriguez seemed to understand the situation less and less. Her comprehension of English had been adequate in the office setting but her verbal and comprehension skills had significantly deteriorated as she became anxious and hypotensive. As a result Mrs Rodriguez' husband became invaluable in translating the doctor's explanations of the procedures being used by the medical team in order to stop the bleeding. As opposed to many situations where family are removed from the room when complications arise, the medical team was relieved to have the patient's husband present in order to keep his wife informed and calm during the crisis. After Mrs Rodriguez went into shock her husband was unable to remain with her. He was left wondering and frightened, his worst fears becoming a reality.

At one point while the doctor was talking to the family, Mr Rodriguez looked at him and asked, 'Is this a normal delivery in your country?'. This question made Dr Holmes realize how different their cultures were. It emphasized for him the importance of clear explanations and taking time to explore the patient's prior healthcare experiences and health beliefs.

Throughout the medical crisis Mr Rodriguez' aunt had maintained a vigil at the baby's layette. In a quiet moment, Dr Holmes approached this sad and despondent-looking woman. Gently, he asked her how she was feeling and if she had any children. She explained to the doctor that she had been a victim of torture in her war-torn homeland; the tragic outcome was a hysterectomy. Her inability to bear children was experienced as a major loss by her family; families of many children were the norm in her country.

Later this information proved to be very valuable in supporting Mr Rodriguez with the difficult news about his wife's hysterectomy and loss of childbearing ability. Dr Holmes was able to understand the family's profound grief and sense of loss.

Sensitivity to the nuances of people's expressions and appropriate responses to key information are essential in the care of individuals and families from other cultures. This case highlights the importance of discovering the context of people's lives – both their family histories and cultural histories. Even in a medical emergency, this information can be of great value to the doctor in helping the family cope with the information given to them.

In summary, this case illustrates how communication in a medical emergency is enhanced by specific qualities of the patient–doctor relationship. Taking time to inquire and understand the patient's cultural context can be invaluable in helping them cope with the emotional sequelae of the trauma.

Component VI: Being Realistic

W Wayne Weston, Judith Belle Brown and Carol L McWilliam

Patient problems are increasingly more complex and multifaceted, time is scarce, resources are at a premium, doctors' physical and emotional energies are constantly taxed and the increasing demands of bureaucracy are often overwhelming. In this component we examine the issue of being realistic in terms of what a practitioner can reasonably expect to achieve in providing patient-centered care, given normal human limitations. We examine issues of time, resources, team building and the importance of wise stewardship.

Time and timing

Patient-centered visits are not necessarily lengthy visits. In studies of communication in primary care, visits in which the patients are active participants in telling about their illness and asking questions are almost identical in length to other visits where this does not happen – 30 minutes in US primary care internal medicine offices (Greenfield *et al.*, 1988) and nine minutes in Canadian family practices (Stewart *et al.*, 1989, 1996).

Furthermore, such visits are likely to be the best use of resources over the long term. Several studies demonstrate that patient-centered interviews result in greater patient satisfaction, better compliance and enhanced physiological recovery (Lipkin *et al.*, 1995; Roter and Hall, 1992). A study of 315 patients of family physicians showed that interviews in which patients perceived that the visit had been patient-centered resulted in only half as many referrals and investigations (Stewart *et al.*, 2000).

We do not suggest that all areas of patient concern be explored in every visit. In fact, one of the advantages of primary care is the opportunity to use several

---

Note: Parts of this chapter were published previously in *Patient-Centered Medicine: transforming the clinical method*, Sage Publications (1995).

visits, over time, to explore complex or deeply personal issues. Often, after a close and trusting relationship has developed, doctor and patient can get to the heart of a matter very quickly. Thus, time and timing are both important.

While it is not realistic to deal with all the problems of every patient in each visit, doctors must be able to recognize when a patient requires more time, even if it means disrupting their office schedules. When a patient presents with a list of symptoms and concerns, the physician must establish which are the most pressing issues at that time. In most cases this can be accomplished by quickly reviewing the list, indicating that time is limited and asking the patient which one or two problems (or more if there is time) are most urgent. Occasionally, patients may not recognize the potential seriousness of one of the problems and may not include it on their urgent list. When the patient's or another's safety may be at risk, the doctor may need to take a more assertive role in this process. For example, child abuse, suicidal ideation, woman abuse or a life-threatening medical situation, such as ketoacidosis or asthma, require immediate attention even if the patient does not recognize the danger.

While patients welcome the opportunity to have their opinions recognized, most do not want their physician to simply provide whatever they ask for – a 'blank check', so to speak. This is a simplistic and mistaken notion of what it means to be patient-centered. In adopting this prioritizing approach, doctors must quickly create an atmosphere in which patients feel heard and understand that the doctor sees their problems as important and worthy of further exploration. If patients leave the office feeling frustrated, they may not pursue their remaining concerns during subsequent visits. Alternatively, patients may feel the need to amplify their symptoms or make several visits to 'prompt' the doctor to hear their worries.

'Doorknob' comments by patients – comments or questions posed just as the patient is about to leave the room – present a particular challenge for the busy clinician. This 'parting shot' may be the patient's last attempt to raise an issue and it often reflects the physician's failure to establish the patient's priorities earlier in the interview. It is important for the doctor to at least acknowledge the patient's concern. If there is time, the problem may be addressed at that moment or arrangements should be made to deal with it later. This problem might have been prevented if the physician had elicited a full list of patient concerns at the outset and then reached common ground about which ones would be dealt with today and which ones later. Often, when physicians are rushed, they seize the first problem the patient mentions and, hoping this is all there is, make a diagnosis, prescribe a treatment and head for the door. It is important to remember that the average patient seeing a primary care physician has 2.5 problems and the first one they offer may not be the most important. Sometimes they 'test' physicians with a simple problem before mentioning a more difficult or embarrassing predicament.

Timing also speaks to the issue of the patient's readiness to share certain concerns or experiences with the doctor. Reluctance to present concerns may arise for many reasons. Here the doctor's knowledge of the whole person can be of vital importance in understanding patients. For example, patients may be reluctant to disclose family problems because it runs counter to family norms and values: 'These problems are our business and no one else needs to know about them!'. Patients may be reticent to share their concerns or problems for fear of reprisal or abandonment by their doctor. They may experience their inability to independently resolve their problems as a failure or a loss of face. As a result, patients often feel shame, embarrassment or anxiety when seeking help. Especially in the primary care setting, it may take them several visits to the doctor, frequently for undifferentiated or vague complaints, before they can reveal the actual source of their concern.

When they finally do share their understanding of the problem with their doctor, it may be when the doctor is pressed for time or emotionally worn by the demands of the practice. Again, it is important for the doctor to acknowledge the patient's concerns and to provide an environment that lends itself to further exploration of the problem. It may not be realistic, or even wise, to delve into the problem at that time. When doctors are exhausted from sleepless nights on call, it is wise to acknowledge their fatigue, both to themselves and to their patients, and ask if the patient would be willing to return when the doctor is rested and better able to help. But it is essential that patients feel understood and know the doctor is prepared to work with them on their problem during future visits. This will be supported and enhanced by the strength of the patient–doctor relationship.

Accessing resources and team building

Expecting doctors to be knowledgeable about every available resource in their community for each specific group that they serve is unrealistic. Nevertheless, they must be prepared to learn about the context in which their patients live and how to access the appropriate resources – for example, who can advocate for their patient about housing; who can recommend an appropriate support group; who can facilitate a referral for rehabilitation.

A collaborative approach to team care is flexible and crosses disciplinary boundaries; it capitalizes on the talents and expertise of all professionals involved. It means that all professionals concerned with the patient's care assume an equal degree of responsibility and accountability for the services being provided. Professional activities may cross traditional roles and functions to provide comprehensive patient care (Schlesinger, 1985). The collaborative approach entails greater blurring of team member roles with involvement premised on who can best meet the patient's needs at that moment. This may be determined by specific knowledge or skills needed by the patient or influenced by the quality of the relationship between the patient and a particular member of the team. Critical to the collaborative approach is the active involvement of patients in all phases of their care – they are viewed as equal participants on the healthcare team.

All team members must be aware of their strengths and weaknesses so that they seek help and support with problems that are baffling or difficult. Requesting assistance or consultation with other professionals should not be viewed as a weakness, but as an opportunity for further learning and growth. This approach may also provide team members with new information and offer a different perspective on the problem. While the team approach is initially time consuming and not particularly cost effective, in the long run it reduces the frustration, confusion and emotional depletion of all team members. Newer methods of payment for physicians, other than fee for service, will make teamwork more attractive.

Wise stewardship

Doctors are challenged, more than ever, by issues of cost containment and increasing bureaucratic demands, all of which infringe on patient-centered practice (Miller, 1993). The doctor is now increasingly pulled by the system to consider the needs of hospitals and other healthcare agencies and of society in general, along with considering the patient's needs. Coping with the growing demands of bureaucracy and its threat to patient-centered care requires constant conscious attention to the realities of the evolving healthcare system. Doctors must ensure that patient-centeredness and the patient–physician relationship do not suffer in the process of making trade-offs.

Physicians are being asked to be gatekeepers for the system (Capen, 1997). This role is consistent with patient-centered care when it means opening the gates to all the healthcare resources needed by the patient. But the 'negative' gatekeeper role is more problematic if it means closing access to expensive modalities of care for one patient to make them more available to others or to save money for the 'system'. This trend is even more troubling if the physician receives financial benefit from reducing patient utilization of expensive forms of care. Managed care is appropriate when it provides incentives for reducing or eliminating unnecessary investigations or treatments. In this situation there is no conflict of interest – all parties benefit from the cost-cutting measures. But managed care is not appropriate when it means withholding potentially beneficial treatments to cut costs without involving the patient in the decision-making process.

Physicians have obligations to each of their patients and to society as a whole; because of the possibility of a conflict of interest, it is wise to keep these obligations separate whenever possible. In their day-to-day work with patients, physicians must 'give primacy to a patient's need, not to the needs of the healthcare system as a whole' (Hebert, 1996). But, at the same time, physicians must not squander resources by 'doing everything humanly possible' for each patient when the chances of benefit are negligible. Where to draw the line cannot be precisely stated; that is the essence of the physician's ethical dilemma. Physicians can fulfill their societal obligations by assisting in the development of care guidelines, by engaging in research for more effective and economical care and by speaking out publicly about the issues.

Conclusion

Being realistic about patient-centered care invokes several elements of the art of medical practice. Selecting the best timing and time allotment for problems is essential. Accessing resources and effective teambuilding also contribute to practicing realistically. Awareness of one's own abilities and priorities both as a practitioner and as a person is critical to orchestrating a team approach. Currently, issues of cost containment and increasing demands of bureaucracy create the need for wise stewardship of the healthcare system's resources.

We do not pretend to have all the answers. This would be impossible given the rapid and radical changes continuously occurring in the healthcare system. The ideas we present are relevant for today but will need to adapt to the changing environment and all the societal, economic, cultural and health issues that confront us in the future.

Preview of the cases

The first case illustrates the complexity of the nurse–physician relationship. Examples of poor collaboration are presented along with an outline of strategies for collaborating more effectively.

The next three cases focus on various aspects of referral and teamwork. The first case demonstrates the importance of clear communication about the purpose of the referral. The second case addresses the need for co-ordinated care when several hospital teams are involved in management. The third case discusses the value of a 'rich' description of the patient, not just a brief summary of their biomedical problems, in communication with specialists at the time of referral.

Two cases illustrate the importance of planning for hospital discharge from the day of admission. The first case teaches us how important it is to prepare patients for possible complications and to educate them about what to do if complications develop. The importance of involving the patient and family physician in the discharge process is highlighted in both cases.

The next two cases discuss the importance of respecting personal and professional boundaries. The importance of looking after oneself and the pitfalls of caring for a friend are illustrated.

The last case in this book, also presented in two parts, is a complex story illustrating all six components of the patient-centered clinical method. The case addresses all four aspects of understanding the whole person – the disease, the illness, the person and the context. Specifically, the story demonstrates the importance of understanding the patient's cultural context as we strive to find common ground. This case also raises issues about prevention and health promotion. The challenges in maintaining a therapeutic patient–doctor relationship are central to the story. Finally, issues of collaboration between hospital and community-based care and engaging alternative healers in the healthcare team emphasize the importance of patient-centered medicine.

Cases Illustrating Component VI: Being Realistic

51

Physician and nurse teams

Toula M Gerace, Judith Belle Brown and W Wayne Weston

Patients are confused when they receive conflicting advice from healthcare professionals providing their care. Doctors and nurses need to work together in a complementary, collaborative way, respecting each other's expertise and communicating effectively to avoid giving conflicting advice.

Mrs Barker was perplexed. Recently, the 40-year-old mother of three asked her doctor about using nutritional supplements, such as vitamins C and D. The doctor said there was no harm in low-dose vitamins and possibly some benefit. With her busy lifestyle, it was possible that she sometimes didn't get all the nutrients she required for good health. Later, she asked the clinic's nurse what type of vitamins she would recommend. The nurse immediately said she didn't believe supplements were necessary and added that the danger of excessive doses of some vitamins outweighed any potential good they might do.

Another time Mrs Barker asked about a weight loss program she was considering enrolling in. The doctor felt that support and encouragement from the program would help her achieve her modest weight loss goal. The nurse, however, advised against commercial programs. In her opinion, a sensible diet and increased exercise was the only route to sustained weight loss.

In the past Mrs Barker had appreciated and respected the assistance of both of these healthcare professionals but now she felt confused. Why didn't they agree? And whose advice should she take?

No matter what the health concerns of the patient, there is the same potential for confusion and conflict of loyalties in a variety of healthcare settings, such as a family practice, specialty care or on the hospital ward. Doctors and nurses should function in a complementary fashion. As co-providers of care they offer a comprehensive package which incorporates expertise from both nursing and

Note: This case description first appeared in the August 1990 issue of the *Ontario Medical Review* and is reprinted with the permission of the Ontario Medical Association.

medicine. Patients should never be caught in the crossfire of discipline disputes or hierarchical battles.

The collaborative model suggested by Alt-White *et al.* (1983) emphasizes nurses and physicians working together in the delivery of care, jointly contributing in a balanced relationship which is characterized by mutual trust. Essential to this model is a non-hierarchical system of communication and responsibility. Physicians and nurses have independent as well as overlapping functions. This results in a mutual commitment to a specific shared practice population.

Devereux (1981) cites three essential components for collaborative practice: communication, competence and accountability. Open and honest communication between professionals is imperative to promote a dialogue that maximizes patient care. Doctors and nurses must be able to rely on and have confidence in each other's clinical knowledge and skills. Accountability entails responsibility for actions regarding patient care decisions. In addition, physicians and nurses are accountable on a personal level, as well as to each other, for patient care decisions made independently or collectively. Other important aspects of collaboration include assertiveness, respect for the other professional's contributions and the ability to negotiate.

For patients, collaborative practice provides more comprehensive care. They benefit from the combined expertise of both the nurse and the physician, in an atmosphere that is supportive and consistent.

As patients interact with the nurse–physician team they may have an opportunity to observe and learn the concepts of good communication, respect, shared responsibility and accountability.

Several strategies can be used to enhance collaboration among team members.

- Establish guidelines for the management of common problems. Regular review and discussion of published guidelines is invaluable. Each discipline brings a unique perspective to patient care; discussing these distinctive points of view enhances the abilities of all team members.
- Regular meetings to discuss individual patients is important to apply the principles to practice. Often, guidelines only become clear when they are applied to individual patients. Knowing when to 'bend the rules' may be as important as understanding the guidelines.
- Explore any cues that suggest that patients have heard mixed messages from the team. Patients tend to be reticent about expressing this directly, consequently all team members must be alert to intercept comments that imply that the team has been inconsistent. Before providing advice to a patient it is wise to ask them what they have already heard or read.
- Don't try to cover up differences of opinion by backtracking or obfuscation. Acknowledge that there is room for honest differences of opinion about many

issues in healthcare. It may help to go back to basic principles and outline the pros and cons of each recommendation and help the patient to make the final decision.

- Good teamwork is not easy; it takes time and effort to develop an effective and efficient team. But in the long run, patients benefit from the comprehensive team approach and team members benefit from the intellectual stimulation and the opportunity to share the work.

52

Communication between physicians

Moira Stewart, Judith Belle Brown and W Wayne Weston

The family physician–consultant relationship is central to exemplary medical practice. The key to a good relationship is good communication and mutual respect between the two physicians.

Nadia, a 25-year-old woman, had presented to her family doctor reporting one incident of bright red rectal bleeding. When the doctor questioned her, she admitted that the incident had occurred after a brief episode of constipation. She had no other symptoms but seemed excessively worried about the bleeding. 'I just know there's something terribly wrong,' she said. Although her doctor reassured her, she insisted on a second opinion.

Her doctor referred her to a gastroenterologist for assessment of rectal bleeding. She arrived with a note from the doctor saying, 'Please see and advise'.

Although the gastroenterologist thought that a serious cause was unlikely, he felt obliged to pursue a full investigation because the patient's family doctor had referred her. Nadia underwent a series of tests, which only made her worry more. Eventually, she received the news that everything was okay.

Failure to clarify the reason for the consultation led to inappropriate investigation which neither physician felt was warranted. It caused increased anxiety and discomfort for the patient as well as increased cost for the system. This issue is an example of 'collusion of anonymity', a situation where decisions are made about patient care with no one taking responsibility for these decisions (Balint, 1964).

A study by Langley and Till (1989) found that family physicians and consultants both cited the family physician–consultant relationship as central to

---

Note: This case description first appeared in the May 1991 issue of the *Ontario Medical Review* and is reprinted with the permission of the Ontario Medical Association.

exemplary medical practice. Important contributions to the relationship by the family physician were:

- communicates well
- follows up
- respects the role of the consultant
- tries to match the consultant to the patient.

Exemplary consultants, according to the study:

- provide prompt, lucid, concise and complete reports
- are approachable for the family physician
- respect the referring physician's role
- do not retain referred patients
- do not re-refer.

In studies by Marshall (1988) and Cybulska and Rucinski (1989), family physicians have been criticized for failing to give the precise reason for referral, for providing notes that are illegible and for failing to mention in the note the patient's current treatment.

The most common criticism of consultants was their failure to provide any follow-up report. Cybulska and Rucinski (1989) found that lack of detail or delay in sending the report affected management in 24% of cases.

Many physicians use pre-printed form letters to facilitate rapid recording of key information by hand. This eliminates the cost and delay of having a secretary prepare a typed letter. The computerized medical record will make this even easier and sending reports by fax or email will reduce delays. But the technology will not help if we are not clear about the reason for referral or do not understand or respect one another's roles (Epstein, 1995; Mold, 1997; Wood and McWilliam, 1996).

53

Communication and co-ordinated care

W Wayne Weston, Judith Belle Brown and Moira Stewart

When a patient is being treated by more than one specialty team, it is essential that one physician or team be responsible for the co-ordination of care. This way, the patient is treated in the context of his or her personal circumstances and needs and any conflicts are resolved in the patient's best interest.

Misha, a 14-year-old boy, was in hospital with multiple injuries after being struck by a truck while riding his bicycle.

Most of his care was being provided by an orthopedic surgeon for a huge hematoma in his buttock and a knee injury. An ophthalmologist was consulted regarding diplopia and a general surgeon was consulted to deal with a small pneumothorax. After several days in hospital, the orthopedic surgeon wanted to get the patient up and walking but the general surgeon suggested inserting a chest tube for the pneumothorax. When the father (himself a physician) questioned the need for a chest tube, the procedure was postponed. Each day, however, the general surgery team recommended inserting the tube. The father asked the orthopedic surgeon for his opinion about the effects of inserting a chest tube on the patient's overall well-being.

'I'm worried,' the father said, 'that a tube is going to cause him more pain. God knows, he's been through enough. And won't it slow down the plans to get him moving again?'

'I'm sorry,' said the orthopedic surgeon, shaking his head. 'The chest problem has been turned over to general surgery. I can't interfere with the surgeon's decision   you know, for political reasons.'

Note: This case description first appeared in the January 1992 issue of the *Ontario Medical Review* and is reprinted with the permission of the Ontario Medical Association.

The father was aghast. These were specialists managing the care of each of his son's injured body parts but no one seemed to be co-ordinating the care. When treatment by one team might interfere with treatment by another, nothing was said because of professional etiquette.

This case illustrates a problem in the overall system of medical care. As medical science has advanced, healthcare has become more complex and physicians have tended to specialize. This may work well for patients with disease in one organ system. But for patients with multiple problems, the lack of co-ordinated leadership and good communication often leads to serious difficulties. Balint (1964) referred to the problem of 'collusion of anonymity'. By this, he meant that decisions were made about patient care but no one took responsibility for these decisions.

Referral to a general surgeon did not absolve the orthopedic surgery team of their responsibility for his overall management. If they had doubts or concerns about the wisdom of inserting a chest tube, it was their responsibility to address these concerns directly with the general surgeon.

The argument might be made that referral was arranged because management of pneumothorax was outside the area of expertise of the orthopedic team; therefore they should not interfere with this aspect of the treatment. But this ignores the importance of context. Treatment that is beneficial for one patient in a particular situation may not be good for another patient with a different set of circumstances. Someone must take responsibility for understanding each patient's unique situation and for tailoring treatments, from all those involved, to suit his or her special needs.

Several approaches can be used to provide more co-ordinated care to patients. Often the family doctor, having known the patient and family for years, is in an ideal situation to provide an understanding of the context. He or she needs to be involved in a meaningful way in the deliberations of the treatment team. One physician (or one team) should take primary responsibility for the patient's care and write all the orders for treatment on the chart. If other physicians are involved, they should record their suggestions on the chart, rather than writing orders. Even better, they should discuss their suggestions with the primary treatment physician or team.

54

Consultation

John Yaphe, Judith Belle Brown and Carol L McWilliam

A family physician is often in a good position to understand not only the disease process but the meaning of an illness to the patient. Sharing both kinds of information with the consultant may lead to more satisfactory and meaningful consultations.

'I'm sorry I couldn't return your call earlier, Dr Sullivan, but I was busy with another angio,' said the cardiologist. 'I noticed that you left two messages with my receptionist. Are you a family member or a friend of the patient?'

Dr Sullivan was somewhat surprised by the cardiologist's question. He explained that he had joined the group practice six months previously and was caring for 70-year-old Mrs Pritchard while her family physician was away on vacation. He had developed a close therapeutic relationship with Mrs Pritchard during several episodes of angina.

'I see,' said the cardiologist. 'Well, I can appreciate how difficult it has been for you to manage her angina. Her cardiac catheterization shows that the three vessels of her bypass graft from eight years ago are blocked. She has good left ventricular function and is a good candidate for repeat bypass. I have called the surgeon who treated her previously and he has agreed to see her again. If he does not feel that surgery is indicated we may try angioplasty.'

Dr Sullivan thanked the cardiologist for his reply and hung up thinking about the consultation. The requested diagnostic procedure, which Dr Sullivan was unable to do, had been performed quickly and skillfully. Both doctor and patient now had a clear explanation for her worsening chest pain. The referring doctor had been given a clear recommendation regarding treatment and follow-up had been arranged. An alternative treatment had also been suggested. Yet, Dr Sullivan felt that something was missing from the consultation, a feeling that was

Note: This case description first appeared in the August 1992 issue of the *Ontario Medical Review* and is reprinted with the permission of the Ontario Medical Association.

triggered perhaps by the cardiologist's question regarding his relationship to the patient. What was missing was a sense of the meaning of the illness and its proposed treatment to Mrs Pritchard.

During previous office visits in the last few months, Mrs Pritchard had described to Dr Sullivan how she had struggled with the death of her husband from cancer five years before. She spoke of the strength of their bond, how they had walked as one person through the years of their marriage. After his death she felt as though she had lost a leg and could not stand straight or move forward. Gradually, after a period of mourning, she had recovered her 'balance'. She discovered a great freedom in being on her own, freedom to do things she had never conceived of doing during her marriage. She enjoyed travelling by car to visit her children and friends out of town. She enjoyed painting and writing. She said she had discovered how to be whole again after his death.

But the recurrence of her angina meant that she was losing her ability to stand alone. Car trips had become very tiring and eventually trips down the hall in her apartment were accompanied by an annoying ache in her jaw and arm. The angina was awful, she said, not because of the pain, which she could bear, but because of the fear that she was losing her independence.

Dr Sullivan had understood and appreciated Mrs Pritchard's concerns, yet he had included nothing of his personal knowledge of the patient in the referral letter. The letter had included accurate descriptions of her pain, a list of her medications, a description of physical findings and the last cardiogram done in the office during a bout of chest pain. The reason for referral had been a clearly posed question regarding angiography and surgery. Why had issues of meaning been excluded from the referral information?

Many factors may impinge upon the quality of referral information. Studies of referral letters from general practitioners to specialists have focused on the lack of information in the letters (Thurston *et al.*, 1982). This phenomenon has been found across specialties (Walsh, 1985) and around the world (Tse, 1987). Hansen and his colleagues (1982) found that increased content of information in the referral letter was correlated with increased information in the consultant's reply.

In an unpublished study of family physician–specialist communication by Bass and Yaphe (1991), both family physicians and specialists agree on the importance of:

- developing a rapport with the referred patient, and
- making the consultation psychologically therapeutic for the patient.

In fact, more specialists rated the psychological value of the consultation as important than family physicians. In the same study physicians were also asked to rate items to be included in a standardized referral letter. The patient's personal and social history was suggested for inclusion by 42% of family physicians and 35% of the specialists. There is an apparent discrepancy between the expectations of family physicians and specialists about the exchange of information on the personal dimension of patients' lives. This suggests that family physicians and specialists need to share ideas and viewpoints on what is valuable in the patient–doctor encounter.

Dr Sullivan felt that it had been a good referral and consultation in terms of meeting the patient's medical needs. But it could have been a better consultation if more attention had been paid to the whole person. Dr Sullivan needed to share with the consultant some of his personal knowledge of the meaning of the illness for this patient. He had taken time to listen to his patient. Now it was time to talk to the consultant.

55

Informing patients

W Wayne Weston, Judith Belle Brown and Moira Stewart

Informing patients about their health problems is much more than simple transmission of information. Physicians need to prepare their patients for possible complications and tell them how to get help if they need it. Doctors and their staff should also remember that sickness often makes people dependent and less able to cope.

Mr Parkinson, a 65-year-old retired male teacher, was having a routine physical examination when his doctor found a firm nodule on his prostate. Following consultation with a surgeon, he was admitted to hospital for a biopsy, which established the diagnosis of carcinoma of the prostate. He unquestioningly submitted himself to the various examinations and procedures required to establish the diagnosis. After a three-day admission and biopsy, he was discharged to await the diagnosis. He was told that the blood in his urine would soon subside and that no complications were anticipated.

Following discharge Mr Parkinson felt well and was not unduly anxious about the possible diagnosis, confident in his surgeon's assessment and the treatment alternatives available. However, within 24 hours he began to experience difficulty voiding. It became more and more difficult to urinate, his sleep was disturbed and his anxiety mounted.

Mr Parkinson had not yet come to grips with the potential seriousness of his problem and his doctor's well-intentioned reassurance increased his denial. He continued to expect his condition to improve. Finally, after 48 hours he contacted the surgeon's office, only to be informed that the doctor was not available and that the next appointment was in two days. This usually articulate man, stunned by the situation and muted by his pain, did not argue. After another 24 hours, he was completely unable to void and was experiencing considerable pain and anxiety. Desperate, he went to the emergency department where a catheter was inserted and pain medication administered.

Note: This case description first appeared in the January 1990 issue of the *Ontario Medical Review* and is reprinted with the permission of the Ontario Medical Association.

Informing patients about their health problems is much more than simple transmission of information. This case illustrates two central issues. First, his physician failed Mr Parkinson by not informing him of possible complications. Physicians need to prepare their patients for what might happen and how they can appropriately obtain the help they need. While we need to be careful in organizing and protecting our time, we must also remain available for the needs of our patients. This highlights the crucial role played by the individuals, such as receptionists or nursing personnel, who answer our phones. There should be a mechanism to differentiate between patients who make demands which are primarily for their own convenience and others who present serious needs or concerns.

Second, it is important for physicians and their staff to be aware that sickness often makes people dependent, even people who, in health, shoulder major responsibilities. Cassell (1976) notes that even patients who are normally bright and articulate regress in their cognitive abilities during a serious illness and may have trouble making sensible decisions. Perhaps in this case, this man's pain and the repercussions of his illness rendered him silent and unable to clearly express his needs.

In conclusion, one of the important duties of physicians is to attend to their patients' sense of vulnerability, to lend them the strength to cope when they are feeling dependent and fearful. We must make sure that the systems that physicians institute to guard their time do not present obstacles for patients who need help.

56

The impact of the health reform

Judith Belle Brown, W Wayne Weston and Moira Stewart

Feelings of uncertainty and apprehension emanating from changes to the healthcare system can often result in a decline in the care provided to patients. Hospital staff must guard against their own emotions, such as frustration, anxiety or fear, being translated into poor patient care.

Eighty-three year old Mrs Gadzig sat stoically in her hospital room awaiting discharge. She had survived the aortic repair, a procedure which she had anticipated with great fear and apprehension. Mrs Gadzig had expected to die on the operating table and was now exuberant with the prospect of living.

Neatly attired, she and her sister waited and waited throughout the morning for the 'official go ahead'. Near noon, two surgical residents suddenly appeared.

'Any questions?' grunted Dr Zwick.

'Well . . . I was wondering about my medication,' began Mrs Gadzig. 'Should I . . . ?' 'You'll be on Lasix,' said Dr Zwick in an abrupt tone of voice. 'Contact your family doctor about continuing them.'

Mrs Gadzig persisted, 'But what about my . . . ?'

Dr Karls interrupted: 'Water pills . . . they're water pills.'

'I'll write out a prescription,' said Dr Zwick.

They turned on their heels and abruptly departed from the patient's room.

Mrs Gadzig felt hurt and confused. She had many more questions to ask. Should she continue with the medications she was taking prior to surgery? Were there any restrictions on her activities? What were the plans for follow-up? Should she see the surgeon again or return to her family physician? While Mrs Gadzig understood the doctors were very busy and had many sick patients to care for, she felt disappointed by their apparent lack of interest and concern.

Note: This case description first appeared in the October 1995 issue of the *Ontario Medical Review* and is reprinted with the permission of the Ontario Medical Association.

Mrs Gadzig considered requesting to speak with the attending surgeon but, anxious not to jeopardize her future care, she dismissed this idea. 'I don't want to cause any trouble for me or anyone else,' she thought. Mrs Gadzig hid her concern from her sister and they silently waited for someone to give her permission to leave the hospital.

Thirty minutes later a nurse appeared. 'So, you are going home,' the nurse stated.

'Well, actually dear, I'm going to the rest home,' responded Mrs Gadzig.

'Who made those arrangements?' the nurse wanted to know. 'We certainly didn't. What a mess, no one told me!'

'I did, I made the plans,' Mrs Gadzig answered meekly. Prior to surgery, she had independently arranged to move to a rest home during her recovery period, recognizing her limitations for self-care. In time she would return to her own home when she had regained her strength.

The nurse stared at Mrs Gadzig. 'How are you getting there?'

With growing agitation Mrs Gadzig responded, 'My sister has kindly offered to drive me to the rest home. They were expecting me this morning. Oh dear, I imagine I have missed lunch by now!'

'Oh,' said the nurse.

'May I go now?' asked Mrs Gadzig.

'Oh, sure, I guess so,' said the nurse. 'I'll see if the discharge papers are ready.' And she turned and left the room.

Now Mrs Gadzig was getting angry.

'This is no way to treat an old lady!' she said to her sister in an exasperated tone. 'Now, I know you're frustrated but we'll be out of here soon,' said her sister reassuringly. 'At the rest home you'll get the care you need.'

A few moments later the nurse returned and officially discharged Mrs Gadzig.

Apparent lack of interest, disrespect and inattention to our patients can cause harm. Patients often feel they are responsible. They question their own actions, wondering what they have done to be the recipients of such behavior. Many patients are reluctant to express their dissatisfaction for fear of reprisal in the form of even less attention. They are also reticent to challenge their caregivers because historically they have not confronted those in authority. This leaves patients in a no-win situation. They are not receiving the care they need and desire but often they do not have a strong enough 'voice' to request better care (McWilliam *et al.*, 1994).

Why would such unsatisfactory interactions occur? The patient was not 'difficult' or 'demanding'; on the contrary, she was most co-operative and had even taken the initiative to make all her own arrangements for discharge. Were the doctors and nurse too busy? It would not have taken any longer for the nurse to talk with the patient in a pleasant tone of voice. The two surgical residents could have split up rounds if they were too rushed to adequately address the patient's questions about discharge. Several possible explanations come to mind.

- The healthcare providers may have been unaware of the importance, for the patient, of thorough discharge planning. Attention to detail is crucial; there are so many things that can go wrong in the transition from hospital to home. Patients need to know what restrictions are being placed on their activities, what diet is appropriate, what medications to take (and when to take each pill), what side effects to watch for and when to follow up with their family doctor and specialist. Some patients will need special arrangements to go to a rest home or for home care support. In this case, discharge planning had been inadequate. Planning for a patient's discharge should involve the whole team and should begin as soon as the patient is admitted. Leaving it all to whoever is on duty when the patient is leaving is unfair to the patient as well as to the healthcare providers left 'holding the bag'. Some of their unhelpful behavior may have reflected this.
- The healthcare providers may have lacked basic communication skills. Simple things make a big difference to patients. A cardinal principle is that the professionals should sit down near the patient for any discussions. This conveys interest and respect and patients are more likely to feel heard and to be satisfied with their care, even if no more time was spent than standing and talking to them. Before ending, ask, 'Is there anything else?'. Busy professionals are reluctant to open the door to more issues but rushing off from a patient who is left with several unanswered questions is not good care. If there is no time to address all the patient's concerns at that time, arrangements need to be made to deal with them later.
- The healthcare providers were 'burned out'. Even though they may not have been rushed off their feet at the time this incident occurred, they may be suffering from extreme fatigue from working for months or years in a situation of chronic overload and lack of sleep. While downsizing our hospitals, we have often added to the workload of people who were already strained close to the limit. Unless we find different ways to organize the work, this situation will become intolerable as our population ages and the demands on the system accelerate. We must attend to the basic human needs of our healthcare professionals for rest and recreation. Also, it is helpful to have opportunities for professionals to share their feelings of frustration, sadness or anger that are common in such high-stress occupations. 'Burnout' is often a euphemism for depression, which can have devastating consequences for healthcare professionals, as well as their patients and families. We owe it to our colleagues and our patients to do what we can to prevent it.

While the above observations are specific to this case presentation they are also transferable to many interactions between patients and healthcare professionals. First, attention and care need to be given to the patient's discharge, involving both the patient and the healthcare team. Second, good communication between the patient and his or her providers is essential to quality care. Finally, we can only care for our patients if we care for ourselves.

57

Personal and professional boundaries

Leslie Rourke, Sharon Graham and Judith Belle Brown

Medicine can be all-consuming, especially in small, closely knit communities where physicians meet their patients in different roles outside the office. It is a challenge to set appropriate professional and personal boundaries.

'Hi Doc, am I ever glad you came into our store! Would you mind taking a quick look at young Trevor? He has had a fever and trouble breathing since last night.'

Dr Gulka groaned inside. It was a beautiful Saturday morning in the heart of summer and he and his family had booked a weekend at a cottage two hours away. They were on their way and had stopped at the corner grocery store in their small town to buy some snacks for the trip. His children, very excited about this special weekend, had already asked, 'How long till we get there, Daddy?'.

Dr Gulka was also looking forward to this weekend. Time with his family had been limited by the demands of work. Since setting up practice four years ago in this small town of 3000, medicine had been all-consuming. Not only was he very busy in his family practice office, but he also had many unpredictable hospital commitments. Between emergency department shifts, assisting at surgery, attending urgent problems with patients in hospital, delivering babies and consulting on some of his colleagues' patients, Dr Gulka's family life was often disrupted. His wife was becoming increasingly angry and his children were starting to ask when Daddy was going to be home. He had promised them this trip for several weeks and it was a commitment he was reluctant to break.

Note: This case description first appeared in the May 1996 issue of the *Ontario Medical Review* and is reprinted with the permission of the Ontario Medical Association.

However, his patient's request raised an ongoing conflict for Dr Gulka. He found practicing medicine in this town stimulating and rewarding and felt quite indispensable. He valued the sense of belonging and involvement in the community and felt he had a deeper understanding of his patients as people through his knowledge of them outside the office.

Dr Gulka found it hard to establish limits. Yet there were times like this that he needed a break. Dr Gulka felt torn. John and Betty, the owners of the store, had been patients since he had started his practice and Dr Gulka had delivered their youngest child. He liked this couple and considered them friends. Their children went to nursery school together, they curled in the same recreational league and volunteered together on several community projects. Dr Gulka knew that John and Betty were under considerable stress, keeping their small business financially viable with the arrival of large grocery chains in the area and caring for Trevor, their eight year old who had cystic fibrosis. He had had many admissions to hospital with pneumonia, including some close brushes with death.

Dr Gulka saw the concern on the parents' faces. It would be easy to go next door and examine Trevor – in fact, he felt obliged. If indeed Trevor required urgent care, Dr Gulka's family would still have their weekend at the cottage; he'd join them later.

Returning to his car, Dr Gulka leaned through the window to his wife. 'Young Trevor is ill, and I need to take a look at him.' He didn't wait to see the reactions on his wife's or children's faces.

Dr Gulka went with Betty through the inner door from the store to the home. It didn't take more than a few minutes to confirm that Trevor was indeed quite ill. He certainly required aggressive treatment in hospital and perhaps transfer to the tertiary care hospital two hours away if he didn't improve. Once again, Dr Gulka experienced conflicting emotions about how to handle this situation. He felt obliged to be with his patient through this illness. He felt it was expected of him. But he also thought of his own family waiting in the car.

Dr Gulka talked with John and Betty about Trevor's condition and the need for hospitalization and told them another doctor would be looking after Trevor this weekend. Dr Gulka made the necessary arrangements by telephone to ensure that the child was well cared for. John and Betty thanked Dr Gulka as he returned to his car. Dr Gulka continued to have mixed feelings, including guilt, but also now some relief at his decision.

'Is Trevor very sick?' his wife asked. Dr Gulka nodded. He saw the disappointment on her face. 'But I've arranged for him to be seen at the hospital. They will look after him there. We're all going to the cottage.'

Over the course of the weekend Dr Gulka and his wife had the opportunity to talk about many issues: their own relationship, their present life and the difficulties of finding the right balance of work and leisure. Dr Gulka realized that this was the first occasion in a long time that he had consciously made a decision to limit his medical involvement for the good of himself and his family. He began to understand the importance of placing limits on the demands of his medical practice. He realized that he could deputize his trusted colleagues to cover his practice at times like these and provide the same service for their patients.

Doctors need to develop self-awareness regarding the pull of their professional responsibilities as well as their personal needs (Linklater and MacDougall, 1993). Establishing professional and personal boundaries can be more difficult in a rural setting, partly because doctors encounter patients frequently outside the office in other day-to-day activities where a chance meeting, as this case illustrates, can occur (Rourke *et al.*, 1993). As well, doctors' relationships with many of their patients are more complex than a purely conventional patient–doctor relationship. Patients include neighbors, colleagues, hospital staff, children's teachers and personal friends, all with access to the physician outside the office. It is often impossible to separate the patient population from personal friends. In small towns the doctor would either have very few patients or very few friends!

In a rural setting, it is crucial to establish personal and professional boundaries. Clear professional boundaries create safety for both patients and physicians by eliminating the opportunity for abuse. It is important to educate patients about the appropriate time and place to discuss their medical problems. A call group of trusted colleagues is invaluable in this regard. It becomes difficult if there are few colleagues or if those available are not like-minded or compatible. Doctors in small communities cannot be all things to all people. If physicians do not set boundaries, they run the risk of 'burnout' or marital and family breakdown, while others move to larger centers where limits are more easily set.

Although some patients are unrealistic in their expectations of the doctor's availability, most readily accept the doctor's limits. Physicians need to ask how they in fact might be giving patients the message that they are available as a doctor to them at all times. For example, a friendly out-of-office greeting of 'Hi, how are you?' can be met with a litany of health problems or requests for results of recent treatments if patients interpret this statement literally. 'Hi, it's nice to see you' is less likely to blur the personal and professional boundaries. Firmly refusing to discuss medical matters at social functions also helps to establish clear limits. Furthermore, it places the medical encounter in the appropriate context where the doctor can give the patient his or her undivided attention.

As this case illustrates, establishing appropriate personal and professional boundaries can be difficult. The challenge is to set boundaries that are both firm yet flexible and to establish limits before the physician's personal and family well-being is compromised.

58

Balancing relationships

Lynne Hughes Marsh, Judith Belle Brown and W Wayne Weston

Fear of illness can result in denial of a medical problem. This denial can be further complicated when the problem is urgent and the person in denial is not your patient, but your friend. The challenge becomes one of facilitating appropriate treatment, while respecting the boundaries between one's professional and personal life.

When Dr Cantor arrived at her friend Barbara's house on Saturday morning, she was looking forward to their exercise class. It had been a hectic week, both at the office and at home. Thankfully she wasn't on call this weekend. It would be wonderful to go for a workout followed by a relaxing chat in the hot tub. She and Barbara had been friends since grade school, both returning to their hometown, Barbara to teach physical education at the district high school and Dr Cantor to practice family medicine.

As they were leaving for the gym, Barbara mentioned that she had been up most of the night with her six-year-old son, Mathieu. Dr Cantor casually inquired about the problem. Barbara went on to elaborate that Mathieu's asthma was 'acting up a little' but he was better this morning after 'using the machine'. Barbara seemed annoyed that she had been up through the night and complained that Mathieu always seemed to be sick. In fact, it was only three days ago that she had taken him to the after-hours clinic with an ear infection. However, Barbara was determined not to miss exercise class. Her husband was away on business and Mathieu would be cared for by their teenage babysitter.

When Mathieu came to say goodbye to his mother, Dr Cantor noticed that he looked pale and short of breath. He had difficulty speaking in full sentences and was coughing frequently. 'Mathieu certainly doesn't look like a child who should be left in the care of a teenager,' thought Dr Cantor. Surprisingly, his mother, Barbara, seemed unconcerned about his condition.

Note: This case description first appeared in the June 1996 issue of the *Ontario Medical Review* and is reprinted with the permission of the Ontario Medical Association.

Dr Cantor felt uncomfortable not attending to this sick child, yet she was not Mathieu's physician. Furthermore, Barbara had not asked for her professional opinion. Dr Cantor was at an impasse. If she hadn't come by this morning, she would have been totally unaware of this situation. Should she refrain from offering her professional advice and hope that Mathieu would be assessed by his own physician once his mother realized that he wasn't getting better? Should she force the issue and tell her friend that her son was seriously ill and needed to be seen? Recognizing that today she was not the doctor but instead the friend, she decided that friends can also express concern.

Cautiously, Dr Cantor inquired when Mathieu had last received an inhalation treatment. Although it had only been an hour ago, the child was clearly in distress. Dr Cantor struggled inwardly with what to do next. She hesitated to question her friend's judgment but Mathieu's condition was not improving. Dr Cantor decided to suggest to her friend that they forego their exercise class, and that together they take Mathieu to be assessed by his physician.

Barbara seemed surprised by her friend's concern and remained insistent that her son would be fine in a few hours. Barbara saw no need to take him to the emergency department to be assessed and suggested that Dr Cantor, her friend, could listen to his chest instead. With her doctor's bag still in the car, Dr Cantor concluded, that, under the circumstances, this was perhaps the best option available.

Listening to Mathieu's chest confirmed Dr Cantor's worst fears: the child was in acute respiratory distress and needed prompt treatment. Dr Cantor again reinforced with Barbara that Mathieu needed to be seen in the emergency department yet Barbara continued to minimize the seriousness of her son's situation, insisting that he would be better soon. Dr Cantor was puzzled by her friend's apparent denial of this precarious situation. Somehow she had to help Barbara understand.

Dr Cantor realized that one way to help Barbara acknowledge the severity of the situation was for her to understand what Barbara was experiencing – what she was thinking and what she was feeling. Dr Cantor reflected to Barbara that although she seemed concerned about Mathieu, she also appeared unwilling to seek further help for her son. Suddenly Barbara burst into tears. Sobbing, she told her friend that she was hoping that when Dr Cantor listened to Mathieu's chest everything would be clear and he would be okay. Barbara, choking back tears, described how the last time she took Mathieu to the emergency department for his asthma, he had been admitted for three days. She had been terrified to learn how seriously ill her only son had become, feeling both responsible and guilty. Once again, Barbara felt responsible that she had 'left it too long' and Mathieu's failing condition was a reflection of her inadequacy as a parent. To admit to herself that he was sick meant facing the possibility that she could lose him. Barbara knew deep in her heart that Mathieu was in need of further treatment and asked her friend to drive them to the emergency department.

On the drive to the hospital, Dr Cantor reflected upon her interaction with her friend and pondered the dilemma that she had faced today and would face again in the future – how to respect the boundary between one's personal and professional life. Clearly, as Barbara's friend, Dr Cantor had been unable to convince her to seek treatment for her son. However, as a physician, Dr Cantor knew it was her responsibility to ensure that medical treatment be obtained. The dilemma was resolved when Dr Cantor achieved a clearer understanding of her friend's denial. By gaining an understanding of Barbara's feelings and fears about her son's illness, it became possible for treatment to be obtained promptly for Mathieu without compromising the integrity of their relationship.

Physicians sometimes find themselves in the difficult position of being asked to provide care for a friend who is not their patient. The dilemma in these instances is one of dealing appropriately with the request without jeopardizing the friendship. With non-urgent requests for the provision of care, the doctor is able to direct the friend to consult her personal physician. In an emergency, the physician's responsibility is clear – to quickly and instinctively maintain the integrity of the individual. Less clear, however, are those times when the request and need are urgent. It is essential to be mindful of the subjective nature of personal relationships. This lack of objectivity, usually found within the professional relationship, may cloud judgment. The key question is 'How can we best help our friend receive the appropriate medical care?'. Whenever possible, the emphasis should be on facilitating the provision of care, rather than providing the care.

It is natural to expect that the physician may experience internal conflict, as she struggles to fulfill her obligations as a friend while recognizing the limitations of becoming the personal physician for that friend. This conflict can be lessened or avoided by open and honest communication between the friends where the issue of personal and professional boundaries is addressed and the parameters established.

In this case, Dr Cantor's responsibility to Mathieu was clear – he was in need of urgent medical attention and the doctor's obligation to this child coincided with her obligation as his mother's friend. Dr Cantor's discomfort was not about what she needed to do but about how to do it without jeopardizing her friendship with his mother. But there are features of this seemingly straightforward case that are potentially more problematic. Why is Barbara so unwilling to recognize the seriousness of Mathieu's illness? What is the father's role in the family and what does he think about the illness? Are there problems in the parents' relationship that make it more difficult for Barbara to come to terms with the problems with her son? Is she depressed and having trouble thinking clearly because of that?

Exploring these areas is usually outside the bounds of ordinary friendship; certainly it is extraordinarily difficult to engage in a therapeutic discussion of such personal problems within a non-professional relationship. Friends may share their personal feelings and a sense of desperation with each other and may provide mutual support and engage in a consideration of what to do about it but this is not psychotherapy. A professional therapist must be able to confront issues that are kept secret from even the closest friends and which may even be unconscious to the patient. Additionally, an effective therapist will share the patient's pain in an empathic relationship but will not become paralyzed by the overidentification that is common among close friends.

The best thing a good friend can do is to be a good friend, not a therapist. At one level it seems easy to be both but, as this case illustrates, medical care is often not as straightforward as it looks; physicians need to be aware of the potential pitfalls of combining the roles of friend and physician.

But there are exceptions to this recommendation. Michael Klein (Klein, 1997a) and his wife Bonnie (Klein, 1997b) describe their remarkable story of coping with a brainstem hemorrhage. Without the many interventions of her physician husband, Bonnie would surely have died. They both present a strong case for involving physicians in the care of their family members. As Michael Klein (Klein, 1997a, p. 55) argues, 'Why should medical professionals check their training and experience at the door when a close family member gets sick?'

59

Integrating Western and traditional medicine: 1

W E Osmun, Judith Belle Brown and Christine Millman

Integrating Western medicine with traditional medicine is a complex and often daunting task. This case illustrates how the two very distinct and separate worlds clashed in one patient's care, resulting in his behavior being misinterpreted and misunderstood.

Mr Walter, a 50-year-old native man, was brought by his family to the emergency department complaining of dizziness, syncope and weakness. In the emergency room he suffered a cardiac arrest, was resuscitated and transferred to the intensive care unit. He was found to have a hemoglobin of 43 g/l and a potassium of 6.2 mmol/l. Mr Walter was known to have type II diabetes mellitus complicated with neuropathy, chronic renal failure, partial blindness secondary to retinopathy and hypertension.

Following his arrest Mr Walter suffered from intermittent confusion, a mild dysarthria and memory loss. His conversation was vague and circumferential. A soft-spoken man, he constantly asked to go home. Becoming more insistent as his confusion diminished, he finally told everyone point-blank, 'I want to go home. I am lonely. I have nobody to talk to.' However, Mr Walter needed a high level of care and required further investigations before he could be safely discharged home.

In desperation, Mr Walter, clad only in pyjamas, 'escaped' into the parking lot during a thunderstorm. Frustrated by his behavior and concerned for his safety, the nurses put up a strap across the doorway to keep him on the ward. Still, Mr Walter wandered outside again. On this occasion the nursing staff found

Note: This case description first appeared in the May 1995 issue of the *Ontario Medical Review* and is reprinted with the permission of the Ontario Medical Association.

him with his arms outstretched against the door frame, while his family tried to get him back into the hospital. Security was eventually called to help return him to his room. The patient was defeated and despondent, again trapped in a foreign environment.

Dr Ornstein, the family doctor, was uncertain of the degree of brain damage suffered by Mr Walter as a result of his arrest. Many of the nurses thought he was demented. Mr Walter would seemingly ignore questions put to him by the doctor, answering with rambling descriptions of his medicine man: 'There is this man . . . who lives on the reserve . . . a ways from here . . . he is a farmer . . . he is a busy man . . . he talks to me, kind of the way you do, asking me how I am doing, what I am eating, that kind of thing, everything about my life.'

Unfortunately, investigations of Mr Walter's anemia discovered a suspicious colon lesion. Before colonoscopy was planned, the physicians involved debated whether he was a surgical candidate. Eventually it was decided that surgical intervention was warranted. Dr Ornstein met with Mr Walter and his family, explaining in detail the probable diagnosis, the need for colonoscopy, the risks of surgery and the necessity for transfer to a tertiary care hospital. The family was worried and uncertain, on one hand realizing that surgery offered the only hope for cure, yet on the other hand fearful of the outcome. Dr Ornstein felt under pressure to make the decision for Mr Walter and his family. Repeated attempts were made to elicit a decision from Mr Walter but he only asked to go home and to see the medicine man.

During one discussion, Mr Walter quietly commented, 'Doctors can make a mistake, maybe the diagnosis is wrong. Perhaps this thing that is growing inside of me will stop growing and go away on its own.' He paused, then continued, 'The medicine man takes care of the whole of me. He can tell what is wrong with the organs inside the body. He has given me a herbal drink that I take three times a day. If the medicine man finds out about this illness and listens to my pouch, he could give me another drink that might cure me.' Mr Walter brought out a small purse to show the doctor. He put the pouch to his ear and gently rocked back and forth as though listening.

Mr Walter's inability to make a decision, coupled with his adamant requests to return home despite concerns for his safety, raised questions about his competency once again. Dr Ornstein arranged to meet with Mr Walter and his family. After a lengthy discussion there was mutual agreement that Mr Walter was competent, understood his situation and could make his own decisions.

Still something about the entire situation did not make sense to Dr Ornstein. Eventually the doctor realized that she was not the patient's primary caregiver: the medicine man was. The medicine man was invested with the trust and respect necessary to help Mr Walter with the decision regarding his treatment.

Mr Walter was discharged with a wheelchair and home care assistance. The family was reassured that Dr Ornstein would be available for Mr Walter at home. They agreed to take him to see the medicine man to explore the idea of surgical treatment. Mr Walter was relieved to be home and to be exercising some control. The medical team awaited his decision.

Throughout Mr Walter's hospitalization the two worlds of medicine, Western and traditional, had severely clashed. No amount of scientific explanation could convince the patient of the need for surgical intervention. His trust and belief rested with the medicine man (Gagnon, 1989). It was not until the family doctor acknowledged the significant role the medicine man played in the patient's healthcare and respected his need to consult the medicine man that common ground could be established. The patient's behavior, frequently interpreted as dementia or obstinacy, was a reflection of his cultural context. For Mr Walter, the medicine man was responsible for his well-being. He had little faith in Western medicine unless it was sanctioned by the medicine man. To ignore the guidance of the medicine man was contrary to the patient's belief system.

To care for people is to hope for the best possible outcome. It is difficult for the patient and the physician when they cannot reach common ground regarding treatment. It was not until the medical team understood and accepted Mr Walter's strongly held beliefs that they were more effective in communicating and caring for their patient and could reach common ground. Mr Walters' story concludes in the next case vignette.

60

Integrating Western and traditional medicine: 2

W E Osmun, Judith Belle Brown and Christine Millman

Through the combination of flexibility, communication and patience a successful resolution was achieved.

After returning home with the provision of home care and mobility aids, Mr Walter's family took him to meet with the medicine man. The medicine man told Mr Walter, 'The surgery will go very well for you.' With the medicine man's support and reassurance, Mr Walter agreed to the colonoscopy and possible surgery.

Concerns remained regarding Mr Walter's medical status: while his diabetes was under control, his cardiac and renal status remained problematic. He continued to have anemia and a high potassium count. There were concerns about Mr Walter's ability to cope with a potential ostomy and his family's comfort in providing care. Most importantly, Dr Ornstein sensed Mr Walter's continuing mistrust of Western medicine. The patient still appeared more comfortable with the medicine man's methods of treating him. Consequently, the doctor was not surprised when Mr Walter did not show up for his surgical admission. The surgical staff, however, were exasperated and confused with the patient's non-compliance and the surgery was cancelled.

Dr Ornstein met with the patient and his family to discuss whether Mr Walter really wanted surgery. She stressed with the family that Mr Walter must assume responsibility for the decision. Characteristically, Mr Walter provided another vaguely affirmative answer and requested to speak to his medicine man again.

Having recognized the significant role the medicine man played in the patient's healthcare, the doctor strongly encouraged Mr Walter to consult the

Note: This case description first appeared in the June 1995 issue of the *Ontario Medical Review* and is reprinted with the permission of the Ontario Medical Association.

medicine man. Dr Ornstein was concerned about Mr Walter's potassium levels, wondering if the herbal teas could be high in potassium. The doctor offered to speak to the medicine man but Mr Walter declined, preferring to communicate personally with the medicine man. Although Mr Walter willingly agreed to return to Dr Ornstein after his visit with the medicine man, 10 days later he did not show for his scheduled appointment.

Dr Ornstein felt frustrated and disappointed, both with herself and her patient. What more could she do? She clearly understood the importance of the medicine man's opinion to Mr Walter and had supported his involvement in her patient's care. She had attempted to find common ground where the needs of Western medicine and traditional medicine could intersect but she had not been successful. Two options seemed apparent: concede to failure or patiently wait for Mr Walter's decision on a course of action. After some internal debate, the doctor decided to remain involved. To abandon Mr Walter now would only reinforce his mistrust of Western medicine.

A few days later Mr Walter called Dr Ornstein to relay the medicine man's reassurance that the teas he was administering were not high in potassium. At this time Mr Walter requested that Dr Ornstein proceed with the arrangements for the surgery and agreed to come to the doctor's office to have his potassium levels and hemoglobin monitored.

After considerable negotiation, the surgery was re-booked. Mr Walter was firmly requested to notify Dr Ornstein if he should alter his decision, stressing the shortage of operating room time and the possibility of another patient filling his spot.

Mr Walter was booked to have an appointment a week prior to surgery. He missed the appointment. Two days before the patient's scheduled surgery Dr Ornstein phoned Mr Walter requesting that he come to the office to have his potassium and hemoglobin checked. The patient's potassium was 6.1 mmol/l. Concerned that Mr Walter required admission to stabilize him prior to surgery, Dr Ornstein called the surgeon who agreed to see the patient in the emergency room. Mr Walter went directly to the hospital and was subsequently admitted.

During the following days, as Mr Walter was prepared and eventually underwent surgery, Dr Ornstein continued to visit and maintain contact. The surgery was successful with complete tumor resection and negative nodes. Mr Walter recovered quickly and was discharged in eight days with home care support. Following surgery his attendance at Dr Ornstein's office remained sporadic.

Working in a crosscultural setting creates new challenges to the practice of medicine, especially when the patient's health beliefs differ from the physician's. The family doctor might have interpreted Mr Walter's choices as a rejection of her care and a judgment of her abilities. In response, she may have removed herself from the care of the patient.

In this case, the doctor remained with the patient, acting as liaison between the patient and hospital. She insured that Mr Walter was aware of his options, keeping them open while he resolved his concerns with the medicine man, his primary caregiver. With openness, flexibility and patience, a balance was achieved between Mr Walter's traditional beliefs and the doctor's Western, scientific system (Gregory, 1989). Communication between the three key players – the family doctor, the patient and the medicine man – was essential in achieving a positive outcome for the patient (Paulette, 1993).

References

Alt-White A, Charno M and Strayer R (1983) Personal, organizational, and managerial factors related to nurse-physician collaboration. *Nurs Admin Quart.* **8**: 8–18.

Anstett R (1981) Teaching negotiating skills in the family medicine centre. *J Family Pract.* **12**: 503–6.

Arborelious E, Bremberg S and Timpka T (1991) What is going on when the general practitioner doesn't grasp the situation? *Family Pract.* **8**(1): 3–9.

Audunsson G (1986) *Preventive Infrastructure in Family Practice.* Iceland Ministry of Health, Reykjavik, Iceland.

Baird M and Grant W (1994) Families and health. In: R Taylor (ed) *Family Medicine – principles and practice* (4e). Springer-Verlag, New York.

Balint M (1964) *The Doctor, His Patient, and the Illness* (2e). International Universities Press, New York.

Bandura A (1986) *Social Foundations of Thought and Action: a social cognitive theory.* Prentice-Hall, Englewood Cliffs, NJ.

Barnes H, Aronson M and Delbanco T (1987) *Alcoholism – a guide for the primary-care physician.* Springer-Verlag, New York.

Barnes P (1990) A new approach to the treatment of asthma. *NEJM.* **321**: 1517–27.

Bass E and Davis L (1988) *The Courage to Heal.* Harper and Row, New York.

Bass M and Yaphe J (1991) Family physician – specialist communication problems: identifying the issues. North American Primary Care Research Group, 19th Annual Meeting, May, Quebec City, Canada.

Bass M, Buck C, Turner L, Dickie G, Pratt G and Robinson H (1986) The physician's actions and the outcome of illness in family practice. *J Family Pract.* **23**(1): 43–7.

Battista R and Lawrence R (eds) (1988) Implementing preventive services. *Am J Prevent Med.* **4** (suppl. 8).

Becker M and Janz N (1990) Practising health promotion: the doctor's dilemma. *Ann Intern Med.* **113**(6): 419–22.

Belenky M, Clinchy B, Goldberger N and Tarule J (1986) *Women's Ways of Knowing: the development of self, voice and mind.* Basic Books, New York.

Berger J and Mohr J (1967) *A Fortunate Man – the story of a country doctor.* Pantheon Books, New York.

Brewin T (1991) Three ways of giving bad news. *Lancet.* **337**: 1207–9.

Britt H, Harris M, Driver B, Bridges-Webb C, O'Toole B and Neary S (1992) Reasons for encounter and diagnosed health problems: convergence between doctors and patients. *Family Pract.* **9**(2): 191–4.

Brod M and Hall S (1984) Joiners and nonjoiners in smoking treatment: a comparison of psychosocial variables. *Addict Behav.* **9**: 217–21.

Brody H (1987) *Stories of Sickness.* Yale University Press, New Haven, CT.

Brody H (1992) *The Healer's Power.* Yale University Press, Hartford, CT.

Brown H (1989) Motivating women to participate in breast cancer detection. *Cancer.* **64**: 2690–3.

Brown J, Lent B, Brett P, Sas G and Pederson L (1996) Development of the woman abuse screening tool (WAST) for use in family practice. *Family Med.* **28**: 350–6.

Brown J, Weston W and Stewart M (1995) The first component: exploring both the disease and the illness experience. In: M Stewart, J Brown, W Weston *et al.* (eds) *Patient-Centered Medicine: transforming the clinical method.* Sage Publications, Thousand Oaks, CA.

Bruce N and Burnett S (1991) Prevention of lifestyle-related disease: general practitioners' views about their role, effectiveness and resources. *Family Pract.* **8**(4): 373–7.

Buckman R (1988) *I Don't Know What to Say: how to help and support someone who is dying.* Key Porter Books, Toronto, ON.

Buckman R and Kason Y (1992) *How to Break Bad News: a practical protocol for health care professionals.* University of Toronto Press, Toronto, ON.

Burge S and Espino D (1990) Spouse and elder abuse. In: R Rakel (ed) *Textbook of Family Practice* (4e). WB Saunders, Philadelphia, PA.

Calhoun K and Atkeson B (1991) *The Treatment of Rape Victims: facilitating psychosocial adjustment.* Pergamon Press, Toronto, ON.

Calnan M (1988) Examining the general practitioner's role in health education: a critical review. *Family Pract.* **5**(3): 217–23.

Canadian Task Force on the Periodic Health Examination (1994) *The Canadian Guide to Clinical Preventive Health Care.* Minister of Supply and Services, Ottawa, ON.

Candib L (1987) What doctors tell about themselves to patients: implications for intimacy and reciprocity in the relationship. *Family Med.* **19**(1): 23–30.

Candib L (1988) Ways of knowing in family medicine: contributions from a feminist perspective. *Family Med.* **20**(2): 133–6.

Capen K (1997) Resource allocation and physician liability. *Canad Med Assoc J.* **156**(3): 393–5.

Carkhuff R (1987) *The Art of Helping VI.* Human Resource Development, Amherst, MA.

Carlsen M (1991) *Creative Aging – a meaning-making perspective.* W W Norton, New York.

Carroll J, Reid A, Woodward C *et al.* (1997) Ontario maternal serum screening program: practices, knowledge and opinions of health care providers. *Canad Med Assoc J.* **156**(6): 775–84.

Carter W, Belcher C and Inui T (1981) Implementing preventive care in clinical practice. II. Problems for managers, clinicians, and patients. *Med Care Rev*. **Winter**: 195–216.

Cassell E (1976) *The Healer's Art*. MIT Press, Cambridge, MA.

Cassell E (1985) *Talking with Patients. II. Clinical technique*. MIT Press, Cambridge, MA.

Cassell E (1991) *The Nature of Suffering and the Goals of Medicine*. Oxford University Press, New York.

Charlton R and Dolman E (1995) Bereavement: a protocol for primary care. *Br J Gen Pract*. **45**: 427–30.

Cohen L and Roth S (1987) The psychological aftermath of rape: longterm effects and individual differences in recovery. *J Social Clin Psychol*. **5**: 525–34.

Connidis I (1989) The subjective experience of aging: correlates of divergent views. *Canad J Aging*. **8**(1): 7–18.

Consumer Reports (1995) How is your doctor treating you? *Consumer Reports*. **60**(2): 81–8.

Cournoyer B (1991) *The Social Work Skills Workbook*. Wadsworth, Belmont, CA.

Courtois C (1988) *Healing the Incest Wound*. W W Norton, New York.

Cybulska E and Rucinski J (1989) Communication between doctors. *Br J Hosp Med*. **41**(3): 266–8.

Cyr M and Wartman S (1988) The effectiveness of routine screening questions in the detection of alcoholism. *JAMA*. **259**(1): 51–4.

Davies B, Reimer J and Martens N (1994) Family functioning and its implications for palliative care. *J Palliative Care*. **10**(1): 29–36.

de Leeuw E (1989) Concepts in health promotion: the notion of relativism. *Social Sci Med*. **29**(11): 1281–8.

Devereux P (1981) Does joint practice work? *J Nursing*. **June**: 39–43.

Doherty W and Baird M (1986) Developmental levels in family centered medical care. *Family Med*. **18**: 153–6.

Donovan J (1951) The menopausal syndrome: a study of case histories. *Am J Obstet Gynecol*. **62**: 1281–91.

Doxiadis S (ed) (1987) *Ethical Dilemmas in Health Promotion*. John Wiley, Toronto, ON.

Dubovsky S (1981) *Psychotherapeutics in Primary Care*. Grune and Stratton, New York.

Dunst C, Trivette C and Deal A (1988) *Enabling and Empowering Families: principles and guidelines for practice*. Brookline Brooks, Cambridge, MA.

Eagle M (1984) *Recent Developments in Psychoanalysis: a critical evaluation*. McGraw-Hill, New York.

Ende J, Kazis L, Ash A and Moskowitz M (1989) Measuring patients' desire for autonomy: decision-making and information-seeking preferences among medical patients. *J Gen Intern Med*. **4**(1): 23–8.

Ende J, Kazis L and Moskowitz, M (1990) Preferences for autonomy when patients are physicians. *J Gen Intern Med.* **5**: 506–9.

Epp J (1986) *Achieving Health for All: a framework for health promotion.* Health and Welfare Canada, Ottawa, ON.

Epstein R (1995) Communication between primary care physicians and consultants. *Arch Family Med.* **4**: 403–9.

Epstein R, Campbell T, Cohen-Cole S, McWhinney I and Smilkstein G (1993) Perspectives on patient–doctor communication. *J Family Pract.* **37**(4): 377–88.

Erikson E (1950) *Childhood and Society.* W W Norton, New York.

Erikson E (1982) *The Life Cycle Completed: a review.* W W Norton, New York.

Evans B, Kiellerup F, Stanley R, Burrows G and Sweet B (1987) A communication skills programme for increasing patients' satisfaction with general practice consultations. *Br J Med Psychol.* **60**: 373–8.

Evans J (1997) Screening for fetal anomalies: old habits, new challenges. *Canad Med Assoc J.* **156**(6): 805–6.

Ewart C, Taylor C, Reese L and DeBusk R (1983) Effects of early postmyocardial infarction exercise testing on self-perception and subsequent physical activity. *Am J Cardiol.* **51**(7): 1076–80.

Ewing J and Mayfield D (1974) CAGE. *Am J Psychiat.* **131**: 1121–3.

Fallowfield L (1993) Giving sad and bad news. *Lancet.* **341**: 476–8.

Farrow J, Deisher R, Brown R, Kulig J and Kipke M (1992) Health and health needs of homeless and runaway youth: a position paper of the society for adolescent medicine. *J Adolescent Health.* **13**: 717–26.

Feldman W, Hodgson C, Corber S and Quinn A (1986) Health concerns and health-related behaviours of adolescents. *Canad Med Assoc J.* **134**(5): 489–93.

Frank A (1991b) *At the Will of the Body: reflections on illness.* Houghton Mifflin, Boston, MA.

Frank S (1991a) Two green tomatoes: a case report regarding religion and health. *Family Systems Med.* **9**(1): 69–75.

Gabel L, Lucas J and Westbury R (1993) Why do patients continue to see the same physician? *Family Pract Res J.* **13**(2): 133–47.

Gagnon Y (1989) Physicians' attitudes toward collaboration with traditional healers. *Native Studies Rev.* **5**(1): 175–86.

Galazka S and Eckert J (1986) Clinically applied anthropology: concepts for the family physician. *J Family Pract.* **22**: 159–65.

Gearhart J, Beebe D, Milhorn H and Meeks G (1991) Alcoholism in women. *Am Family Physician.* **44**(3): 907–13.

Germain C (1984) *Social Work Practice in Health Care: an ecological perspective.* Free Press, New York.

Giefer M and Nelson C (1981) A method to help new fathers develop parenting skills. *J Obstet Gynecol Neonatal Nurs.* **10**: 455–7.

Gillis A (1993) Determinants of a health-promoting lifestyle: an integrative review. *J Adv Nurs.* **18**: 345–53.

Godkin M and Catlin R (1984) Office design. In: R Rakel and H Conn (eds) *Textbook of Family Practice* (3e). W B Saunders, Philadelphia, PA.

Goldbloom R and Lawrence R (eds) (1990) *Preventing Disease – beyond the rhetoric.* Springer-Verlag, New York.

Good B and Good M (1981) Meaning of symptoms: a cultural-hermeneutic model for clinical practice. In: L Eisenberg and A Kleinman (eds) *Relevance of Social Science for Medicine.* Reidel, Boston, MA.

Green S, Goldberg R, Goldstein D and Liehenluft E (1988) *Limit Setting in Clinical Practice.* American Psychiatric Press, Washington, DC.

Greenfield S, Kaplan S and Ware J (1985) Expanding patient involvement in care – effects on patient outcomes. *Ann Intern Med.* **102**: 520–8.

Greenfield S, Kaplan S and Ware J (1988) Patients' participation in medical care – effects on blood sugar control and quality of life in diabetes. *J Gen Intern Med.* **3**: 448–57.

Gregory D (1989) Traditional Indian healers in Northern Manitoba: an emerging relationship with the health care system. *Native Studies Rev.* **5**(1): 163–74.

Gupta K (1993) Alcoholism in the elderly. Uncovering a hidden problem. *Postgrad Med.* **93**(2): 203–6.

Haezen-Klemens I and Lapinska E (1984) Doctor–patient interaction, patients' health behaviour and effects of treatment. *Social Sci Med.* **19**: 9–18.

Hall E (1986) The art of cross-cultural care. *Canad Family Physician.* **32**: 1317.

Hansen J, Brown S, Sullivan R and Muhlbaier L (1982) Factors related to an effective referral and consultation process. *J Family Pract.* **15**: 651–6.

Haug M and Lavin B (1983) *Consumerism in Medicine: challenging physician authority.* Sage Publications, Beverly Hills, CA.

Heaton P (1981) Negotiation as an integral part of the physician's clinical reasoning. *J Family Pract.* **6**: 845–8.

Hebert P (1996) *Doing Right – a practical guide to ethics for medical trainees and physicians.* Oxford University Press, Toronto, ON.

Hepworth D and Larsen J (1990) *Direct Social Work Practice: theory and skills* (3e). Wadsworth, Belmont, CA.

Herbert C (1991) Family violence and family physicians. *Canad Family Physician.* **37**: 385–90.

Herth K (1993) Hope in the family care giver of terminally ill people. *J Adv Nurs.* **18**(4): 538–48.

Hoffmaster B (1992) Values: the hidden agenda in preventive medicine. *Canad Family Physician.* **38**: 321–7.

Holt S, Skinner H and Israel Y (1981) Early identification of alcohol abuse: clinical and laboratory indicators. *Canad Med Assoc J.* **124**: 1279–99.

Hopayian K, Horrocks G, Garner P and Levitt A (1983) Battered women presenting in general practice. *J Roy Coll Gen Pract.* **33**: 506–7.

Hurowitz J (1993) Toward a social policy for health. *NEJM.* **329**(2): 130–3.

Illich I (1976) *Medical Nemesis: the expropriation of health.* Pantheon, New York.

Jeffrey R, Bjornson-Benson W, Rosenthal B *et al.* (1984) Correlates of weight loss and its maintenance over two years of follow-up among middle-aged men. *Prevent Med.* **13**(2): 155–68.

Jenkins L (1987) Self-efficacy: new perspectives in caring for patients recovering from myocardial infarction. *Professional Cardiovasc Nurs.* **2**(1): 32–5.

Jordan J, Kaplan A, Miller J *et al.* (1991) *Women's Growth in Connection: writings from the Stone Center.* Guilford Press, New York.

Kaplan R, Atkins C and Reinsch S (1984) Specific efficacy expectations mediate exercise compliance in patients with COPD. *Health Psychol.* **3**(3): 223–42.

Kaplan S, Greenfield S and Ware J (1989a) Assessing the effects of physician-patient interactions on the outcomes of chronic disease. *Med Care.* **275**: 5110–27.

Kaplan S, Greenfield S and Ware J (1989b) Impact of the doctor–patient relationship on outcomes of chronic disease. In: M Stewart and D Roter (eds) *Communicating with Medical Patients.* Sage, Newbury Park, CA.

Katon W and Kleinman A (1981) Doctor–patient negotiation and other social science strategies in patient care. In: L Eisenberg and A Kleinman (eds) *Relevance of Social Science for Medicine.* Reidel, Boston, MA.

Klein B (1997b) *Slow Dance – a story of stroke, love and disability.* Knopf, Toronto, ON.

Klein M (1997a) Too close for comfort? A family physician questions whether medical professionals should be excluded from their loved one's care. *Canad Med Assoc J.* **156**(1): 53–5.

Kleinman A (1988) *The Illness Narratives. Suffering, healing and the human condition.* Basic Books, New York.

Kleinman A, Eisenberg L and Good B (1978) Culture, illness and care. *Ann Intern Med.* **88**: 251–8.

Kruse J and Phillips D (1987) Factors influencing women's decision to undergo mammography. *Obstet Gynecol.* **70**(5): 744–8.

Langley G and Till J (1989) Exemplary family physicians and consultants: empirical definition of contemporary medical practice. *Canad Med Assoc J.* **141**: 301–7.

Lantz P, Remington P and Soref M (1990) Self-reported barriers to mammography: implications for physicians. *Wisconsin Med J.* **602**(89): 605–6.

Lent B (1986) Diagnosing wife assault. *Canad Family Physician.* **32**: 547–9.

Letchky O (1992) There are easy ways to deal with difficult patients, MDs say. *Canad Med Assoc J.* **146**(10): 1793–5.

Linklater D and MacDougall S (1993) Boundary issues: what do they mean for family physicians? *Canad Family Physician.* **39**: 2569–73.

Lipkin M Jr, Putnam S and Lazare S (eds) (1995) *The Medical Interview – clinical care, education, and research.* Springer-Verlag, New York.

Longhurst M (1980) Angry patient, angry doctor. *Canad Med Assoc J.* **123**: 597–8.

Longhurst M (1989) Physician self-awareness: the neglected insight. In: M Stewart and D Roter (eds) *Communicating with Medical Patients.* Sage, Newbury Park, CA.

Loxterkamp D (1991) Being there: on the place of the family physician. *J Am Board Family Pract.* **4**(5): 354–60.

Malterud K (1994) Key questions – a strategy for modifying clinical communication. *Scand J Primary Health Care.* **12**: 121–7.

Marshall J (1988) How to make consultations work. *Postgrad Med.* **84**: 253–7.

Marshall K (1996) Prevention. How much harm? How much benefit? 4. The ethics of informed consent for preventive screening programs. *Canad Med Assoc J.* **155**(4): 377–83.

Marteau T (1990) Screening in practice: reducing the psychological costs. *BMJ.* **301**: 26–8.

Marteau T, Kidd J and Cook R (1990) Hospital-based doctors and nurses presenting a routine screening test to patients: practice observed. International Conference on Health Communication, Oxford, England.

Mathers N and Gask L (1995) Surviving the 'heartsink' experience. *Family Pract.* **12**(2): 176–83.

Maurer J and Strasberg P (1989) *Building a New Dream – a family guide to coping with chronic illness and disability.* Addison-Wesley, Reading, MA.

Mayeroff M (1971) *On Caring.* Harper and Row, New York.

McDaniel E, Campbell T and Seaburn D (1990) *Family-Oriented Primary Care: a manual for medical providers.* Springer-Verlag, New York.

McGinnis J and Hamburg M (1988) Opportunities for health promotion and disease prevention in the clinical setting. *Western J Med.* **149**: 468–74.

McIntyre K, Lichtenstein E and Mermelstein P (1983) Self-efficacy and relapse in smoking cessation: a replication and extension. *J Consult Clin Psychol.* **51**: 632–3.

McNeil C (1991) From migration to palliation: uncharted waters. *J Palliative Care.* **7**(4): 26–30.

McPhee S and Schroeder S (1987) Promoting preventive care: changing reimbursement is not enough. *Am J Public Health.* **77**: 780–1.

McPhee S, Richard R and Solkowit S (1986) Performance of cancer screening in a university internal medicine practice. *J Gen Intern Med.* **1**: 275–8.

McWhinney I (1972) Beyond diagnosis. *NEJM.* **287**: 384–7.

McWhinney I (1997) *A Textbook of Family Medicine.* Oxford University Press, New York.

McWilliam C (1993) Health promotion: strategies for family physicians. *Canad Family Physician.* **39**: 1079–85.

McWilliam C, Brown J, Carmichael J and Lehman M (1994) A new perspective on threatened autonomy: the disempowering process. *Social Sci Med.* **38**(2): 327–38.

Miller B and Bowen S (1982) Father-to-newborn attachment behavior in relation to prenatal classes and presence at delivery. *Family Relations.* **31**(1): 71–8.

Miller J (1992) *Coping with Chronic Illness – overcoming powerlessness* (2e). F A Davis, Philadelphia, PA.

Miller W (1993) Physicians, patients, and third parties: everybody's talking but is anybody listening? *J Family Pract.* **37**(4): 331–3.

Miller W, Yanoshik M, Crabtree B and Reymond W (1994) Patients, family physicians, and pain: visions from interview narratives. *Family Med.* **26**(3): 179–84.

Miller W and Rollnick S (1991) *Motivational Interviewing – preparing people to change addictive behavior.* Guilford Press, New York.

Mishler E (1984) *Discourse of Medicine: dialectics of medical interviews.* Ablex, Norwood, NJ.

Mishne J (1993) *The Evolution and Application of Clinical Theory. Perspectives from four psychologies.* Free Press, New York.

Mold J (1997) The healthcare system. In: M Mongel and W Holleman (eds) *Fundamentals of Clinical Practice – a textbook on the patient, doctor, and society.* Plenum, New York.

Montgomery C (1993) *Healing Through Communication: the practice of caring.* Sage Publications, Newbury Park, CA.

National Research Council, Committee on Risk Perception and Communication (1989) *Improving Risk Communication.* National Academy Press, Washington, DC.

Nattinger A, Panzer R and Janus J (1989) Improving the utilization of screening mammography in primary care practices. *Arch Intern Med.* **149**: 2087–92.

Needleman J (1985) *The Way of the Patient.* Arkana Penguin, London.

Ney P (1987) Grief work for adolescents: how the family physician can help. *Psychiat Canada.* **1**(3): 93–107.

Nicki R, Remington R and MacDonald G (1984) Self-efficacy, nicotine-fading/self-monitoring and cigarette smoking behaviour. *Behav Res Ther.* **22**: 477–85.

Norton K and Smith S (1994) *Problem with Patients – managing complicated transactions.* Cambridge University Press, Cambridge.

Paulette L (1993) A choice for K'Aila. *Humane Med.* **9**(1): 13–17.

Payer L (1988) *Medicine and Culture.* Penguin Books, New York.

Perlman H (1979) *Relationship: the heart of helping people.* University of Chicago Press, Chicago, IL.

Pommerenke F and Dietrich A (1992) Improving and maintaining preventive services. Part 1: Applying the patient model. *Family Pract.* **34**(1): 86–91.

Pullen D, Lonie C, Lyle D, Cam D and Doughty M (1995) Medical care of doctors. *Med J Aust.* **162**: 481–4.

Quill T (1983) Partnerships in patient care: a contractual approach. *Ann Intern Med.* **98**: 228–34.

Quill T (1989) Diagnosis and treatment: recognizing and adjusting to barriers in doctor–patient communication. *Ann Intern Med.* **111**: 51–7.

Quill T and Brody H (1996) Physician recommendations and patient autonomy: finding a balance between physician power and patient choice. *Ann Intern Med.* **125**(9): 763–9.

Ransom D (1993) The family in family medicine: reflections on the first 25 years. *Family Systems Med.* **11**: 25–9.

Riccardi V and Kurtz S (1983) *Communication and Counseling in Health Care.* Charles C Thomas, Springfield, IL.

Rogers C (1961) Significant learning. In: C Rogers (ed) *On Becoming a Person.* Houghton Mifflin, Boston, MA.

Rolland J (1989) Chronic illness and the family life cycle. In: B Carter and M McGoldrick (eds) *The Changing Family Life Cycle: a framework for family therapy.* Allyn and Bacon, Boston, MA.

Roter D and Hall J (1992) *Doctors Talking with Patients/Patients Talking with Doctors – improving communication in medical visits.* Auburn House, Westport, CT.

Roter D, Hall J, Kern D *et al.* (1995) Improving physicians' interviewing skills and reducing patients' emotional distress: a randomized clinical trial. *Arch Intern Med.* **155**: 1877–84.

Rourke J, Smith L and Brown J (1993) Patients, friends and relationship boundaries. *Canad Family Physician.* **39**: 2557–64.

Rubin J and Brown B (1975) *The Social Psychology of Bargaining and Negotiation.* Academic Press, New York.

Rush B (1989) The use of family medical practices by patients with drinking problems. *Canad Med Assoc J.* **140**: 35–9.

Sanson-Fisher R and Maguire R (1980) Should skills in communicating with patients be taught in medical schools? *Lancet.* **2**: 523–6.

Schlesinger E (1985) *Health Care Social Work Practice.* Times Mirror/Mosby, Toronto, ON.

Schwenk T and Romano S (1992) Managing the difficult physician–patient relationship. *Am Family Physician.* **46**(5): 1503–9.

Sensky T and Catalan J (1992) Asking patients about their treatment. *BMJ.* **305**: 1109–10.

Sherwin S (1992) *No Longer Patient: feminist ethics and health care.* Temple University Press, Philadelphia, PA.

Siegel B (1975) Helping children cope with death. *Am Family Physician.* **31**(3): 175–80.

Skinner H, Holt S and Israel Y (1981) Early identification of alcohol abuse: critical issues and psychosocial indicators for a composite index. *Canad Med Assoc J.* **124**: 1141–52.

Stachtchenko S and Jenicek M (1990) Conceptual differences between prevention and health promotion: research implications for community health programs. *Canad J Public Health.* **81**(1): 53–9.

Starfield B, Steinwachs D, Morris I, Bauer G and Siebert S (1979) Patient–doctor agreement about problems needing follow-up visit. *JAMA*. **242**: 344–6.

Starfield B, Wray C, Hess K *et al.* (1981) The influence of patient–practitioner agreement on outcome of care. *Am J Public Health*. **71**(2): 127–32.

Stein H (1985) *The Psycho-Dynamics of Medical Practice. Unconscious factors in patient care.* University of California Press, Berkeley, CA.

Stephens G (1982) *The Intellectual Basis of Family Practice.* Winter, Tuscon, AZ.

Stephens G (1993) Patients on patienthood: new voices from the high-tech area. *J Am Board Family Pract*. **6**(2): 224–6.

Stewart M (1995) Effective physician–patient communication and health outcomes: a review. *Canad Med Assoc J*. **152**(9): 1423–33.

Stewart M and Roter D (1989) *Communicating with Medical Patients.* Sage Publications, Newbury Park, CA.

Stewart M, Brown J and Weston W (1989) Patient-centred interviewing. Part III: Five provocative questions. *Canad Family Physician*. **35**: 159–61.

Stewart M, Brown J, Weston W *et al.* (1995) *Patient-Centered Medicine: transforming the clinical method.* Sage Publications, Thousand Oaks, CA.

Stewart M, Brown J, Donner A *et al.* (1996) *The Impact of Patient-Centred Care on Patient Outcomes in Family Practice.* Thames Valley Family Practice Research Unit, London, ON.

Stewart M, Brown J, Donner A *et al.* (2000) The impact of patient-centered care on outcomes. *J Family Pract*. **49**(9): 796–804.

Stoudmeire A and Rhoads J (1983) When the doctor needs a doctor: special considerations for the physician-patient. *Ann Intern Med*. **98**(1): 654–9.

Suchman A and Matthews D (1988) What makes the patient–doctor relationship therapeutic? Exploring the connexional dimension of medical care. *Ann Intern Med*. **108**: 125–30.

Szasz T and Hollender M (1956) The basic models of the doctor–patient relationship. *Am Med Assoc Arch Intern Med*. **97**: 585.

Thurston C, Mitchell R and Little K (1982) A study of the contents of referral letters from general practitioners to an accident and emergency department. *Health Bull*. **40**: 120–4.

Tong K and Spicer B (1994) The Chinese palliative patient and family in North America: a cultural perspective. *J Palliative Care*. **11**(1): 26–8.

Toombs S (1992) *The Meaning of Illness – a phenomenological account of the different perspectives of physician and patient.* Kluwer Academic, Boston, MA.

Tse M (1987) How badly are referral letters written? A study of referral letters received by a specialist clinic. *Hong Kong Practitioner*. **9**: 2302–6.

Tuckett D, Boulton M, Olson C and Williams A (1985) *Meetings Between Experts. An approach to sharing ideas in medical consultations.* Tavistock, New York.

US Preventive Services Task Force (1996) *Guide to Clinical Preventive Services: Report of the US Preventive Services Task Force* (2e). Williams and Wilkins, Baltimore, MD.

Veatch R (1972) Models for ethical medicine in a revolutionary age. *Hastings Center Report.* **2**: 5.

Wall J (1989) *The Second International Conference on Health, Law, and Ethics.* Society for Law and Medicine, London.

Walsh M (1985) A study of the content of referral letters from general practitioners for acute surgical admissions to a district general hospital. *Health Bull.* **43**(2): 64–71.

Waters E and Goodman J (1990) *Empowering Older Adults: practical strategies for counsellors.* Jossey-Bass, San Francisco, CA.

Waters I, Watson W and Wetzel W (1994) Genograms: practice tools for family physicians. *Canad Family Physician.* **40**: 282–7.

Watson J (1984) *Health – a need for new direction. A task force on the allocation of health care resources.* Canadian Medical Association, Ottawa, ON.

Watson J (1985) *Nursing: human science and human care.* Appleton-Century-Crofts, Norwalk, CT.

Weston W and Brown J (1989) The importance of patients' beliefs. In: M Stewart and D Roter (eds) *Communicating with Medical Patients.* Sage Publications, Newbury Park, CA.

Weston W and Lipkin J (1989) Doctors learning communication skills: developmental issues. In: M Stewart and D Roter (eds) *Communicating with Medical Patients.* Sage Publications, Newbury Park, CA.

Weston W, Brown J and Stewart M (1989) Patient-centred interviewing part I: understanding patients' experiences. *Canad Family Physician.* **35**: 147–51.

Weyrauch K (1994) The personal knowledge of family physicians for their patients. *Clin Res Methods.* **26**(7): 452–5.

Wood M (1991) Naming the illness: the power of words. *Family Med.* **23**(7): 534–8.

Wood M and McWilliam C (1996) Cancer in remission – challenge in collaboration for family physicians and oncologists. *Canad Family Physician.* **42**: 899–910.

Woods M and Hollis F (1990) *Casework: a psychosocial therapy.* McGraw-Hill, New York.

Woolf S, Jonas S and Lawrence R (eds) (1996) *Health Promotion and Disease Prevention in Clinical Practice.* Williams and Wilkins, Baltimore, MD.

World Health Organization (WHO) (1986a) *Health Promotion: a discussion document on the concept and principles* (ICP/HSR 602). Regional Office for Europe, Copenhagen.

World Health Organization (WHO) (1986b) *Health Promotion: concept and principles in action – a policy framework.* Regional Office for Europe, Copenhagen.

Index